Angela Lee

Bilingualism, Multiculturalism, and Second Language Learning

The McGill Conference in Honour of Wallace E. Lambert

Edited by
Allan G. Reynolds
Nipissing University College

LEA LAWRENCE ERLBAUM ASSOCIATES, PUBLISHERS
1991 Hillsdale, New Jersey   London

Lawrence Erlbaum Associates, Inc., Publishers
365 Broadway
Hillsdale, New Jersey 07642

Library of Congress Cataloging-in-Publication Data

Bilingualism, multiculturalism, and second language learning: the
  McGill conference in honour of Wallace E. Lambert / edited by Allan
  G. Reynolds.
        p.   cm.
  Includes bibliographical references and indexes.
  ISBN 0-8058-0694-6
  1. Education, Bilingual — Congresses. 2. Intercultural education —
Congresses. 3. Second language acquisition — Congresses.
I. Reynolds, Allan G., 1944-   . II. Lambert, Wallace E.
III. McGill University.
LC3705.B55   1990
371.97 — dc20   90-43370
                                                                 CIP

Printed in the United States of America
10   9   8   7   6   5   4   3   2

For Wally

Contents

Preface

In the early summer of 1988, Bob Gardner, Fred Genesee, Al Paivio, Dick Tucker, and I appointed ourselves as an Organizing Committee to plan a conference in honour of Wallace E. Lambert on the occasion of his "official" retirement from McGill University after 35 years of exceptional teaching and distinguished research. We invited a number of scholars to prepare presentations on topics that we felt were reflective of Wally Lambert's profound influence on psycholinguistics, language education, and social psychology.

The conference took place on May 10-12, 1989, at l'Hôtel Estérel, north of Montreal. The audience was comprised of people from social psychology, education, sociology, psychometrics, cognitive psychology, neuropsychology, psychiatry, and linguistics, and included such distinguished guests as M. Pierre-Étienne Laporte (of the Office de la langue française) and Ms. Kathryn Manzer (President of Canadian Parents for French). Ten papers, plus a conference overview by Lambert, were presented. Unlike a traditional *Festschrift,* which is primarily retrospective, the papers presented dealt with issues of current theoretical significance and also pointed to areas for future theoretical and empirical investigation; the eleven chapters in this volume are expansions of the talks given at l'Estérel. In addition to the scholarly presentations, there were also addresses by Mr. Peter Rainboth, the Canadian Deputy Commissioner of Official Languages, and Mr. Keith Fitzpatrick, Directeur du service éducatif aux anglophones du Ministère de l'Education (Province du Québec).

Not all of the three days of the conference was spent on academic pursuits; like everything else connected with Wally Lambert, there was time for fun, too. Like athletes before a game, we took breaks from polishing our papers to shoot pool or swim or just socialize with old friends. The social highpoint of the conference was a banquet in honour of Wally attended by the conference participants, a large contingent of McGill friends, and Wally's entire family, including his wife Janine, his daughter Sylvie, his son Philippe (and his family from France), and his brother Bill (and his family). But then, that night, we were all members of Wally's "family" and, as at any family gathering, old (sometimes ribald) anecdotes were shared again as Wally was "roasted" royally by a cross section of friends, and toasted as well (champagne courtesy of Harry Triandis). In fact, the whole conference was more like a family reunion than a stuffy academic affair. For example, many of the presentations were given by former Lambert PhD students, and almost all of Wally's former PhD students were present at the conference (see the group photo).

No conference of this magnitude can be held without financial support. We extend our thanks to the McGill Psychology Department, McGill's Faculty of Graduate Studies and Research, the Fonds pour la Formation de Chercheurs et l'Aide à la Recherche du Québec (FCAR), the Social Sciences and Humanities Research Council of Canada, and the Gouvernement du Québec (Ministère de l'Education, de l'Enseignement supérieur et de la Science et le Ministère responsable de l'application de la Charte de la langue française) for their generous support. As well, thanks go to the Laurentian University Research Fund, the Nipissing Research Institute, the Ontario Ministry of Colleges and Universities, and the Department of the Secretary of State of Canada for financial and technical support for the preparation and dissemination of this volume.

It is always a pleasure to thank publicly people who have unselfishly aided you in a project in whose worth you all believe. First, thanks to Jim Ramsay, the-then chairman of the McGill Psychology Department for his enthusiastic support for the conference; Barbara Outerbridge and Janet Smart were tireless in ensuring that the conference itself ran smoothly; Kate Williams' participation and advice guaranteed excellent media coverage of the

Picture this: l'Estérel, Québec, May 11, 1989 — Wallace E. Lambert and most of his ex-doctoral students.

conference; Lynn Buckley, Chantal Coulombe, Christine Gentile, Suzanne Richard, and Charlene Tremblay were my faithful editorial assistants during the preparation of this volume; Jim Mroczkowski gave us some invaluable suggestions for the cover design. My sincere appreciation is also given to the staff at LEA, especially Judi Amsel and Art Lizza.

I reserve my last thank-you for Anne Roussell, our Conference Coordinator— words cannot express our gratitude. Anything that went wrong (and very little did) was fixed immediately by Anne. Most of what went right was due to her. She was responsible for almost everything: choosing the conference site, travel arrangements, correspondence with all the participants, coordinating the fundraising, local arrangements, etc., etc. Through an entire year of dealing with an Organizing Committee spread among four separate cities, she was unflappable, generous, and a joy to work with. Without her, there would undoubtedly have been a conference, but it would not have been the success it was.

North Bay, Ontario   A. G. R.
November 1990

Biographical Sketches Of Contributors

Nikolas Coupland received his PhD from the University of Wales in 1981; he is Director of the Centre for Applied English Language Studies at the University of Wales College of Cardiff where he has taught since 1976. He is author of *Dialect in Use* (1988), and editor of *Styles of Discourse* (1988) and *Welsh English: Diversity, Conflict and Change* (1989). Forthcoming books include *Problem Talk and Problem Contexts, Contexts of Accommodation, Old Talk Young Talk,* and *Communication, Health and Ageing.* With Howard Giles, he has codirected an interdisciplinary ESRC research program entitled "Communication and the Elderly." For the 1989-1990 academic year, he was Visiting Professor and Fulbright Scholar at the University of California, Santa Barbara.

Robert C. Gardner received his PhD from McGill University in 1960; he is a Professor of Psychology at the University of Western Ontario. He has written the books *Attitudes and Motivation in Second-language Learning* (with W. E. Lambert, 1972), and *Social Psychology and Second Language Learning: The Role of Attitudes and Motivation* (1985), and has coedited with R. Kalin the book *A Canadian Social Psychology of Ethnic Relations* (1981). In addition, he has published numerous articles on language learning, ethnic stereotypes, psycholinguistics, and statistics. He is a former editor of the *Canadian Journal of Behavioral Science*.

Fred Genesee is a member of the Psychology Department of McGill University, from which he received his PhD in 1974. He has carried out extensive research on alternative forms of bilingual education, in particular second language immersion for majority language students. His other research interests include social psychology and cognitive and neuropsychological aspects of bilingualism. He is the author of *Learning Through Two Languages: Studies in Immersion and Bilingual Education* (1987) and is currently working with Jack Upshur on a book on second language evaluation for teachers.

Howard Giles obtained his PhD from the University of Bristol in 1971. He has published in many areas: second language learning, intergenerational communication, and ethnolinguistics; in 1982, with E. Ryan he edited a book on attitudes toward language variation. He is founding editor of two journals, the *Journal of Language and Social Psychology* and the *Journal of Asian Pacific Communication*. He is on the editorial boards of many language journals and is general editor of several social psychology and interdisciplinary language book series. In 1978 he won the British Psychological Society's Spearman Medal, and he was awarded the Society's 1989 President's Award for his contribution to the study of language and communication within social psychology. He is currently at the University of California, Santa Barbara.

D. Geoffrey Hall had a distinguished undergraduate career at McGill University; upon graduation, he was the recipient of the Governor General's Gold Medal. He is currently pursuing graduate studies at Harvard University. His research interests include cognitive development, language acquisition, and bilingualism.

Josiane F. Hamers received her PhD from McGill University in 1973; she is a Professor in the Department of Linguistics at Laval University and a researcher at Laval's International Center for Research on Bilingualism. She has published three books: *Child-rearing Values: A Cross-national Study* (1979, coauthored with W. E. Lambert and N. Frasure-Smith), *Bilingualité et Bilinguisme* (1983, coauthored with M. Blanc), and *Bilinguality and Bilingualism* (1989, coauthored with M. Blanc). Her research interests include models of bilingual development, social psychological aspects of second language learning and cultural exchange programs, and cross-cultural research on language development in minority and bilingual children in Canada and Africa.

Sharon Lapkin received her PhD from the University of Toronto in 1974; she is an Associate Professor in the Department of Curriculum/Modern Language Centre at the Ontario Institute for Studies in Education. Her research interests include French as a second language education, with particular reference to immersion education, second language test development, and second language writing. Most of her publications are in the area of evaluating bilingual education programs, especially in terms of second language outcomes.

Allan Paivio received his PhD from McGill University in 1959; he was Wallace Lambert's first doctoral student. He is a Professor of Psychology at the University of Western Ontario. His research interests include imagery, memory, language, and cognition, and the testing and development of a general theory of cognition (dual coding theory). His numerous publications include three books: *Imagery and Verbal Processes* (1971, reprinted in 1979), *The Psychology of Language* (1981, coauthored with I. Begg), and *Mental Representations: A Dual-coding Approach* (1986). He is a Fellow of the Royal Society of Canada, former president and honourary president of the Canadian Psychological Association, recipient of the Queen's Silver Jubilee Medal, and a recipient of the Canadian Psychological Association Award for Distinguished Contributions to Psychology as a Science.

Allan G. Reynolds received his PhD from McGill University in 1970. His research interests include memory, bilingualism, educational psychology, and cognitive psychology. He is the coauthor (with P. W. Flagg) of the book *Cognitive Psychology* (1977, 1983). He taught at Dartmouth College and the University of Regina before joining the faculty of Nipissing University College, where he is an Associate Professor of Psychology.

Merrill Swain received her PhD from the University of California at Irvine in 1972; she is a Professor in the Department of Curriculum at the Ontario Institute for Studies in Education and Director of the Modern Language Centre as well as being cross-appointed to the Department of Linguistics at the University of Toronto. Her interests include classroom research (particularly in the context of French immersion education), second language testing, and the development of bilingual proficiency; she has published extensively on these topics. She coauthored *Bilingualism in Education* (1986) with J. Cummins.

Donald M. Taylor is a Professor of Psychology at McGill University; he received his PhD from the University of Western Ontario in 1969. His research interest is in intergroup relations, including such topics as ethnic stereotypes, intergroup communication, ethnic identity, and multicultural societies. His research has been conducted in diverse regions of the world, including the United States, Canada, Britain, and Southeast Asia. He has contributed numerous articles to Canadian, American, European, and Asian journals; he coauthored a major work on multiculturalism titled *Multiculturalism and Ethnic Attitudes in Canada* (with J. W. Berry and R. Kalin, 1977), a book with F. M. Moghaddam titled *Theories of Intergroup*

Relations (1987), and, in 1990, a book with W. E. Lambert entitled *Coping with Cultural and Racial Diversity in Urban America*.

G. Richard Tucker, who received his PhD from McGill University in 1967, is President of the Center for Applied Linguistics in Washington, DC. He has served as a Project Specialist with The Ford Foundation at language centers in Southeast Asia and in the Middle East. He has conducted research and provided technical assistance to Ministries of Education and planning agencies in numerous countries. For the past 20 years, he has been particularly concerned with the development, implementation, and evaluation of language education policy in the Philippines.

Jyotsna Vaid was Wallace Lambert's last doctoral student. She received her PhD from McGill University in 1982 and then worked as a research associate at the Salk Institute for Biological Studies from 1983 to 1985. Since 1986 she has been on the faculty of Texas A & M University, teaching and doing research in psycholinguistics and neuropsychology. She has published a number of research and review papers on the neuropsychology of bilingualism, and edited the 1986 book *Language Processing in Bilinguals: Psycholinguistic and Neuropsychological Perspectives*.

A Few Words About
Wallace E. Lambert

The scientific investigator and the scholar has his own peculiar rewards. He finds a few like-minded persons to cooperate with him because scientific research is not simply a solitary indulgence of infrequent and eccentric individuals. Little drops of knowledge coalesce into bigger drops, and odds and ends of detailed information gradually get shifted into patterns of great interest and beauty.

James Harvey Robinson

Who is Wallace Earl Lambert? First, he is a scientist and scholar. By way of background, he received his undergraduate education at Brown University, his MA from Colgate University, and his PhD from the University of North Carolina. Since 1954, he has been on the faculty of the Department of Psychology at McGill University, although he has taught occasionally at Cornell University, Columbia University, Stanford University, the University of Michigan, and many other schools. A prolific researcher, his *curriculum vitae* lists some 160 published articles and eight books on problems ranging from the social psychology of second language learning, to cross-cultural aspects of child-rearing practices, to the cognitive and neuropsychological characteristics of the bilingual mind. Besides the diversity of his interests, what is most striking about his contributions to these areas is that they have invariably been seminal.

His large body of research on bilingualism, second language learning, and related topics is marked by both scientific rigour and social and educational relevance. Rigour and relevance are combined especially well in his widely known, pioneering research on the effectiveness of second language immersion education. Beginning in 1965 as an experiment in enhancing French education for English-speaking children in St. Lambert, Quebec, the immersion approach proved so successful that it has spread first across

Canada, then across the United States, and now is an educational approach used around the world. It is a superb example of the practical educational benefits that can arise when a well-controlled experimental study is done on a complex problem in a real life social setting. The scientific rigour and dedication to a program of research, for which Lambert is famous, are further demonstrated by his involvement in the continuing and longitudinal evaluation of the effectiveness of French immersion. This ongoing commitment places in sharp perspective his adherence to the value of scientific rigour within an applied context.

His honours and awards include the presidency and honourary presidency of the Canadian Psychological Association, a Fellowship at the Stanford Center for Advanced Study in the Behavioral Sciences, a Fellowship in the Canadian Royal Society, membership in The National Academy of Education of the United States, honourary doctorates from Laurentian University, York University, and the University of Western Ontario, the Queen's Silver Jubilee Medal, the Distinguished Alumni Award from the University of North Carolina, and the Canadian Psychological Association Award for Distinguished Contributions to Psychology as a Science. In addition, as one wag pointed out, he is the only person to have ever been made a saint in his lifetime and then have a city named after him.

Who is Wallace E. Lambert? He is a gifted teacher and more— a true mentor. It is interesting, and maybe only a coincidence, that when the Nova Scotia-born Lambert came to McGill, he joined two other distinguished Nova Scotian teachers, George Ferguson and Don Hebb. It is worth noting that the majority of his publications have been coauthored with undergraduate or graduate students; he teaches by participation in the research enterprise. As well, he teaches about more than psychology; any of his younger colleagues would gladly confirm that Lambert "taught me more about life than I ever learned in PhD school." The key characteristic that sets Lambert the teacher apart from many other gifted instructors is illustrated by a quotation from Douglas Adams' *The Hitchhiker's Guide to the Galaxy:* "He attacked everything in life with a mixture of extraordinary genius and [naïveté] and it was often difficult to tell which was which."

Who is Wallace Lambert? He is a family man, in several senses. His professional career and his life with his nuclear family are indistinguishable. His marriage to a French girl and the raising of bilingual/bicultural children in Montreal sensitized him to issues of language and culture and the barricades to self-fulfillment they can create. His professional family is a large one (and even overlaps with his biological one: Wally and his brother Bill coauthored an influential textbook on social psychology); it includes ex-students, educators, and researchers world-wide. Wallace Lambert is the center of a community of friends and scholars, a "community of those who seek the truth . . . . the true friends" (Allan Bloom).

Who is Wally Lambert? He is a humanist with a vision, a vision that is a product of his own make-up— half *savant,* half "regular guy." It is a simple yet profound vision of a just world where people are not restricted by barriers of culture and language. Through his work, he has endeavoured to help human beings of all races and classes move freely across the boundaries imposed by culture and language. By demonstrating in both his work and his life that people can become bilingual and bicultural, he has helped create a social and intellectual atmosphere where the benefits of bilinguality and biculturalism are no longer the craving of only a privileged minority, but can be the aspiration of all. Wally Lambert imagines a world in which we can all be ourselves, but a world in which those selves will be the best they can be.

1 The Social Psychology of Racial and Cultural Diversity: Issues of Assimilation and Multiculturalism

Donald M. Taylor
McGill University

How newcomers, established ethnic groups, and native peoples accommodate to, and are accommodated by, the dominant group in society is an enduring question that lies at the heart of national unity. Until the early 1960s, in the United States and, to some extent, Canada, politicians and the public alike, supported by theory in the social sciences, envisaged a single inevitable outcome to the integration process— assimilation. But in the middle 1960s (1965 in the USA and 1967 in Canada), dramatic changes in immigration policy placed the integration question at the core of national identity. The policy changes involved removing race and nationality as criteria for qualifying as an acceptable immigrant. The result was a dramatic increase in the number of newcomers from Third World nations, thereby multiplying the mix of colours and very different cultures. The impact was, and is, to test the very limits of human tolerance in terms of dealing with cultural and racial diversity. As we approach the year 2000, politicians, everyday citizens, and social scientists must confront the challenge of understanding the integration process, and of forging a social climate where human diversity and harmony can coexist.

The focus of theory and research on the integration process has revolved around two contrasting ideological positions. At one extreme is *assimilation,* the belief that cultural groups should give up their "heritage" cultures and take on the host society's way of life. At the opposite pole is *multiculturalism,* the view that these groups should maintain their heritage cultures as much as possible.

In this chapter the history of theory and research into racial and cultural diversity will be reviewed in the context of this debate over assimilation and multiculturalism. The debate is truly a multidisciplinary one; to date, sociologists, economists, and political scientists have made the major contributions to the field. Psychology, as a discipline, has only begun to focus on the issues that are central to the debate. The present chapter affords a rare opportunity to review the perspectives of different disciplines in order to place, in a broader context, the direction that psychological theory and research might take.

In the first part of the chapter the preoccupation with an assimilation perspective will be explored. The focus of the next section is on the dramatic shift to a multiculturalism orientation in the form of an almost universal revival of ethnic nationalism. Finally, the current status of these contrasting perspectives is examined, with a view to specifying two key areas that might serve as a focus for social psychological theory and research.

THE PREOCCUPATION WITH ASSIMILATION

The classic assimilationist perspective is presented here not merely for its historical interest but because assimilationist theory in one form or another "continues to be the primary theoretical framework for sociological research" (Hirschman, 1983, p. 401). Assimilationist thinking is captured in the idealized image of the "melting pot," the title of an influential 1914 Broadway play by Zangwill. The theme was that America is becoming a superior society because of the new product that arises from numbers of cultures and races being stirred and melted in the societal pot.

But the melting pot image points to an important confusion in the definition of assimilation. The implication of the image is that every cultural group contributes to the final product: "American." Thus every cultural group, old or new, large or small, melts together and the final product is unique, unlike any of the cultural ingredients that went into the pot initially. To quote Zangwill's play: "Into the crucible with you all! God is making the American."

This view of assimilation allows for every cultural group to make its unique contribution to the final product. Unfortunately, this egalitarian view is not the meaning usually associated with the assimilationist perspective. The definition, when actually put into theoretical practice, is much more unidirectional, such that cultural groups are expected to give up their heritage culture and adopt the "way of life" of the host culture. In this sense cultural groups do not contribute to the definition of national character. Instead, they are "swallowed up by" or "conform to" the dominant host group. It is this implicitly unidirectional conception of assimilation that guided much of the early theory and research in the field of racial and cultural diversity.

The assimilationist perspective as we have defined it here dominated theory and research until the 1960s. Indeed, this view was so predominant that the focus was not so much on validating assimilation as the end product as it was on theorizing about its course.

For example, Park and Burgess, pioneers in the field who dominated thinking in the early decades of the twentieth century, introduced the "contact hypothesis," which held that "as social contact initiates interaction, assimilation is its final perfect product" (Park & Burgess, 1969, p. 361). But Park (1950) was much more concerned with the process of assimilation and so hypothesized the race relations cycle that involved four key stages: contact, competition, accommodation, and, finally, assimilation.

Another driving force behind the assimilationist perspective was the fundamental meritocracy ideology that lay at the heart of modernization and industrialization. An economy based on efficiency and productivity with an emphasis on *individual* effort and ability was incompatible with a society organized in terms of racial and cultural groups (Kerr, Dunlop, Harbison, & Myers, 1964; Myrdal, 1944). That is, the meritocracy ideology emphasizes individual performance as a basis for advancement, and thus racial or cultural affiliation are explicitly discounted as either an advantage or disadvantage for getting ahead in society.

A conceptually more sophisticated view of assimilation was provided by Gordon (1964) who distinguished among seven types of assimilation: cultural, structural, marital, identificational, attitude receptional (prejudice), behavioural receptional (discrimination), and civic. These distinctions allowed for a better understanding of the assimilation process in that not all dimensions of assimilation need, nor indeed would, be expected to proceed at the same pace. Thus, for example, Gordon felt that cultural assimilation proceeds relatively rapidly, but structural assimilation, in terms of the primacy of interactions with one's own cultural group, evolves at a much slower pace.

Hirschman (1983), in his thoughtful analysis, argued that it is extremely difficult to assess the empirical evidence offered as support for the assimilation perspective. As he noted, given the multidimensional nature of assimilation, trends in the direction of assimilation may vary widely from dimension to dimension. Beyond this, for any given dimension the evidence is likely to be equivocal because the theory is meant to apply to every conceivable group, from the Western European immigrant to visible minorities to native peoples. To highlight the equivocal support for assimilation, Hirschman focussed his review of empirical evidence on four aspects of assimilation: socioeconomic, residential segregation, intermarriage, and attitudes.

The review of the evidence in the economic domain led Hirschman to conclude that "this reading of the evidence on trends in socioeconomic inequality provides general support for the melting pot thesis for European ethnics, but not for black Americans" (p. 406). In terms of residential segregation, he noted that black-white segregation is pervasive, but levels of Hispanic-Anglo segregation are lower and seem to be moderating over time.

Intermarriage is an especially important barometer of assimilation because of the personal and intimate nature of the relationship itself. Unfortunately, the evidence is equivocal. Intermarriage across religious barriers appears to be quite prevalent (see, for example, Alba, 1981); however, mixed racial marriages remain infrequent.

Finally, focussing on intergroup attitudes as an index of assimilation is problematic. There seems to be consistent evidence for a steady decline in racial intolerance over the past few decades. However, there is controversy over the measures used in surveys of racial attitudes (see Taylor, Wright, Moghaddam, & Lalonde, 1990) and there are those who argue that "symbolic racism" has replaced more blatant forms but that in reality little has changed in terms of racism itself (Sears, 1988).

In summary, Hirschman's (1983) review of the evidence indicates a general pattern that, over time, newcomers do assimilate to the dominant, host culture. The evidence, however, is always equivocal and of such a nature that assimilation theory is never put to the critical test. Where the evidence is contrary to assimilation, theorists in this tradition can claim that the assimilation process is ongoing but as yet incomplete. With more time, they argue, the assimilation process will be completed. Anti-assimilationists argue, of course, that all it requires is one exception to the inevitable drift toward assimilation for the entire theory to be invalidated. Thus, any indication that even one group does not assimilate, or that assimilation does not proceed swiftly on all dimensions, is enough for them to discount assimilation theory.

Psychology and assimilation. The issue of assimilation has never been a major focus for theory and research in the field of psychology and so has not been directly addressed. The two mainstream areas of social psychology that until the mid-1960s most closely related to the present concerns were the areas of interpersonal attraction and ethnic stereotypes. Interestingly, the principles underlying each are entirely consistent with the assimilation perspective. In the field of interpersonal relations the dominant theme was that of a strong relationship between similarity and attraction (e.g., Byrne, 1971; Newcomb, 1961). This relationship holds true across a wide variety of dimensions, including similarity of attitudes, physical attraction, and, of significance for the present context, ethnic group (Kandel, 1978; Simard, 1981). The implication is clear: The type of culturally homogeneous society that arises in the case of pure assimilation is conducive to interpersonal harmony.

In terms of ethnic and racial stereotypes the theme is similar. Stereotypes that reflect cultural differences have been viewed as inferior cognitive processes that are usually wrong (Taylor, 1981; Taylor & Moghaddam, 1987). For this reason psychologists have felt they should be eradicated. Wiping out stereotypes, of course, is consistent with the assimilationist perspective because discounting stereotypes involves denying the cultural differences upon which stereotypes might be built.

THE ETHNIC REVOLUTION

Beginning in the middle 1960s, theory took a dramatic turn. Key social scientists such as Glazer and Moynihan (1970), Greely (1974), and Novak (1972), to name but a few, challenged the assumptions of assimilation, and the "revival of ethnicity" school was born (Hirschman, 1983). Labels such as ethnic diversity, pluralism, and multiculturalism surfaced, and romantic images such as mosaic, tossed salad, and patchwork quilt replaced the melting pot image.

But this revival was not one spearheaded by social scientists. Rather, it was everyday people struggling with the concrete realities of "getting ahead" in society who made phrases such as Black power, Red power, Hispanic, Latino, Québecois, anglophone, allophone, and every conceivable ethnic label a part of North American vocabulary. What really confronted the political and academic establishment was the reality that ethnicity would not go away. The ethnic revolution was especially surprising in North America because all of the conditions that should favour assimilation were present. North America offered newcomers a chance to escape political and economic oppression, the potential for equality of opportunity, and above all, freedom. The only requirement seemed to be that the individual give up the "old" ways and make a commitment to the new national identity. Despite all these forces favouring assimilation, cultural identity persisted, and indeed was becoming more prevalent. Heritage culture, it seems, would not or could not be assimilated.

The ethnic revolution was reflected at both the political and academic levels. Politically in Canada, for example, it gave rise to an official policy of multiculturalism in 1971 whereby ethnic groups would be encouraged to retain their heritage culture and language. Evidence in both the United States (e.g., Glazer & Moynihan, 1970; Greely, 1974) and Canada (Berry, Kalin, & Taylor, 1977; O'Bryan, Reitz, & Kuplowska, 1976) supported the view that ethnic groups were motivated to retain their heritage culture, and indeed that majority groups were mildly receptive to heritage culture maintenance.

This new multiculturalism perspective that had been dominated by sociologists and political scientists began to intrigue psychologists like Lambert who had been working extensively in the field of bilingualism. Lambert (1981, 1984; Lambert & Tucker, 1972) was aware early in his research on second language learning that language and culture were intimately connected. His theory was that bilingualism could be an additive process, one that afforded the individual a dual perspective rather than a confined or incomplete intellectual and social development. And he believed bilingualism was achievable by all.

For Lambert, what was true for language should be equally applicable to culture. Hence he argued that multiculturalism could be a reality that allowed the person to retain his or her heritage culture while at the same time being culturally sophisticated in terms of the host society. Lambert believed that, as with bilingualism, the acquisition of a new culture would breed respect for that culture, and vice versa.

As a psychologist, naturally Lambert's focus was on the implications of multiculturalism from the individual's perspective. The multiculturalism theme also influenced two other social psychologists at about the same time. Berry (1987) conceptualized the integration process as one that resulted from two separate attitudes, the individual's attitude toward the heritage culture and his or her attitude toward the host culture. Assimilation, according to Berry's scheme, arises when the individual has a positive attitude toward the host culture and a negative attitude toward the heritage culture. Multiculturalism, or what Berry labelled as integration, is characterized by a positive attitude toward both the host and heritage culture.

In the same vein, Taylor and his colleagues (Taylor, 1981; Taylor & Lalonde, 1987; Taylor & Simard, 1979) were redefining the traditional social psychological concept of the ethnic stereotype. Consistent with an assimilation ideology, racial and ethnic stereotypes had traditionally been defined as undesirable, oversimplified images of a group; in other words, they are the prototype of prejudice. Taylor argued that stereotypes are a normal cognitive process that need not be socially undesirable. Specifically, where there are two groups, each having an auto-stereotype and a stereotype of the other group, two conditions are required for a pattern of stereotypes to be socially desirable. First, each group must positively value the attributes they associate with their own group, and second, each group must respect the attributes that are stereotypic of the other group. Taylor (1981) described this condition as socially desirable stereotyping in the sense that both groups maintained their ethnic identity but were positively disposed to the unique attributes of the other group.

The empirical evidence in support of the multicultural perspective would appear to lend credence to the notion of a revival of ethnicity. A number of studies have been reported from a social psychological point of view, and these have two features in common. First, the issue of heritage culture maintenance was approached by asking members of different ethnic groups, in both Canada and the United States, directly about their perceptions and feelings. Second, these studies have all posed the issue to respondents in the form of a societal debate over assimilation on the one hand and heritage culture maintenance on the other, and asked respondents to indicate on a Likert scale where they stand on the debate. Samples have included various cultural and racial groups in the United States, such as Albanian Americans, Arab Americans, black Americans, Mexican Americans, Polish Americans, Puerto Rican Americans, and white Americans (see Lambert & Taylor, 1988). In the Canadian context the focus has been on Greek Canadians (Lambert, Mermigis, & Taylor, 1986), Southeast Asian women (Moghaddam & Taylor, 1987), Iranian Canadians (Moghaddam, Taylor, & Lalonde, 1987), Haitian Canadians, and Jewish Canadians (Taylor, Moghaddam, & Tchoryk-Pelletier, 1989).

The consistent finding from all of these studies is that members of newly arrived ethnic minority groups, long established ethnic groups, and majority "host" groups all support, albeit in varying degrees, heritage culture maintenance. For example, the results for a variety of groups from a predominantly lower workingclass urban centre in the United States are presented in Figure 1-1.

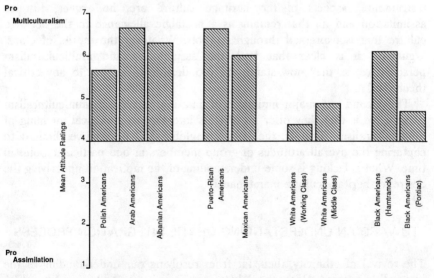

Fig. 1-1. Mean responses on the debate over assimilation versus multiculturalism. (Adapted from Lambert & Taylor, 1990)

As the results in Figure 1-1 indicate, there is a strong endorsement for multiculturalism and an apparent rejection of assimilation. The results of Canadian studies are equally consistent in their support for heritage culture maintenance; however, like the data from the United States there are wide variations in the degree of endorsement.

Despite this apparent universal support for multiculturalism there are two fundamental limitations to these studies that make it premature to draw any concrete conclusions about the role of assimilation and multiculturalism in the integration process. First, the data in support of heritage culture maintenance do not take into account its many dimensions. For example, Taylor et al. (1989) have found that, in terms of specific dimensions, group members seem particularly motivated to retain the heritage language, but teenagers representing various ethnic groups are more interested in assimilation when it comes to relations between the sexes. Just as Gordon (1964) postulated various dimensions to the assimilation process that operate in different ways, so too will it be necessary to specify different dimensions of heritage culture and understand how they operate.

An illustration of the lack of precision associated with both the assimilation and multiculturalism perspectives is Gans' (1979) theoretical analysis. His response to the revival of ethnicity phenomenon is to reject it out of hand. It is his contention that the ethnic revival is superficial and that basically the assimilation process is running its normal course. Gans counters evidence in favour of heritage culture maintenance by arguing that what newcomers maintain is only "symbolic ethnicity." The more fundamental and instrumental aspects of the heritage culture are, he argues, lost to assimilation and all that remains is a nostalgic allegiance to the heritage culture that is expressed through symbols. Whatever the merits of Gans' argument, it is clear that both the assimilation and multiculturalism perspectives, as they now stand, are too flexible to be put to any critical theoretical test.

The second and major limitation of data that support a multiculturalism perspective is that they offer no insights into the psychological meaning of multiculturalism. That is, the data are global and descriptive, limited to capturing the overall attitudes of group members at one particular point in time. What is lacking is some understanding of the motivation underlying the desire for heritage culture maintenance.

TOWARD AN UNDERSTANDING OF THE INTEGRATION PROCESS

The revival of ethnicity, then, far from resolving our understanding of the integration process, places the debate over assimilation and multiculturalism squarely in the forefront. Both perspectives receive some empirical support, but the evidence will always be equivocal. Assimilationists will dismiss evidence for heritage culture maintenance with the claim that with more time the assimilation process will ultimately be completed. Similarly, multiculturalists can accommodate evidence in favour of assimilation by arguing that only certain dimensions of the heritage culture have gone the way of assimilation, whereas other more important ones have not.

What is needed then is a shift in the central question away from the debate per se to the issue of what motivates people to retain or shed aspects of the heritage culture. A survey of current research in the social sciences would indicate two broad categories of motives for assimilation or heritage culture maintenance: economic and political motives on the one hand and psychological motives on the other.

Economic and Political Motivations

Economic motivations. Newcomers may well be motivated to give up their heritage culture or, alternatively, maintain it, depending upon which strategy offers the greater economic rewards. An analysis in such straightforward economic terms is problematic, however, because the question of who benefits economically in any particular situation is not always apparent. For example, if a member of an ethnic group maintains the heritage culture and is thereby virtually guaranteed employment in a particular occupation, whose interests are being served? It may be that the ethnic group member *chose* to emphasize culture as a mechanism for personal achievement, but it is also possible that the dominant group used its power to impose cultural maintenance with a view to satisfying the needs of the dominant group, not those of the ethnic individual.

This possibility is captured in economic theories of internal colonialism, reactive-ethnicity (see Hechter, 1975, 1978), or in Porter's (1965) terms, the *vertical mosaic*. Ethnic groups, according to these theories, are not permitted the option of assimilating. Rather they are forced to retain their heritage culture and to live and work in ethnic enclaves. This strategy by the dominant group is designed to exploit the resources of the ethnic group, always with a view to serving their own economic interests.

Another theory associated with the concentration of ethnic groups in particular occupations is one involving a cultural division of labor. The notion here is not that dominant groups pressure ethnic groups into particular occupational niches, but rather that ethnic networks facilitate employment possibilities for members of their own group. The motivation here is quite different but the outcome is the same: Heritage culture maintenance is encouraged through ethnically linked jobs.

Extrapolating from behaviour to motive then is very difficult in the case of ethnic concentrations in particular occupations. McEvoy's (1987) analysis of

Asian retailers in three British cities is illuminating on this point. An analysis of Asian retailers is especially relevant since, in both North America and Britain there is a growing stereotype that Asians "own all the corner stores" in the neighbourhood. McEvoy's results indicate that Asian retailers are part of an ethnic enclave, where there is heavy reliance on same ethnic clientele. The myth is that Asians have taken over small businesses and are reaping great economic wealth; in short, heritage culture maintenance is a matter of choice, and a wise choice from an economic point of view. However, McEvoy paints a very different scenario. For him the "proliferation of Asian businesses represents a move into a high-risk, low reward activity with few opportunities for expansion" (p. 28). The implication is that Asians are being forced into risky, small retail businesses involving long hours of work, thus leaving open the question of whether heritage culture maintenance is by choice or default.

In summary, there would seem to be two possible motives underlying the oft-cited relationship between ethnicity and specific categories of occupation, and in both cases heritage culture maintenance is reinforced. On the one hand, dominant groups may force ethnic groups into particular economic niches. The heritage culture is maintained through shared experience and social interaction, but it would not be valid to conclude that ethnic group members were themselves motivated to maintain their heritage culture.

Alternatively, ethnic groups may concentrate in distinct occupational categories that are equal in status both with other ethnic groups and, at times, the "dominant" group itself. The motivation for heritage culture maintenance in this case would seem to be more one of choice for economic advantages rather than one of imposition (see Olzak, 1983).

The need to incorporate these motivational economic dimensions is highlighted by recent findings from a study of ethnic groups in Detroit (Lambert & Taylor, 1988). Respondents representing a variety of ethnic groups (see Figure 1-1) were asked about the costs and rewards associated with bilingualism involving their heritage language and English. Not surprisingly, respondents judged being fluent in the heritage language as well as English to be associated with increased pride in ethnic identity and solidarity within the family. Strikingly, however, they also believed that bilingualism was associated with economic advancement in terms of school performance and job opportunity. Thus, maintaining the heritage language was linked directly to bread and butter issues, not only to the quality of social relationships.

What is not clear, however, is why there is a perceived link between bilingualism and economic advancement. Is it that bilingual group members can function effectively with a wider array of people including both their own group and those from the dominant group? Or does it mean that the ethnic group member is pressured, by exclusion from the dominant group, to function exclusively with the ingroup, and thus maintain the heritage language as an economic necessity?

Political motivations. A simple principle to be gleaned from the variety of political analyses related to ethnic groups is simply that motivation for heritage culture maintenance is associated with advancing the individual's self-interest. This apparently simple proposition has the effect of blurring many of the distinctions that arise in the literature. For example, Nagel (1987) contrasts pluralism and segregation as political ideologies for dealing with diversity. A pluralist strategy is best exemplified by notions of "consociational democracy" (Lijphart, 1968) whereby the composition of governing bodies is proportional to the *ethnic* composition of the electorate. Thus, ethnic divisions are formally recognized, they have their own leadership, and the emphasis is on negotiation and accommodation rather than conflict.

Nagel (1987) includes under the segregation category both genocide and apartheid. But she points out that included here would be policies that involve forced migration and relocation. The treatment of native peoples by the dominant group, involving land seizures, relocation, and reservations, would fall into this category (Bantum, 1983).

The theme common to both pluralist policies and segregation is the exercise of power via ethnic solidarity. In consociational democracy, ethnic affiliation is associated with the protection and enhancement of self-interest. In the case of segregation the situation is reversed. The dominant group *imposes* heritage culture maintenance precisely so that it can subordinate all those who are identified with that ethnic category. This theme is even more explicit in Esman's (1987) analysis of ethnic politics and economic power. He notes that in many societies a minority elite economically dominates the majority who are economically disadvantaged. Among his examples Esman cites the francophone majority in Quebec. His thesis is that disadvantaged groups in these instances capitalize on their majority numerical status to gain political control. Then, by expropriation and nationalization they set about to redress the disadvantaged economic status of the majority ethnic group. Again, the theme is that ethnic identity is evoked as a political tool, not for its own sake.

Striking parallels arise from our analysis of economic and political motives. In both cases the question of the extent to which heritage culture maintenance is a matter of choice is raised. And, in most cases, heritage culture maintenance emerges by default as the only mechanism for reacting to perceived injustice.

DIRECTIONS FOR SOCIAL PSYCHOLOGICAL
THEORY AND RESEARCH

One of the dramatic outgrowths of the extent to which heritage culture maintenance is motivated by economic and political subordination is the concept of affirmative action. Affirmative action arises out of collective pressures by minority groups to redress historical injustices in the economic and political spheres. The term "affirmative action" is a complex one and Young (1986, p. 10) has defined four categories of approaches to discrimination that have been given the label affirmative action:

1. *Passive nondiscrimination*. This approach means that the employer refrains from racial or sexual discrimination when choosing among the applicants for a position.

2. *Active nondiscrimination*. This term implies that the employer will aggressively recruit black, brown, female, and other minority applicants before making an employment decision on the basis of merit.

3. *Restitutional nondiscrimination*. This term implies that the employer has been guilty of racial, ethnic, or sexual discrimination in the past; in the future, preference will be given to applicants from groups previously discriminated against in order to compensate for past actions.

4. *Reverse discrimination*. Here, the employer may not have been guilty of past discriminatory practices, but as a matter of policy gives preference in hiring to the members of targeted groups which have experienced discrimination in American society in the past.

As the label implies, *affirmative* action is not a passive approach and thus, most often, and in the present analysis, affirmative action will refer to the second, third, or fourth of Young's categories.

Affirmative action regarding racial and ethnic minority groups has received government-mandated support in such areas as employment, the civil service, and education, giving rise to such controversial programs as employment quotas, school bussing, and bilingual education. Affirmative action, however, is much more than a specific policy designed to deal with a particular problem. It is a broadly based philosophy of justice that contrasts dramatically with the meritocracy or equity based justice that is the cornerstone of Western democracy.

Gordon (1981) has been most articulate in defining the different assumptions underlying meritocracy (liberal pluralism) and corporate (affirmative action) pluralism. In North American meritocracy-based justice, no formal recognition is given to categories of people based on their race or culture; the focus is exclusively on the *individual*. Every individual in theory has an equal opportunity and rewards are allocated on the basis of individual merit.

In contrast, affirmative action focuses not on the individual but explicitly on a specified *collectivity,* defined by a racial, cultural, or other grouping. Justice is defined as an allocation of rewards such that the various collectivities within any institution are rewarded in proportion to their numbers in society at large.

Meritocracy and affirmative action based rules of societal justice then are not merely different, they are in direct ideological conflict; both exist simultaneously in society, and one discounts group membership while the other emphasizes it.

One important element in these mutually incompatible systems of justice is the role of time. A meritocracy-based system places responsibility squarely in the hands of the individual and his or her own performance. Thus, people are not accountable for the deeds of their ancestors. With affirmative action, groups are held responsible for past injustices against other groups.

This distinction is important because it points to an often-evoked resolution to these two incompatible ideologies. Specifically, affirmative action programs can be viewed as temporary steps to redress past collective injustices. The implication is that once collective justice has been restored, there will be a return to a meritocracy-based ideology of justice.

What are the implications for heritage culture maintenance? If affirmative action becomes entrenched as a mechanism whereby members of cultural groups can maximize their own rewards, then heritage culture maintenance will be greatly reinforced. But this presupposes that dominant groups will support affirmative action. This is by no means assured, and resistance can surface on at least two levels. First, dominant groups may oppose specific applications of affirmative action when they threaten their own position directly, and second, they may resist because it involves an ideology that fundamentally opposes the meritocracy ideology. It is crucial then, from the point of view of heritage culture maintenance, that the concept of affirmative action be examined from a psychological perspective. How is it perceived and rationalized by cultural minority groups and dominant groups? These perceptions are especially important because they refer not only to specific policies but to fundamental personal and societal values and ideologies. An understanding of these perceptions may well provide insights into what motivational role heritage culture maintenance plays for economic and political participation and advancement.

PSYCHOLOGICAL MOTIVES FOR
HERITAGE CULTURE MAINTENANCE

Interestingly, Canada's multiculturalism policy mentions psychological motives directly in its rationale for the policy itself. The explicit argument is that only when members of a group feel secure in their own identity will they feel open and charitable towards others. This is a particularly bold premise since it belies the basic tenants of ethnocentrism (LeVine & Campbell, 1972; Sumner, 1906). According to the principle of ethnocentrism, group members favour their own group to rival outgroups, and use their own group as a frame of reference for all judgements. Promoting a strong ingroup identity through heritage culture maintenance then might only exacerbate a pattern of ethnocentric attitudes.

What remains undefined at this stage, however, is the meaning of a *secure* group identity, the form of identity that would be associated with positive attitudes toward other groups rather than the negative outgroup attitudes associated with ethnocentrism. What needs to be understood is the specific role that the individual's cultural group plays for personal identity. And, of all the social sciences, psychology should be best suited to address this fundamental question.

Whenever the issue of cultural identity is raised in the scientific literature, the normal rules of conceptual clarity and operational definition become inoperative. To quote Greely (1974): "The striking thing . . . is that they [Isaacs (1964), Geertz (1963), and Shils (1957)] all use a rhetoric that is uncommonly poetic for the social sciences" (p. 14). Greely's explanation for this is that "they are dealing with something so basic and so fundamental in the human condition that academic prose is not altogether adequate to deal with it" (p. 14).

It may be instructive at this point to return to Gans' (1979) treatise on symbolic ethnicity. His main thesis is that assimilation remains the integration strategy of choice for ethnic minorities, and that evidence for heritage culture maintenance is really more symbolic than real. This symbolic ethnicity is really an expression of ethnic identity with little or no substance or instrumentality to it.

At first glance, Gans' notion of symbolic ethnicity would seem to be trivializing heritage culture maintenance. Roberts and Clifton (1982) agree with Gans, but recognize that symbolic ethnicity is not superficial or unimportant. As they note:

> Those who possess a "symbolic ethnicity" command the flexibility necessary to participate and benefit as members of a complex industrialized society while also feeling that they belong to a smaller community. This flexibility exists because symbolic ethnicity is a psychological rather than a social construct; it services

individual rather than community needs, and, as such, is less subject to forces
beyond an individual's control. (p. 19)

The psychological needs that are met through symbolic ethnicity, then,
may be fundamental. And they lie at the core of social psychological
processes, whether one examines Asch's (1955) basic distinction between
physical and social reality in his classic conformity experiment, the
emergence of social comparison as a basic process (Festinger, 1954), or the
traditions of symbolic interaction (see Manis & Meltzer, 1978; Stryber &
Stathon, 1985). The conclusion is that commerce with one's social
environment defines reality— and what reality is more fundamental than
the individual's understanding of his or her self? It is interaction with
significant others that provides the basic data that allow the individual to
answer two basic questions: Who am I? Am I worthwhile? These are the
primary schemata that allow the individual to understand the social
environment and his or her place in it. It is the basic blueprint for action and
self worth.

The blueprint requires that interaction with others provide continual
feedback to the individual that is relatively consistent and structured. Where
better to look for such consistency than to a shared culture that provides not
only continuity and structure but a consistent context for thinking, feeling,
and acting; in short, these are the essential ingredients for a personal identity
offering a framework for effective commerce with the social environment.

Thus, the ethnicity of the newcomer to North America or the long-term
resident or the native person should not be judged in terms of its faithfulness
to the "original" culture. The "original" context has changed and so too will
the content, meaning, and expression of cultural identity. What remains is a
fundamental context upon which to build a self-image, a collective
commitment that provides the context for gaining a sense of mastery over the
social environment.

CONCLUSION

From our analysis of economic, political, and psychological motives for
heritage culture maintenance, two broad conclusions can be drawn that bear
directly on the integration process. First, it would seem that, for the most
part, what motivates minority group members to maintain the heritage
culture in the economic and political sphere is collective action designed to
redress perceived injustice. The tactic would seem to be successful because,
in concert with other disadvantaged groups, notably women, government-
sponsored affirmative action programs have been instituted widely. Such
programs are ideologically opposed to the North American meritocracy with

its focus on the individual, equality of opportunity, and the notion of merit. The rationale for affirmative action, then, is that it won't be necessary once economic and political justice have been achieved. If such an ideal state is indeed reached, then heritage culture maintenance would not be necessary as a mechanism for achieving economic and political justice. Thus it may be useful to view heritage maintenance in the economic and political sphere as temporary and it is hoped, in the long run, unnecessary.

By contrast, heritage culture maintenance for the purposes of self identity would seem to be fundamental. Moreover, maintaining the heritage culture for identity purposes is socially constructive, providing the individual with a framework from which to understand and act effectively in the social environment.

The primacy of culture for self identity may explain, in part, the paradox of the so-called ethnic revival that surfaced in the 1970s. Why were people seeking a more "local" ethnic identity at a time when, because of advanced technology in communication, the world was becoming a "global village"? It may well be that with the information explosion comes the need for a consistent well-structured framework to form the basis of self identity. Culture would seem well-suited to such a purpose.

If the major function of culture is to provide a framework for self identity, this has implications for the integration process. First, it does not require that the cultural framework for ethnic newcomers be true to the "original." That is, "heritage culture" for the second and third generation Greek, Italian, Cuban, or Native person need not, nor is it likely to be, identical to those cultures as they exist in the country of origin, or in some past era. What is important is that the individual be socialized, through a "culture" that provides for a framework from which to define and evaluate "self."

Second, if personal identity is the key issue, then we would not expect ethnicity to be instituted formally in political, economic, and educational institutions. At the same time a cultural framework for identity must provide values that allow the individual to interact effectively with these primary institutions, and these institutions must in turn be respectful of cultural diversity in order to provide an environment for cultures to contribute positively to identity.

Thus, society's major institutions will be reflective of a modern industrialized state with its complex bureaucracy, market economy, high technology, and values based on meritocracy. Ethnic minorities would seem no less committed to such a society than anyone else. From the point of view of heritage culture, then, it would not seem applicable to society's primary institutions, with two major exceptions. First, to the extent that heritage cultures enrich and add new dimensions to "modern technological culture" they must be embraced and, second, every societal institution must be open to the "expression" of culture, or how else can any culture have a positive impact on self identity?

ACKNOWLEDGEMENTS

The preparation of this chapter was supported in part by research grants from the Social Sciences and Humanities Research Council of Canada and the Spencer Foundation.

REFERENCES

Alba, R. D. (1981). The twilight of ethnicity among American Catholics of European ancestry. *Annals of the American Academy of Political Social Science, 454,* 86-97.

Asch, S. E. (1955, November). Opinions and social pressure. *Scientific American,* pp. 31-35.

Bantum, M. (1983). *Racial and ethnic competition.* Cambridge: Cambridge University Press.

Berry, J. W. (1987). Finding identity: Separation, integration, assimilation, or marginality? In L. Driedger (Ed.), *Ethnic Canada: Identities and inequalities.* Toronto: Copp Clark Pitman.

Berry, J. W., Kalin, R., & Taylor, D. M. (1977). *Multiculturalism and ethnic attitudes in Canada.* Ottawa: Minister of Supply and Services.

Byrne, D. (1971). *The attraction paradigm.* New York: Academic Press.

Esman, M. J. (1987). Ethnic politics and economic power. *Comparative Politics, 19,* 395-417.

Festinger, L. (1954). A theory of social comparison processes. *Human Relations, 7,* 117-140.

Gans, H. (1979). Symbolic ethnicity: The future of ethnic groups and culture in America. *Ethnic and Racial Studies, 2,* 1-20.

Geertz, C. (1963). The integrated revolution. In C. Geertz (Ed.), *Old societies and new societies.* Glencoe, IL: The Free Press.

Glazer, N., & Moynihan, D. P. (1970). *Beyond the melting pot* (2nd ed.). Cambridge, MA: MIT Press.

Gordon, M. M. (1964). *Assimilation in American life.* New York: Oxford University Press.

Gordon, M. M. (1981). Models of pluralism: The new American dilemma. *The Annals of the American Academy of Political and Social Science: America as a Multicultural Society, 454,* 178-188.

Greely, A. M. (1974). *Ethnicity in the United States: A preliminary reconnaissance.* New York: Wiley.

Hechter, M. (1975). *Internal colonialism: The Celtic fringe in British national development.* Berkeley: University of California Press.

Hechter, M. (1978). Group formation and the cultural division of labor. *American Journal of Sociology, 84,* 293-318.

Hirschman, C. (1983). America's melting pot reconsidered. *Annual Review of Sociology, 9,* 393-423.

Isaacs, H. (1964). Group identity and political change. *Bulletin of the International House of Japan, April,* 24-25.

Kandel, D. B. (1978). Similarity in real-life adolescent friendship pairs. *Journal of Personality and Social Psychology, 31,* 306-388.

Kerr, C., Dunlop, J. T., Harbison, F., & Myers, C. A. (1964). *Industrialism and industrial man.* New York: Oxford University Press.

Lambert, W. E. (1981). Bilingualism and language acquisition. In H. Winitz (Ed.), *Native language and foreign language acquisition.* New York: The New York Academy of Sciences.

Lambert, W. E. (1984). An overview of issues in immersion education. In *Studies in immersion education: A collection for United States educators.* Sacramento: State Department of Education.

Lambert, W. E., Mermigis, L., & Taylor, D. M. (1986). Greek Canadians' attitudes towards own group and other Canadian ethnic groups: A test of the multiculturalism hypothesis. *Canadian Journal of Behavioral Science, 18*(1), 35-51.

Lambert, W. E., & Taylor, D. M. (1988). Assimilation versus multiculturalism: The views of urban Americans. *Sociological Forum, 3,* 72-88.

Lambert, W. E., & Taylor, D. M. (1990). *Coping with cultural and racial diversity in urban America.* New York: Praeger.

Lambert, W. E., & Tucker, G. R. (1972). *Bilingual education of children: The St. Lambert experiment.* Rowley, MA: Newbury House.

LeVine, R. A., & Campbell, D. T. (1972). *Ethnocentrism: Theories of conflict, ethnic attitudes and group behavior.* New York: Wiley.

Lijphart, A. (1968). *The politics of accommodation: Pluralism and democracy in the Netherlands.* Berkeley: University of California Press.

Manis, J. G., & Meltzer, B. N. (1978). *Symbolic interaction: A reader in social psychology* (3rd. ed.). Boston: Allyn & Bacon.

McEvoy, D. (1987, July). Two views of British Asian retailing in a time of recession. *British Business,* pp. 15-30.

Moghaddam, F. M., & Taylor, D. M. (1987). The meaning of multiculturalism for visible minority immigrant women. *Canadian Journal of Behavioural Science, 19,* 121-136.

Moghaddam, F. M., Taylor, D. M., & Lalonde, R. N. (1987). Individualistic and collective integration strategies among Iranians in Canada. *International Journal of Psychology, 22,* 301-313.

Myrdal, G. (1944). *An American dilemma.* New York: Harper.

Nagel, J. (1987). The ethnic revolution: Emergence of ethnic nationalism. In L. Driedger (Ed.), *Ethnic Canada: Identities and inequalities.* Toronto: Copp Clark Pitman.

Newcomb, T. M. (1961). *The acquaintance process.* New York: Holt, Rinehart and Winston.

Novak, R. D. (1972). *The rise of the unmeltable ethnics.* New York: Macmillan.

O'Bryan, K. G., Reitz, J. G., & Kuplowska, O. (1976). *Non-official languages: A study in Canadian multiculturalism.* Ottawa: Minister Responsible for Multiculturalism, Government of Canada.

Olzak, S. (1983.) Contemporary ethnic mobilization. *Annual Review of Sociology, 9,* 355-374.

Park, R. E. (1950). *Race and culture.* Glencoe, IL.: Free Press.

Park, R. E., & Burgess, E. W. (1969). *Introduction to the science of sociology.* Chicago: University of Chicago Press. (Original work published 1921)

Porter, J. (1965). *The vertical mosaic.* Toronto: University of Toronto Press.

Roberts, L. W., & Clifton, R. A. (1982). Exploring the ideology of Canadian multiculturalism. *Canadian Public Policy, VII:1,* 88-94.

Sears, D. O. (1988). Symbolic racism. In P. A. Katz & D. A. Taylor (Eds.), *Eliminating racism: Profiles in controversy.* New York: Plenum Press.

Shils, E. (1957). Primordial, personal, sacred, and civil ties. *British Journal of Sociology, June,* 130-145.

Simard, L. M. (1981). Cross cultural interaction: potential invisible barriers. *Journal of Social Psychology, 113,* 171-192.

Stryber, S., & Stathon, A. (1985). Symbolic interaction and role theory. In G. Lindzey & E. Aronson (Eds.), *Handbook of social psychology* (3rd. ed., Vol. 1). New York: Random House.

Sumner, W. G. (1906). *Folkways.* New York: Ginn.

Taylor, D. M. (1981). Stereotypes and intergroup relations. In R. C. Gardner & R. Kalin (Eds.), *A Canadian social psychology of ethnic relations.* Toronto: Methuen.

Taylor, D. M., & Lalonde, R. N. (1987). Ethnic stereotypes: A psychological analysis. In L. Driedger (Ed.), *Ethnic Canada: Identities and inequalities.* Toronto: Copp Clark Pitman.

Taylor, D. M., & Moghaddam, F. M. (1987). *Theories of intergroup relations: International social psychological perspectives.* New York: Praeger.

Taylor, D. M., Moghaddam, F. M., & Tchoryk-Pelletier, P. (1989). *Dimensions of heritage maintenance in Québec.* Unpublished manuscript, McGill University, Montreal.

Taylor, D. M., & Simard, L. M. (1979). Ethnic identity and intergroup relations. In D. J. Lee (Ed.), *Emerging ethnic boundaries.* Ottawa: University of Ottawa Press.

Taylor, D. M., Wright, S. C., Moghaddam, F. M., & Lalonde, R. N. (1990). The Personal/Group discrimination discrepancy: Perceiving my group, but not myself, to be a target for discrimination. *Personality and Social Psychology Bulletin, 16,* 254-262.

Young, R. (1986). Affirmative action and the problem of substantive racism. In M. W. Combs & J. Gruhl (Eds.), *Affirmative action: Theory, analysis, and prospects.* Jefferson, NC: McFarland.

2 Language Attitudes: Discursive, Contextual, and Gerontological Considerations

Howard Giles
University of California, Santa Barbara
Nikolas Coupland
University of Wales College of Cardiff

Prior to the 1970s, the study of language in its social context was conducted primarily by sociolinguists, sociologists, ethnographers, and anthropologists, having various degrees of influence upon each other (see, for example, Giglioli, 1972; Gumperz & Hymes, 1972; Pride & Holmes, 1972). In the late 1970s, a "social psychology of language" clearly emerged in its own right (e.g., Giles & St. Clair, 1979; Markova, 1978) and is now beginning to have an influence not only on the aforementioned language and society disciplines (e.g., Fasold, 1984; Trudgill, 1986) but also in the development of social psychology itself (e.g., Hewstone, Stroebe, Codol, & Stephenson, 1988; Hogg & Abrams, 1988). A considerable proportion of the social psychology of language is, arguably, devoted to the study of language attitudes, the origins of which, in large part, can be found in the Lambert, Hodgson, Gardner, and Fillenbaum (1960) study introducing the matched-guise technique (MGT). Put another way, many of the roots of the social psychology of language and, in turn, its influence in social science, can be traced to this seminal investigation.

In this chapter, then, we overview the MGT and the subsequent contributions made to its development by Lambert and his associates, as well as others, empirically and methodologically. We discuss the recent attention given to theoretical matters in the language attitudes domain pointing to various lacunae as they appear to us. In this regard, we introduce a process model of the matched-guise paradigm highlighting some limitations and laying down priorities for the future. Finally, we consider the MGT in gerontological context, arguing that the role of language in intergenerational communication is but another facet of biculturalism and bilingualism, an understanding of which affords us some insights into the psychosociolinguistic construction of the lifespan.

THE MATCHED-GUISE TECHNIQUE: ITS DEVELOPMENT AND VALUE

Lambert was interested initially in interethnic attitudes in Montreal, more specifically, how French and English Canadians perceived each other. Having been disinclined to taking people's overt ascriptions to him in public (via direct questionnaire procedures) as a true reflection of their privately held views, he formulated the MGT as an attempt to elicit the latter. The procedure was built on the assumption that speech style can trigger certain social categorizations which will lead to a set of group-related trait inferences. In other words, hearing a voice which is classified as French-Canadian will predispose listeners to inferring he or she is of a particular kind of personality. Hence, balanced bilinguals were tape recorded reading a standard passage of prose in French and in English. These "guises" were transferred to a stimulus tape and each speaker's versions were placed in nonadjacent positions on the tape so as to avoid identification of the same speaker. Care was taken to ensure that the guises were perceived to be authentic; in other words, independent listeners should believe the English guise to derive from an English Canadian and not from a French Canadian speaking in English. In the MGT, considerable care is thus expended on issues of stimulus control. Paralinguistic features of voice (such as pitch and speech rate) are uniform throughout the recordings, as are reading style and expressed personality. Thus, it is argued that reactions to the speakers are dependent solely on social expectations based on language cues.

Listener judges are asked to listen to a series of *different* speakers on audiotape, form an impression of these speakers (if they can) after they have heard each passage, and frame these appraisals along a series of person perception rating scales (e.g., competence traits such as intelligence, ambition, and confidence, and social attractiveness-integrity traits such as sincerity, friendliness, and generosity) provided for them on a questionnaire. Judges are asked to undertake this task in the same way as people gaining first impressions about speakers they hear (but cannot see) in, say, a bar behind them or on the radio. In the original Lambert et al. study, the judges were French- and English-Canadian students and the guises representative of these groups. Although there were many facets to this study, and hence a variety of findings emerged, for our purposes the main results were that

English-Canadian listeners judged speakers of their own group more favorably on half of the 14 traits, whereas the French-Canadian listeners not only went along in the same evaluative direction, but accentuated this to the tune of favoring this "outgroup" over their own on 10 of 14 traits.

The value of this initial MGT study is at least sevenfold. First, Lambert and his associates invented a rigorous and elegant method for eliciting private attitudes (see Lambert, Anisfeld, & Yeni-Komshian, 1965) which controlled for many extraneous variables. Second, the findings underscored the important role of language (and code- and dialect-choice) in impression formation. Third, the study laid the foundations for an interface between sociolinguistics and sociopsychological analyses of language and was an important factor in establishing the cross-disciplinary field of "language attitudes" (Shuy & Fasold, 1973). Indeed, Labov's (1966) exploration into this arena by means of his "subjective reaction test" owes much to the innovations of Lambert. Fourth, the original study spawned an enormous number of studies worldwide, particularly in Wales (Giles, 1989), Australia (Callan & Gallois, 1986), the United States (Sebastian & Ryan, 1985; Williams, 1976), and more recently in Spain (Woolard, 1989), and The Netherlands (van Hout & Knops, 1988). Indeed, an array of journal special issues (Cooper, 1974, 1975; Giles & Edwards, 1983) and reviews in texts for the field (Edwards, 1989; Giles & Powesland, 1975; Ryan & Giles, 1982; Ryan, Giles, & Hewstone, 1988) have since emerged, and the importance of the Lambert et al. paper can be gauged by the fact that Tajfel (1959) published a critique of it a year before the original was published! Fifth, the investigation fuelled study on the "ubiquitous Québecois" in the ethnic literature of the 1960s and 1970s and assisted in laying down the foundations also for a distinctive Canadian social psychology (Gardner & Kalin, 1981). Sixth, the dependent variables utilized in the study gave rise to the now pervasive and relabelled judgmental clusters of status versus solidarity traits (see Edwards & Jacobsen, 1987) as well as fuelling the notion of "group denigration." Finally, but not least, the study and its empirical aftermath inspired a series of productive and innovative scholars to pursue research in the social psychology of language.

THE MATCHED-GUISE TECHNIQUE: LATER EMPIRICAL AND THEORETICAL DEVELOPMENTS

The value of the initial study notwithstanding, it was not a "one-time" affair. Lambert and his colleagues were fully involved in a whole program of research involving the MGT over the years, and nurtured its development in many ways. For instance, Lambert examined the roles of listener variables such as age (Anisfeld & Lambert, 1964; Lambert, Frankel, & Tucker, 1966) as well as reported on interactions between speakers' and listeners' ethnicity and gender (see Lambert, 1967). He moved beyond "static" varieties of speech styles towards evaluations of language shifts as manifested in convergence and divergence (Bourhis, Giles, & Lambert, 1975) and showed how language could affect other forms of social decision-making in an educational context (Frender, Brown, & Lambert, 1970; Frender & Lambert, 1972; Seligman, Tucker, & Lambert, 1972). In addition, the original effects were monitored from time to time to appraise the influence of changing sociocultural and historical climates in quasi-replication studies (Genesee & Holobow, 1989; Marzurkewich, Fister-Stoga, Mawle, Somers, & Thibaudeau, 1986), and the generalized role of language in social evaluation was substantiated by introducing variants of the technique across a range of black (Tucker & Lambert, 1969), French (Lambert, Giles, & Albert, 1976; Lambert, Giles, & Picard, 1975), and Jewish (Anisfeld, Bogo, & Lambert, 1962) communities in the United States, and in Israel (Lambert et al., 1965) and the Philippines (Tucker, 1968).

In the 1970s, there came an explosion of empirical interest in the matched-guise technique across the world and many (interdependent) elements of it were diversified from the original paradigm as exemplified in Figure 2-1 (for explicit reviews, see Bradac, 1990; Giles, Hewstone, Ryan, & Johnson, 1987).

Albeit diversified in one way or another (see Figure 2-1), work in the basic MGT mold continues today and much of it, as can be expected, is descriptive to the extent it lays out valuable baseline data about intergroup attitudes in particular sociolinguistic communities. As essential as such groundwork is, the area was, arguably (Giles, Hewstone, & Ball, 1983), being

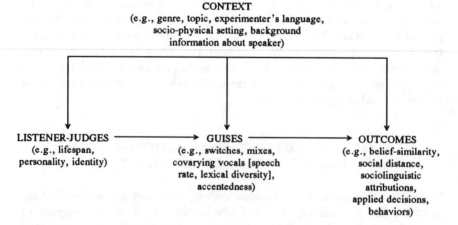

Fig. 2-1. Examples of MGT variables recently studied.

overrepresented by unrelated studies in vastly different cultures, sociolinguistic conditions, and situational and procedural domains, making other than very generalized principles (see Bradac, 1990) impossible to infer. In large part as a reaction to this atheoretical trend, the 1980s witnessed the development of an array of diverse models which either focussed on language attitude issues per se or incorporated their complexity into frameworks oriented towards larger communication concerns. To date, these models have not been overviewed *critically*. Space herein precludes following this important quest, yet we can provide some conceptual order into the evergrowing theoretical elaborations by overviewing the essence of these models in terms of five overarching questions that they have (for the most part, implicitly) been addressing. These are:

1. Are there other possible generative mechanisms operating other than the original conception (see also Robinson, 1972) of language $\longrightarrow$ social categorization $\longrightarrow$ trait inferences? Berger and Bradac (1982) contended that there were indeed four other models operating, some more cognitively complex than others; each one was dedicated to the pursuit of "uncertainty reduction" (UCR in Figure 2-2). These scholars argue that an important social objective in initial interactions is to reduce uncertainty about what the other is like psychologically, and how to respond to them appropriately. Language cues are used therefore as a means of increasing predictability (e.g., "She sounds rather informal and hence I can act more casually here.") with perceived similarity being an important mediator in all cases. Gudykunst and Ting-Toomey (1990) have suggested that these models are operative in different social contexts (see Figure 2-2) and can be located in the two-dimensional space of "interindividual" (high vs. low) and "intergroup" (high vs. low) social interactions. One extreme is where interaction is based solely on the moods, personalities, and temperaments of the participants, whereas the other extreme is dependent entirely on their social group characteristics (see Tajfel & Turner, 1979). Some interactions, as for example between spouses, can be based on their own idiosyncratic attributes or on their gender-linked characteristics, or on both.

2. Are language cues hierarchically perceived and evaluated? Gallois, Callan, and Johnstone (1984) argued that different situations induce us to afford different vocal cues salience over others. Their model suggests that in intercultural situations, ethnolinguistic cues usually assume primacy over others, especially when social distance between the groups is perceived to be high. When social distance, however, is medium or low, attributes such as gender and contextual considerations assume greater importance, especially when expectations and appropriacy are violated. In other words, this model attends to which cues assume importance, when, and how.

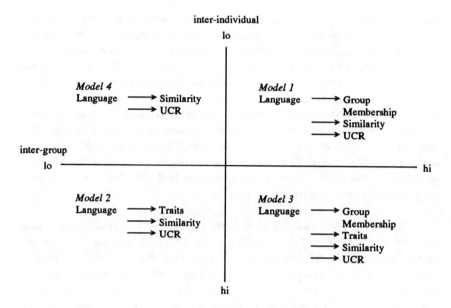

Fig. 2-2. Impression formation process models. (Schematized from Gudykunst & Ting-Toomey, 1990)

3. Can language attitude situations be organized meaningfully in terms of large-scale social forces? Ryan, Giles, and Sebastian (1982) speculated that language attitude "situations" could be placed in a dynamic and interrelated, two-dimensional space of standardness-nonstandardness and vitality (increasing vs. decreasing). The latter dimension refers to sociostructural factors (status, demography, and institutional support) which can be to a group's advantage or not. Hence, for example, language attitude situations located in the quadrant "decreasing vitality and nonstandard" might include the Welsh, Breton, and many ethnolinguistic minorities in the United States.

4. Are there different language attitude profiles, and if so, are they a function of perceptions of the intergroup forces prevailing, and the nature of immediate situations? From the literature, these same authors (Ryan et al., 1982) identified four different patterns of the social evaluation of contrastive speech styles in majority/minority settings in terms of the dependent variables of status and solidarity. Pattern A is where there is a preference by both groups for the dominant group's speech patterns and Pattern B is where there is a status preference for the dominant group and a solidarity preference for the ingroup. Pattern C is characterized by ingroup preferences by both parties and Pattern D occurs where there is a consensually agreed upon status preference for the dominant group and a solidarity preference for the subordinate group. Subsequently, Ryan, Hewstone, and Giles (1984)

associated these patterns (and other finer distinctions within them) with different historical phases of the relationships between groups in contact. An important point emerging from this rather complex analysis was that the same profile may function sociopsychologically quite differently for the groups involved, and that different members of the same social group could express the patterns variously (see also Giles & Johnson, 1987). Regarding situational specificity, more recently it has also been argued (Giles & Johnson, 1986) that such patterns are dependent on messages' relationships to listeners' social identities (central vs. peripheral) as well as the group-stressingness of the evaluative context in which they occur (Giles & Ryan, 1982).

5. Are language attitudes meaningfully related to other levels of analysis and/or forms of communicative behavior? Bradac (1990) has also related specific language attitudes towards different forms of language behaviors (see Figure 2-3). He hypothesizes that speakers' convergences towards listeners on normatively valued dimensions will be favorably perceived on dimensions of status and solidarity, whereas the complete opposite will happen when divergence accrues on nonnormatively valued dimensions. Street and Hopper (1982) have also offered a conceptual model wherein such accommodations not only affect reception and social judgements but also influence the kinds of accommodative tactics the recipients will evince in return in context. Finally, Giles and Street (1985) argued that language attitudes often mediate communicative acts so as to effect positive self-presentations on many occasions, valued ingroup presentations on others, and even healthy "couple-presentations" (see Giles & Fitzpatrick, 1984) on still others; Hewstone and Giles (1986) developed this in a more relationally declining direction by modelling intergroup communication breakdown as being mediated by sociolinguistic stereotypes (i.e., language attitudes).

| | SPEAKER'S LINGUISTIC | |
	CONVERGENCE	DIVERGENCE
NORMATIVE ADHERENCE	+ve status and +ve solidarity	+ve status but -ve solidarity
NON-ADHERENCE	-ve status but +ve solidarity	-ve status and -ve solidarity

Fig. 2-3. Language attitude outcomes as a function of interpersonal accommodation tactics and norm adherence-nonadherence. (Schematized from Bradac, 1990)

The inductive and deductive validity of some of the aforementioned models, and the dire need for related empirical explorations notwithstanding, we have seen a much needed advance in the development of language attitude theory to complement the plethora of descriptive studies which have emerged over the years. Elsewhere, we have tried to integrate these language attitude models with other intercultural phenomena and processes with a view to providing a cohesive and predictive theoretical framework (Giles, Leets, & Coupland, 1990).

THE MATCHED-GUISE TECHNIQUE
AS A STAGED DISCURSIVE EVENT

Given our caricature of the current and healthy state-of-the-art, whither next, constructively? The MGT has not been without its critics over the years and we have been found among them (Giles & Ryan, 1982) as well as among its advocates (Giles & Bourhis, 1976). Questions have, legitimately, been raised about the technique's sterility in terms of its task and relational requirements, the lack of programmatic, longitudinal work and/or linguistic sophistication, the ignoring of the role of message content, and so forth. While these limitations could be addressed in individual methodological modifications, we believe exciting and innovative prospects for the future are possible if, at least as an alternative design, we embrace a *discursive* perspective; we should adopt an approach whereby social meanings (and in this case, language attitudes) are assumed to be inferred by means of *constructive, interpretive* processes drawing upon social actors' reservoirs of contextual and textual knowledge. This is a perspective which has, of course, much in common with constructivist (O'Keefe & Delia, 1985) and pragmatic (Austin, 1962) orientations. Indeed, the MGT researchers seem to have been reluctant to move beyond a static, input-output, mechanistic framework; perhaps scholars have been blinkered in part by the real-time design characteristic of the traditional methods, such as the practice of having listener-judges commence their evaluations a matter of seconds after hearing a stimulus voice (see Williams, 1976). The discursive approach would attend to *processes* of meaning generation and the way we come to construct our language attitudes, inside and beyond established MGT practices, and would explore alternative (undoubtedly less elegant) methods, through which these processes are amenable to analysis.

In this vein, we would wish to re-explore the MGT paradigm as a *series of interlocking processes* operating under the constraints and influences of macro- and micro-contextual factors, as in Figure 2-4. This figure does not establish detailed flow paths through the systems, but merely seeks to highlight relevant psychosociolinguistic considerations. It invites us also to consider processes in the *production* of vocal stimuli— the sociolinguistic heartland of the MGT. In our experience, the "quality" of guises in most MGT studies is remarkably high in the sense of being reliably convincing and authentic-sounding to audiences who are not informed initially of the guising subterfuge. But given that speech style is a multidimensional configuration of phonological forms, prosodic, paralinguistic, and rhetorical selections, questions arise as to *what it may be* in the stimulus materials that possibly generates social evaluations. It is apparent that the control imposed by the reading of a prepared text is far from total. Whatever the source data, the construction of a guise implicates the full range of discursive encoding processes, with the reader/speaker actively building a contextualized performance. Figure 2-4 suggests that this constructive process is necessarily carried through by virtue of an actor-guiser's social, linguistic, and cultural competence (both at recognizing and producing stereotyped social and stylistic categories) to invoke a *persona* adequately matched to the task requirements.

Let us take the case of genre, that by its unfolding also underscores the point (see feedback loops in Figure 2-4) that these processes are not mutually exclusive. MGT designs have variously presented vocal stimuli as "naturally occurring speech," or "readings," while almost invariably actually deriving stimuli from the reading of prepared written texts. Though it may be true that highly skilled readers and actors can approximate many critical characteristics of spontaneous speech working from a written text, the disparities between the two modes (reading aloud and spontaneous speech) are widely recognized (see, for example, Labov, 1972, who takes these two modes to distinguish key stylistic varieties). Our point is again not to quibble about the "realism" of read-as-if-spoken stimuli. Rather, it seems important to recognize that generically different texts are, conventionally in our literacy-fetishist society, subject to quite different *evaluative* considerations. Where a spoken text is known (or guessed) to derive from a written source, it enters an evaluative paradigm wherein quite different expectations are held of its encoding, in terms of phrasing, intonation, fluency, and possibly rate characteristics. Predictably, read texts will attract higher or lower competence evaluations along quite different dimensions from spontaneous spoken texts, perhaps reflecting the social norms for "good reading." (Reading aloud is, in fact, a highly restricted contemporary cultural genre, and its pedagogic associations may account for our evaluations of it.) Much more broadly, however, we should anticipate that considerations of genre will *always* impinge upon social evaluations of stimulus materials. Utterances cannot be heard devoid of a supposed (if not known) generic context— desultory conversation, personal narrative, public lecture, confession, account,

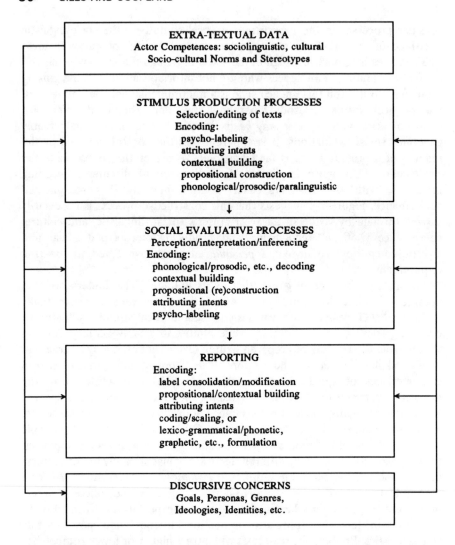

Fig. 2-4. A model of discursive processes in MGT designs.

etc.— and stylistic characteristics such as rate or dialect naturally cross-reference with the goals and demands associated with each of these.

A precondition for vocal evaluative research must in future, therefore, be to determine how stimulus speakers operationalize vocal dimensions, and to transcend mere "checking" of stimulus materials for authenticity. In fact, the guising of social categories (by actors and lay people alike) deserves to become an independent research area. Until this is done, it may even be, for example, that the instruction to stimulus producers to "increase rate" may be operationalized by readers as a need to increase perceptual dynamism, or efficiency, or competence along dimensions that even they are not conscious of manipulating. Take age as another example. Vocal features which can mark advanced age (e.g., perturbation of fundamental frequency, creaky or "thin" voices; see Helfrich, 1979) appear to carry within them inferences of weakness and incapacity. Those creating aged guises by these means render the evaluative task precisely circular; a guise is created to invoke frailty which is then mapped onto an age categorization as an evaluative attribute. Only more rigorous attention to the goals and strategies of guise producers, to the social psychology and sociolinguistics of their art, can clarify the first discursive phase of the MGT upon which the entire enterprise rests.

Moving to the second process in Figure 2-4, it is an established tenet of discourse analysis that meanings arise from the interplay of communicative acts and the full range of factors in their contextualization (see also, Bransford & Johnson, 1973; Loftus, 1975; Loftus & Loftus, 1976; Thorndyke, 1977). Another is that texts are never *neutral;* note from our introduction that this is an avowed and valued control feature of the MGT! Texts inevitably seek to establish or subvert, through complex and often inconsistent means, rhetorical, political, and ideological positions. This may seem an exaggerated claim in the case of texts we researchers may have composed *explicitly* to be uncontroversial or even trivial, and to be politically and socially inert. But to take a case in point, how is it possible to generate a text that is "age-neutral"?

Recently, we tried to do precisely this in a matched-guise study (Giles, Coupland, Henwood, Harriman, & Coupland, 1989) which required listeners to evaluate speakers varying in terms of speech rate (fast, medium, or slow), accent (standard or nonstandard), and age (young adult vs. elderly). The passage spoken was supposedly an extract from an interview where the speaker was talking at length about his car. Adopting the traditional rating measures, we found that few effects emerged for speaker's age. However, in addition, we asked textually-interpretative and attributionally-qualitative questions. We found when providing listeners with extracts from the text such as the speaker saying, "I didn't know what to think," they interpreted this variously depending on the speaker's age. Hence, this was more likely to be attributed to his being "confused" if elderly (therein, perceived to be in his early 60s), but if young (early 30s), then it was much more likely to be attributed to his wishing to withhold judgment given the complexity of issues at hand. In other words, listeners are interpreting the same utterances in schema-consistent fashion, and agistly so. When asked why they rated the speaker as they had done, despite the fact that he said exactly the same thing in each condition, he was described as: "arrogant and pompous" when a young standard speaker; "trying to impress" or "using the words of others" when nonstandard and young; "egocentric, living in the past, and talking of trivia" when standard and elderly; and even "stupid, and losing his grip" when nonstandard and elderly. Even more interestingly, when invited to substantiate these accounts by recourse to pinpointing textual information, respondents would very often highlight exactly the *same* speaker utterances to justify their (very disparate) claims!

Texts themselves therefore, no less than the vocal styles that may realize them, can never be neutral; they are interpreted and subsequent actions accounted for on the basis of preexisting social schemata. It seems clear then that whatever "social evaluations" are produced in relation to "stimuli" may be better conceived of as responses to textual and contextual interconnections, as indeed would be the case in any face-to-face encounter. It is also significant that attempts to minimize or deny the contextualization of stimuli are likely to fail given the natural propensity of communicators to *generate* contextual dimensions, implicatures, or propositional bridges as an inevitable component of the interpretation of texts. Hence, language attitudes are not simply passive reactions to blocks of vocal sounds, as listener-judges are cognitively active at processing messages according to activated social representations. It follows then that the more denuded a stimulus text is of contextual specificity, the more assiduous, variable, and creative will be the contextual inventiveness of listener-judges.

The evaluative process, as indicated in Figure 2-4, needs to be separated conceptually from its "reporting" as language attitudes are, after all, appraisals conveyed in a particular context. Indeed, the reporting can come about in many different forms, and may in reality never have been transmitted or even mindfully appraised (Palmerino, Langer, & McGillis, 1984). Recent work in Britain has begun to challenge— if not deconstruct— the very notion of "attitude" as currently measured and conceptualized in social psychology. This is the very bedrock upon which language attitude studies are based. Potter and Wetherell (1987) point not only to the variability inherent in people's social attitudes when they are expressed in talk (even within the same conversation), but also question whether attitudes *can* be rarified in the minds of individuals *away* from the assumed objects to which they are targeted in the "outside world." As we know from a myriad of studies in the social psychology of language (Street & Hopper, 1982), our judgements about how people actually sound and speak— the object of language attitudes— can involve a constantly redefining, social construction process and be dependent on social cognitive biases (Thakerar & Giles, 1981). Hence, "language varieties" on the one hand, and "attitudes" on the other, are *symbolically* related in a subjective sense, and are *not* really dichotomous entities as they are caricatured in the MGT paradigm. Billig (1987) also considers attitudes in a wider historical context *as positions in an argument* and embedded in particular social controversies. Attitudes in *this* sense are not only explicit appraisals pro or con a position but also include an implicit stance against a counterposition. Moreover, justifications and criticism are viewed as part-and-parcel of attitudes— and not epiphenomena derived from them— and should become sharpened and modified as the argumentative context changes. Although not directed originally in any sense towards MGT studies explicitly, developing further these two approaches for our present "reporting" phase should elucidate how we negotiate our language attitudes rhetorically and interactively, and should lead to more discourse-based and observational studies to complement the traditional MGT design.

In summary, we have paid, arguably, too little attention to the processes of guise construction and selection, have had too little appreciation of the cognitive activities involved in recipiency, and have had too little understanding of the complex interrelationships between language and attitudes, and the functions of these in discourse. Furthermore, we have paid insufficient attention to the role of *emotional* construals and expressions in MGT contexts (cf. Bowers, Metts, & Duncanson, 1985; Scherer, 1988). The affective connotations associated with linguistically triggered self- and other-categorizations (Dijker, 1987, and Garza & Henniger, 1987, respectively) and the emotionally-linked attributions we make about speakers who are either stigmatized (Weiner, Perry, & Magnusson, 1988) or illegitimated, or advantaged or privileged, may have considerable mediating significance in formulating language attitude patterns. That said, the future suggests exciting, radical shifts in the study of language attitudes in the direction of discourse and rhetoric, and a new generation of MGT studies aimed at elucidating ongoing interpretive processes (Giles, Henwood, Coupland, Harriman, & Coupland, 1989).

THE MGT IN GERONTOLOGICAL CONTEXT: AGING AS A MULTICULTURAL PROCESS

At various stages in the foregoing, age has been mentioned as a variable and we have seen the potential listeners have for agist processing of messages. Indeed, much of the social psychology of language and sociolinguistics is agist in its dominant emphases (Giles & Ryan, 1986) and this is manifest in traditionally youthful guises, and youthful listeners (see, however, Ryan & Cole, 1990). Moreover, when age is attended to, it often derives from a deficit and decremental model (Coupland & Coupland, 1990). But our intention is not simply to score ready-made "gerontological points." Rather, this forum allows us to make the case that following through with the matched-guise paradigm in gerontological settings has convinced us that aging across the lifespan is a continuous *interculturing* process. More specifically, when we talk of intergenerational communication we are talking of intercultural relations: different (internally differentiated) cultural groups who possess different values and beliefs about talk (Giles, Coupland, & Wiemann, in press), different social and existential agendas (Coupland, Coupland, Giles, Henwood, & Wiemann, 1988), and different language codes (Coupland & Coupland, 1990). Yet, few attempts at (if you like) "bilingualism" involving different adult age groups are apparent. When the young do take the initiative in speaking the language of the elderly, it can often be misguided and can have disturbing consequences, both at the individual and collective levels.

The aphoristic cartoon by Ashleigh Brilliant (1986, p. 67) below perhaps reflects folklinguistic wisdom, in many Western cultures anyway, about how a thoughtful, sensitive young person needs to attune communicatively when interacting with his or her elders. We and others have observed that some young people "overaccommodate" to the elderly (e.g., Caporael & Culbertson, 1986; Coupland, Coupland, Giles, & Henwood, 1988): They become overly polite, warm, and grammatically and/or ideationally simple. This of course can cause some elderly people irritation, anger, and frustration, and, despite the often nurturing intentions of the young, can lead to severed communication. On the other hand, we have also found, admittedly in a limited data set, that many elderly people spend about one-sixth of their time in initial intergenerational encounters disclosing personally painful information about themselves (Coupland, Coupland, Giles, Henwood, & Wiemann, 1988). Although this is textually managed quite well by young interlocutors, at least in procedural terms, and often solicited by them in the

© ASHLEIGH BRILLIANT 1985.

POT-SHOTS NO. 3501.

WHEN YOU PLAN
A JOURNEY
FROM
YOUR MIND
INTO MINE,

REMEMBER
TO
ALLOW FOR
THE
TIME
DIFFERENCE.

first place, it is often evaluated by young people in ways that we would interpret as being "underaccommodative" and attributed negatively as elderly egocentrism, social insensitivity, and the like. That said, we believe there is much functional significance in this elderly lack of accommodation as it translates into their garnering social control and eliciting outwardly sympathetic, supportive, and flattering responses from the young: It can be viewed as self-handicapping (Arkin & Baumgardner, 1985), though it is often a rational reflection of their life circumstances and the events (very often painful) they have endured (Coupland, Coupland, Giles, Henwood, & Wiemann, 1988).

Another potential process intrudes here and this derives theoretically from Turner's (1987) self-stereotyping theory. When group identity (in our case, elderliness) becomes salient for whatever contextual reason, people not only depersonalize and stereotype a relevant outgroup, they also stereotype themselves. In other words, they take on characteristics they believe (rightly or wrongly) to be prototypical of the social group to which they themselves belong. In pilot studies with Lindsay St. Clair, we have observed that when age is made salient (e.g., by overaccommodating to the elderly, making visible a magazine attending to aging decrements) elderly folk will, compared to a control condition, look, move, sound, think, talk, and account "older"; this is a self-stereotyping phenomenon we call "instant aging." Of course, societal cues abound beyond the interactional linguistic cues which make age constantly salient for the elderly and, more often than not, in negative ways (cf. processes in the telling and eliciting of chronological age; see Coupland, Coupland, & Giles, 1989). Hence, as attributional principles would attest, hearing enough and different people in various contexts inform you indirectly by overaccommodations that "you're past it," will ultimately induce many a susceptible recipient to come to accept this as reality.

By the time we reach retirement age many folk will have been well primed to accepting the above sociolinguistically framed messages. As Baker's (1985) data show, young people (in the United States anyway) feel that a person's societal status decreases linearly from 30 years of age until the mid-80s, and we have shown recently that seeking information from others is also linearly related to the target's age (Franklyn-Stokes, Harriman, Giles, & Coupland, 1988; Ng, Giles, & Moody, 1989). Stereotypes of the middle-aged also impute negative competence and in a recent study with Azja Henzle we found not only that young undergraduates had a tremendous reservoir of stereotypes of middle-aged people, but that the majority of them pertained to sensory and physical decrement, as well as the keen desire of middle-aged people to look younger than they were! But agist assumptions about energy and competence are also not infrequent among the over-30s (see Giles & Condor, 1988) and more than some of us collude in proffering such myths through humor, accounting for others' and our own disappointments, failures, and so forth.

This self-generating collusion is doubtless an important (de)constructive element in our physical and psychological decline and demise.

Hence, language attitudes mediate *both* the young's conceptions of the elderly's interpretive and cognitive competences as well as the elderly's construals of their own capacities. As regards the young, this can be manifest in overaccommodations, the sociolinguistic meanings of which fuel elderly helplessness, a negative personal and social identity, and perceived, actual, and "instant" aging. It can also be manifest perhaps in the solicitation of painful self-disclosures from the elderly within the precincts of behavioral confirmation (see Snyder, 1981). Both these processes and especially also the spontaneous evocation of elderly painful self-disclosure will transactively result in a vicious psychosociolinguistic circle. Exceptions obviously exist and the collective Grey Panthers may be a case in point. Nevertheless, the plain truth of the matter is that language attitudes are a potent force in the construction of aging, and indirectly hasten mortality. If we reexamine Ashleigh Brilliant's cartoon, we can see that taking "account of time" should be acknowledging that the generational groups derive from different cultures, and that time does not necessarily have to equate with "decay." Indeed, acknowledgement of biculturalism should put us on the road at least to effective bilingualism.

EPILOGUE

The MGT has blossomed into a massive area now cross-disciplinarily and is at the core of the social psychology of language which has its tendrils in many subdisciplines of the study of language in society. The area as we have reviewed it has exploded empirically and theoretically, and many exciting prospects, discursively, rhetorically, and no doubt in other directions, are open to us. Lambert (e.g., 1980) always counselled us about investing our academic energies in solving real social problems. One of the issues we have to confront as lay individuals is how to cope with a finite lifespan and our transient and ambiguous role in reality. We are forced unwittingly into a succession of invisible, cultural stages, and few of us become multicultural in this sense or have the "hardiness" to construe achieving it as a challenge (cf. Kobasa & Puccetti, 1983). Even if this is beyond our remedial telescope at present, we must become more bilingual between generations, and more urgently, now that our society is becoming "greyer." Indeed, consideration of intercultural communication models of immigrants' adaptation into a host culture may be theoretically valuable for pursuing our lifespan concerns here (see Kim, 1988).

Yet the last thing Lambert probably had in mind when he conceived of the MGT was the sociolinguistic construction of aging and death, but this diversity is the legacy which seminal contributions attract; and as this volume attests, it is but one of them in so many grossly different areas of bilingualism. But put another way, we can see that psychosociolinguistic studies are not simply paper-and-pencil, mike-and-recorder tasks. They can tackle life and death issues, as voice may be as potent a cue to psychosociological and context age (Rubin, 1986) as ever it has been to chronological age, and thereby have enormous implications for trait attribution, social decision-making, and interactional strategies. Indeed, as we have argued, language in both reception and production can, bluntly, be a killer. This allows us nearer to having the courage and persistence which Lambert wants us to have, to prepare ourselves to offer solutions to important problems. Increasing the quality as well as the quantity of life demands its place on this agenda.

ACKNOWLEDGEMENTS

This chapter is based, in part, on research funded by the Economic and Social Research Council (ESRC, UK) Ref. #G00222002. Ashleigh Brilliant epigrams, Pot-Shots, and Brilliant Thoughts used by permission of the author, Ashleigh Brilliant, 117 West Valerio St., Santa Barbara, CA 93101. We are extremely grateful to Allan Reynolds for his thorough editorial feedback and suggestions.

REFERENCES

Anisfeld, M., Bogo, N., & Lambert, W. E. (1962). Evaluational reactions to accented English speech. *Journal of Abnormal and Social Psychology, 65*, 223-231.

Anisfeld, M., & Lambert, W. E. (1964). Evaluational reactions of bilingual and monolingual children to spoken languages. *Journal of Abnormal and Social Psychology, 69*, 89-97.

Arkin, R. M., & Baumgardner, H. (1985). Self-handicapping. In J. H. Harvey & G. Weary (Eds.), *Attribution: Basic issues and applications*. Orlando, FL: Academic.

Austin, J. L. (1962). *How to do things with words*. New York: Oxford University Press.

Baker, P. M. (1985). The status of age: Preliminary results. *Journal of Gerontology, 40*, 506-508.

Berger, C. R., & Bradac, J. J. (1982). *Language and social knowledge*. London: Edward Arnold.

Billig, M. (1987). *Arguing and thinking: A rhetorical approach to social psychology*. Cambridge: Cambridge University Press.

Bourhis, R. Y., Giles, H., & Lambert, W. E. (1975). Social consequences of accommodating one's style of speech: A cross-national investigation. *International Journal of the Sociology of Language, 6*, 55-72.

Bowers, J. T., Metts, S. M., & Duncanson, W. T. (1985). Emotion and interpersonal communication. In M. L. Knapp & G. R. Miller (Eds.), *The handbook of interpersonal communication*. Beverly Hills: Sage.

Bradac, J. J. (1990). Language attitudes and impression formation. In H. Giles & W. P. Robinson (Eds.), *The handbook of language and social psychology*. Chichester: Wiley.

Bransford, J. D., & Johnson, M. K. (1973). Considerations of some problems of comprehension. In W. G. Chase (Ed.), *Visual information processing*. New York: Academic.

Brilliant, A. (1986). *All I want is a warm bed and a kind word and unlimited power: Even more brilliant thoughts*. Santa Barbara: Woolbridge Press.

Callan, V. J., & Gallois, C. (1986). Anglo-Australians' and immigrants' attitudes toward language and accent: A review of experimental and survey research. *International Migration Review, 11*, 48-69.

Caporael, L. R., & Culbertson, G. H. (1986). Verbal response modes of baby talk and other speech at institutions for the aged. *Language and Communication, 6*, 99-112.

Cooper, R. L. (Ed.). (1974). Language attitudes: I. *International Journal of the Sociology of Language, 3*.

Cooper, R. L. (Ed.). (1975). Language attitudes: II. *International Journal of the Sociology of Language, 6*.

Coupland, N., & Coupland, J. (1990). Language and later life: The diachrony predicament. In H. Giles & W. P. Robinson (Eds.), *The handbook of language and social psychology*. Chichester: Wiley.

Coupland, N., Coupland, J., & Giles, H. (1989). Telling age in later life: Identity and face implications. *Text, 9*, 129-151.

Coupland, N., Coupland, J., Giles, H., & Henwood, K. (1988). Accommodating the elderly: Invoking and extending a theory. *Language in Society, 17*, 1-41.

Coupland, N., Coupland, J., Giles, H., Henwood, K., & Wiemann, J. (1988). Elderly self-disclosure: Interactional and intergroup issues. *Language and Communication, 8*, 109-133.

Dijker, A. J. M. (1987). Emotional reactions to ethnic minorities. *European Journal of Social Psychology, 17*, 305-325.

Edwards, J. R. (1989). *Language and disadvantage* (2nd. ed.). London: Cole & Whurr.

Edwards, J. R., & Jacobsen, M. (1987). Standard and regional standard speech: Distinctions and similarities. *Language in Society, 16*, 369-380.

Fasold, R. W. (1984). *The sociolinguistics of society*. Oxford: Blackwell.

Franklyn-Stokes, A., Harriman, J., Giles, H., & Coupland, N. (1988). Information seeking across the life span. *Journal of Social Psychology, 128*, 419-421.

Frender, R., Brown, B. L., & Lambert, W. E. (1970). The role of speech characteristics in scholastic success. *Canadian Journal of Behavioral Sciences, 2*, 299-306.

Frender, R., & Lambert, W. E. (1972). Speech style and scholastic success: The tentative relationship and possible implications for lower class children. In R. Shuy (Ed.), *Monograph series on language and linguistics*. Washington, DC: Georgetown University Press.

Gallois, C., Callan, V. J., & Johnstone, M. (1984). Personality judgements of Australian Aborigine and white speakers: Ethnicity, sex, and content. *Journal of Language and Social Psychology, 3*, 39-57.

Gardner, R. C., & Kalin, R. (1981). *A Canadian social psychology of ethnic relations*. Toronto: Methuen.

Garza, R. T., & Henniger, L. G. (1987). Social identity: A multidimensional approach. *Journal of Social Psychology, 127*, 299-308.

Genesee, F., & Holobow, N. E. (1989). Change and stability in intergroup perceptions. *Journal of Language and Social Psychology, 8*, 17-38.

Giglioli, P. P. (Ed.). (1972). *Language and social context*. Harmondsworth: Penguin.

Giles, H. (1989). The social meanings of Welsh-English. In N. Coupland (Ed.), *English in Wales: Diversity, conflict, and change*. Clevedon: Multilingual Matters.

Giles, H., & Bourhis, R. Y. (1976). Methodological issues in dialect perception: Some social psychological perspectives. *Anthropological Linguistics, 18,* 294-304.

Giles, H., & Condor, S. (1988). Aging, technology, and society: An introduction and future priorities. *Social Behavior: An International Journal of Applied Social Psychology, 3,* 59-70.

Giles, H., Coupland, N., Henwood, K., Harriman, J., & Coupland, J. (1989). The social meaning of RP: A intergenerational perspective. In S. Ramsaran (Ed.), *Studies in the pronunciation of English: A commemorative volume in honor of A. C. Gimson.* London: Routledge.

Giles, H., Coupland, N., & Wiemann, J. (in press). "Talk is cheap . . ." but "my word is my bond": Beliefs about talk. In K. Bolton & H. Kwok (Eds.), *Sociolinguistics today: Eastern and Western perspectives.* London: Routledge.

Giles, H., & Edwards, J. R. (Eds.). (1983). Language attitudes in multilingual settings. *Journal of Multilingual and Multicultural Development, 4*(2 & 3).

Giles, H., & Fitzpatrick, M. A. (1984). Personal, group, and couple identities: Towards a relational context for the study of language attitudes and linguistic forms. In D. Schiffrin (Ed.), *Meaning, form, and use in context: Linguistic applications.* Washington, DC: Georgetown University Press.

Giles, H., Henwood, K., Coupland, N., Harriman, J., & Coupland, J. (1989). *Language attitudes and cognitive mediation.* Manuscript submitted for publication.

Giles, H., Hewstone, M., & Ball, P. (1983). Language attitudes in multilingual settings: Prologue and priorities. *Journal of Multilingual and Multicultural Development, 4,* 81-100.

Giles, H., Hewstone, M., Ryan, E. B., & Johnson, P. (1987). Research on language attitudes. In U. Ammon, N. Dittmar, & K. J. Mattheier (Eds.), *Sociolinguistics: An international handbook of the science of language and society* (Vol. 1). Berlin: de Gruyter.

Giles, H., & Johnson, P. (1986). Perceived threat, ethnic commitment and interethnic language behavior. In Y. Kim (Ed.), *Interethnic communication: Current research.* Beverly Hills: Sage.

Giles, H., & Johnson, P. (1987). Ethnolinguistic identity theory: A social psychological approach to language maintenance. *International Journal of the Sociology of Language, 68,* 69-99.

Giles, H., Leets, L., & Coupland, N. (1990). Minority language group status: A theoretical conspexus. *Journal of Multilingual and Multicultural Development, 11,* 1-19.

Giles, H., & Powesland, P. F. (1975). *Speech style and social evaluation.* London: Academic Press.

Giles, H., & Ryan, E. B. (1982). Prolegomena for developing a social psychology theory of language attitudes. In E. B. Ryan & H. Giles (Eds.), *Attitudes towards language variation: Social and applied contexts.* London: Edward Arnold.

Giles, H., & Ryan, E. B. (Eds.). (1986). Language, communication, and the elderly. *Language and Communication, 6*(1 & 2).

Giles, H., & St. Clair, R. N. (Eds.). (1979). *Language and social psychology.* Oxford: Blackwell.

Giles, H., & Street, R. L., Jr. (1985). Communicator characteristics and behavior: A review, generalizations, and model. In M. Knapp & G. R. Miller (Eds.), *The handbook of interpersonal communication.* Beverly Hills: Sage.

Gudykunst, W., & Ting-Toomey, S. (1990). Ethnic identity, language, and communication breakdowns. In H. Giles & W. P. Robinson (Eds.), *The handbook of language and social psychology.* Chichester: Wiley.

Gumperz, J. J., & Hymes, D. (Eds.). (1972). *Directions in sociolinguistics: The ethnography of communication.* New York: Holt, Rinehart and Winston.

Helfrich, H. (1979). Age markers in speech. In K. R. Scherer & H. Giles (Eds.), *Social markers in speech*. Cambridge: Cambridge University Press.

Hewstone, M., & Giles, H. (1986). Social groups and social stereotypes in intergroup communication: A review and model of intergroup communication breakdown. In W. B. Gudykunst (Ed.), *Intergroup communication*. London: Edward Arnold.

Hewstone, M., Stroebe, W., Codol, J-P., & Stephenson, G. M. (Eds.). (1988). *Introduction to social psychology*. Oxford: Blackwell.

Hogg, M. A., & Abrams, D. (1988). *Social identifications*. London: Routledge.

Kim, Y. Y. (1988). *Communication and cross-cultural adaptation*. Clevedon: Multilingual Matters.

Kobasa, S. C. O., & Puccetti, M. C. (1983). Personality and social resources in stress resistance. *Journal of Personality and Social Psychology, 45*, 839-850.

Labov, W. (1966). *The social stratification of English in New York City*. Washington, DC: Center for Applied Linguistics.

Labov, W. (1972). *Sociolinguistic patterns*. Philadelphia: University of Pennsylvania Press.

Lambert, W. E. (1967). A social psychology of bilingualism. *Journal of Social Issues, 23*, 91-109.

Lambert, W. E. (1980). The social psychology of language: A perspective for the 1980s. In H. Giles, W. P. Robinson, & P. M. Smith (Eds.), *Language: Social psychological perspectives*. Oxford: Pergamon.

Lambert, W. E., Anisfeld, M., & Yeni-Komshian, G. (1965). Evaluational reactions of Jewish and Arab adolescents to dialect and language variations. *Journal of Personality and Social Psychology, 2*, 84-90.

Lambert, W. E., Frankel, H., & Tucker, G. R. (1966). Judging personality through speech: A French-Canadian example. *Journal of Communication, 16*, 305-321.

Lambert, W. E., Giles, H., & Albert, A. (1976). Language attitudes in a rural community in Northern Maine. *La Monda Linguo-Problemo, 5*, 129-144.

Lambert, W. E., Giles, H., & Picard, O. (1975). Language attitudes in a French-American community. *International Journal of the Sociology of Language, 4*, 127-152.

Lambert, W. E., Hodgson, R., Gardner, R. C., & Fillenbaum, S. (1960). Evaluational reactions to spoken languages. *Journal of Abnormal and Social Psychology, 60*, 44-51.

Loftus, E. F. (1975). Leading questions and the eyewitness report. *Cognitive Psychology, 7*, 560-572.

Loftus, G. R., & Loftus, E. F. (1976). *Human memory: The processing of information*. Hillsdale, NJ: Lawrence Erlbaum Associates.

Markova, I. (Ed.). (1978). *Language in its social context*. Chichester: Wiley.

Marzurkewich, I. F., Fister-Stoga, D., Mawle, D., Somers, M., & Thibaudeau, S. (1986). A new look at language attitudes in Montreal. *Genetic, Social, and General Psychology Monographs, 112*, 201-217.

Ng, S. H., Giles, H., & Moody, J. (1989). *Information-seeking triggered by age*. Manuscript submitted for publication.

O'Keefe, B. J., & Delia, J. G. (1985). Psychological and interactional dimensions of communicative development. In H. Giles & R. N. St. Clair (Eds.), *Recent advances in language, communication, and social psychology*. London: Lawrence Erlbaum Associates.

Palmerino, M., Langer, E., & McGillis, D. (1984). Attitudes and attitude change: Mindlessness-mindfulness perspective. In J. R. Eiser (Ed.), *Attitudinal judgement*. New York: Springer-Verlag.

Potter, J., & Wetherell, M. (1987). *Discourse and social psychology*. London: Sage.

Pride, J. B., & Holmes, J. (Eds.). (1972). *Sociolinguistics*. Harmondsworth: Penguin.

Robinson, W. P. (1972). *Language and social behavior.* Harmondsworth: Penguin.

Rubin, A. M. (1986). Television, aging, and information seeking. *Language and Communication, 6,* 125-138.

Ryan, E. B., & Cole, R. L. (1990). Evaluative perceptions of interpersonal communication with elders. In H. Giles, N. Coupland, & J. M. Wiemann (Eds.), *Communication, health, and the elderly* (Fulbright Colloquia Series 8). Manchester: Manchester University Press.

Ryan, E. B., & Giles, H. (Eds.). (1982). *Attitudes towards language variation: Social and applied contexts.* London: Edward Arnold.

Ryan, E. B., Giles, H., & Hewstone, M. (1988). The measurement of language attitudes. In U. Ammon, N. Dittmar, & K. J. Mattheier (Eds.), *Sociolinguistics: An international handbook of the science of language and society* (Vol. 2). Berlin: de Gruyter.

Ryan, E. B., Giles, H., & Sebastian, R. J. (1982). An integrative perspective for the study of attitudes toward language variation. In E. B. Ryan & H. Giles (Eds.), *Attitudes toward language variation: Social and applied contexts.* London: Edward Arnold.

Ryan, E. B., Hewstone, M., & Giles, H. (1984). Language and intergroup attitudes. In J. R. Eiser (Ed.), *Attitudinal judgement.* New York: Springer-Verlag.

Scherer, K. R. (1988). On the symbolic functions of vocal affect expression. *Journal of Language and Social Psychology, 7,* 79-100.

Sebastian, R. J., & Ryan, E. B. (1985). Speech cues and social evaluation: Markers of ethnicity, social class, and age. In H. Giles & R. N. St. Clair (Eds.), *Recent advances in language, communication, and social psychology.* London: Lawrence Erlbaum Associates.

Seligman, C., Tucker, G. R., & Lambert, W. E. (1972). The effects of speech style and other attributes on teachers' attitudes toward pupils. *Language in Society, 1,* 131-142.

Shuy, R. W., & Fasold, R. W. (Eds.). (1973). *Language attitudes: Current trends and prospects.* Washington, DC: Georgetown University Press.

Snyder, M. (1981). On the self-perpetuating nature of social stereotypes. In D. Hamilton (Ed.), *Cognitive processes in stereotyping and intergroup behavior.* Hillsdale, NJ: Lawrence Erlbaum Associates.

Street, R. L., Jr., & Hopper, R. (1982). A model of speech style evaluation. In E. B. Ryan & H. Giles (Eds.), *Attitudes towards language variation: Social and applied contexts.* London: Edward Arnold.

Tajfel, H. (1959). A note on Lambert's "Evaluational reactions to spoken language." *Canadian Journal of Psychology, 13,* 86-92.

Tajfel, H., & Turner, J. C. (1979). An integrative theory of intergroup conflict. In W. G. Austin & S. Worchel (Eds.), *The social psychology of intergroup relations.* Monterey, CA: Brooks/Cole.

Thakerar, J. N., & Giles, H. (1981). They are — so they speak: Noncontent speech stereotypes. *Language and Communication, 1,* 251-256.

Thorndyke, P. W. (1977). Cognitive structures in comprehension and memory of narrative discourse. *Cognitive Psychology, 9,* 77-110.

Trudgill, P. (1986). *Dialects in contact.* Oxford: Blackwell.

Tucker, G. R. (1968). Judging personality from language usage: A Filipino example. *Philippine Sociological Review, 16,* 30-39.

Tucker, G. R., & Lambert, W. E. (1969). White and Negro listeners' reactions to various American-English dialects. *Social Forces, 47,* 463-468.

Turner, J. C. (1987). *Rediscovering the social group: A self-categorization theory.* Oxford: Blackwell.

van Hout, R., & Knops, U. (Eds.). (1988). *Language attitudes in the Dutch language area.* Dordrecht: Foris.

Weiner, B., Perry, R. P., & Magnusson, J. (1988). An attributional analysis of reactions to stigmas. *Journal of Personality and Social Psychology, 55,* 738-748.

Williams, F. (1976). *Explorations of the linguistic attitudes of teachers.* Rowley, MA: Newbury House.

Woolard, K. A. (1989). *Double talk: Bilingualism and the politics of ethnicity in Catalonia.* Stanford: Stanford University Press.

3 Attitudes and Motivation in Second Language Learning

Robert C. Gardner
University of Western Ontario

The intent of this chapter is to provide an overview of the literature concerned with the role of attitudes and motivation in second language acquisition. It is fitting, I believe, to have a chapter devoted to this topic in a *Festschrift* for W. E. Lambert because the topic itself represents a significant chapter in Wally's life. My recollection of my interest in this topic dates back to 1956 when, as a new graduate student at McGill University, I was searching for a thesis topic and a supervisor. Being monolingual, the topic of bilingualism wasn't particularly meaningful to me, nor particularly interesting for that matter, but Dr. Lambert, as I referred to him then, was a very open, welcoming individual who was always available to discuss research ideas, and who always seemed to suggest novel interpretations and solutions. My memory is that one afternoon we were discussing the importance of language aptitude in second language learning, and I countered that, if you didn't like the other language community, you could never really learn their language. At which time he responded with something like, "Hey, man, that sounds like an interesting thesis." After all this time, I'm not certain that this is precisely the sequence of events. I do know, however, that the idea didn't originate with me. It is easily documented that this "original" idea on my part actually had appeared in a publication of Wally's a year earlier (Lambert, 1955) and was an important aspect of his PhD dissertation.

There has been considerable research conducted on the topic of attitudes and motivation in second language learning, and it is simply not possible to review it all here. I intend to be highly selective and to emphasize certain aspects of the research, largely studies from my own laboratory. One thing that I have noted, however, is that despite the considerable amount of research that has been conducted, much of the relevant conceptual development can, in fact, be traced back to Wally's seminal work on this topic. The major research objectives and underlying theoretical concepts can generally be found expressed in a number of articles published by him (see, for example, Lambert, 1955, 1956a, 1956b, 1956c, 1963a, 1967, 1974). I hope that these links become clear in the presentation to follow.

Although there were some studies and commentaries linking attitudes to second language acquisition conducted before then, the study that initiated the program of research under discussion here was, in fact, W. E. Lambert's PhD dissertation. In an article based on this research, Lambert (1955) discussed the case of two American graduate students who measured as French dominant on various indicators of bilingualism. Interviews with these students led him to conclude that they were intensely motivated to learn French, and that such motivation was responsible for their high level of competence in their second language. One of the students (G1) evidenced what Lambert referred to as "a biographical picture of cultural malcontent" (p. 199). Lambert states that G1 "was certain that he did 'more thinking in French,' had recently spent a year in France, and was planning to return as soon as possible. A friend volunteered the information that G1 'reacted against' anything which was non-European and 'only read' French materials" (p. 199). The other student was a woman who had taught French in high school, and who was working toward a graduate degree in French. Lambert pointed out: "Her career demanded that she work and think in French" (p. 199). As can be seen, these two individuals are clear exemplars of the integrative and instrumental orientations that ultimately became important concepts in discussions of the role of attitudes and motivation in second language learning.

SOME HISTORICAL BACKGROUND

There were other researchers who had postulated that language learning would be influenced by attitudes, and some research had been conducted along these lines. In fact, in his review of the literature on bilingualism conducted to that time, Arsenian (1945) had raised a number of questions about possible affective factors. In a listing of "Problems for Research," for example, he proposed two questions that directly involve attitudinal/motivational variables. He asked: "In what way do affective factors, such as social prestige, assumed superiority, or — contrariwise — assumed inferiority, or enforcement of a language by a hated nation, affect language learning in a child?"; and, "How do victor and vanquished nations look at each other's language? Under what conditions may one learn the language of the other?" (p. 85). Even prior to this, Jordan (1941) had investigated the correlation of grades in various subjects with attitudes toward these subjects and reported that a measure of attitudes toward learning French was a significant correlate of grades in French.

In a similar vein, Jones (1950b) found that a measure of attitudes toward learning Welsh correlated significantly with proficiency in Welsh. Moreover, Jones (1950a, 1950b) demonstrated that such attitudes varied with the linguistic background of the parents, indicating that parental variables could play a role in the language learning process through the students' attitudes. Finally, Dunkel (1948) argued that motivation was an important factor in language learning, and he differentiated between two aspects. One, the *kind* of motivation, referred to the purposes of language study, and the other, the *intensity* of motivation, referred to the effort expended in learning the language. Moreover, in what appears to have been the first laboratory-based study investigating practical aspects associated with the learning of a second language (Persian), he studied the effects of financial inducements on vocabulary learning. Although he failed to obtain significant effects, he proposed "that the observed differences might be educationally significant even if not statistically significant" (p. 103).

The first "multivariate" investigation of the relation among indices of language aptitude, attitudes, and motivation, and second language proficiency was conducted by Gardner and Lambert (1959). They factor-analyzed a matrix of correlations obtained from assessments made of Grade 11 students and obtained two orthogonal factors, each of which shared variance in common with the one index of French achievement: teacher ratings of oral proficiency and aural comprehension. They defined one factor as *Linguistic Aptitude* and the other as *Motivation*. It was emphasized, however, that this latter factor described "a motivation of a particular type, *characterized by a willingness to be like valued members of the language community*" (Gardner & Lambert, 1959, p. 271). A subsequent factor analytic study conducted in 1959-1960 using more indices of French achievement and attitudes and motivation tended to confirm this general finding (see Gardner & Lambert, 1972, Reading Number 2). A normalized Varimax rotation of the nine factors obtained in this study demonstrated that achievement in French itself was multidimensional. French achievement measures contributed to six of the factors. More importantly, however, one of these factors, identified as *School French Achievement*, also received contributions from indices of language aptitude (and two motivational measures), while another, referred to as an *Integrative Motive Dimension*, was defined by measures of attitudes and motivation as well as French achievement. Thus, as before, the two major components, attitudes and motivation on the one hand, and language aptitude on the other, were shown to be relatively independent correlates of aspects of French proficiency. As might be expected, however, when many more measures are included in the factor matrix, aspects of French achievement also contributed to other dimensions, indicating that proficiency has other correlates as well.

Similar complexity was demonstrated in a study conducted by Anisfeld and Lambert (1961). They investigated Grade 8 and 9 Jewish students of Hebrew and found that, whereas indices of intelligence and language aptitude were relatively stable correlates of achievement in Hebrew from one class to another and from one socio-cultural context to another, the correlations between attitudinal variables and achievement in Hebrew were somewhat more variable. In fact, although a measure of anti-semitism correlated negatively with various indices of Hebrew achievement in different classes, only 5 of the 10 correlations were significant. A dichotomous measure distinguishing between instrumental and integrative orientations evidenced eight negative correlations, indicating that an instrumental orientation tended to be associated with a high level of achievement, and two positive correlations. Only three of these correlations were significant, however, and of these, two were negative and one was positive! Anisfeld and Lambert presented other data and arguments suggesting that these inconsistencies reflected what it meant to learn Hebrew for Jewish students in different socio-cultural contexts in Montreal.

The effects of the socio-cultural context were investigated further in 1960-1961 with samples of students in Maine, Louisiana, and Connecticut, though this material was not published in its complete form until 1972 (Gardner & Lambert, 1972). This project actually was concerned with five different samplings of high school students. Three of these were described as American students, in that they came from English-speaking homes where they had no experience with the French language. The other two samples consisted of French Americans (in Maine and Louisiana) where at least one parent regularly used French in the home. As it turned out, the majority of French American students from Louisiana had little experience in reading French, while many of those in Maine were more fully bilingual. All students, however, took their major schooling in English and were fluent in English. The factor structures varied considerably from sample to sample, though clear relationships between both language aptitude and attitudinal/motivational characteristics and French proficiency were noted. The conclusions to be drawn from these early studies then was that two relatively independent factors, language aptitude and social motivation, were related to achievement in a second language.

In a series of articles, Lambert (1963a, 1963b, 1967, 1974) provided the theoretical rationale which is still central to much of the subsequent research in this area, and is important as well for later theoretical formulations. In 1963, Lambert published two articles dealing with the psychology of second language learning. In the first (Lambert, 1963a), he discussed a number of psychological theories relevant to language learning (but primarily those of Hebb, 1949, and Skinner, 1957), and reviewed the concept of language aptitude as proposed by Carroll (see Carroll & Sapon, 1959). In the second article (Lambert, 1963b), he described his "social psychology of second-language learning" and his "psychology of bilingualism." His theoretical orientation is best summarized in his own words:

> This theory, in brief, holds that an individual successfully acquiring a second language gradually adopts various aspects of behavior which characterize members of another linguistic-cultural group. The learner's ethnocentric tendencies and his attitudes toward the other group are believed to determine his success in learning the new language. His motivation to learn is thought to be determined by his attitudes and by his orientation toward learning a second language. The orientation is "instrumental" in form if the purposes of language study reflect the more utilitarian value of linguistic achievement, such as getting ahead in one's occupation, and is "integrative" if the student is oriented to learn more about the other cultural community as if he desired to become a potential member of the group. It is also argued that some may be anxious to learn another language as a means of being accepted in another cultural group because of dissatisfactions experienced in their own culture while other individuals may be equally as interested in another culture as they are in their own. However, the more proficient one becomes in a second language the more he may find his place in his original membership group is modified at the same time as the other linguistic-cultural group becomes something more than a reference group for him. It may, in fact, become a second membership group for him. Depending upon the compatibility of the two cultures, he may experience feelings of chagrin or regret as he loses ties in one group, mixed with the fearful anticipation of entering a relatively new group. (p. 114)

This basic theoretical position was maintained and broadened somewhat in later review/theoretical articles. Thus, in addition to considering social psychological aspects of second language learning, Lambert (1967) also discussed social reactions to bilingual speakers and the adjustments bilinguals must make in terms of potentially conflicting cultural allegiances. In a later article (Lambert, 1974), he again expanded on these notions and introduced into the literature on second language learning the distinction between additive and subtractive bilingualism. He argued that additive bilingualism involved the acquisition of proficiency in the second language with no major loss in first language proficiency or allegiance to the original cultural group. Additive bilingualism, he felt, tended to be applicable primarily to majority group members learning a minority language. Subtractive bilingualism, on the other hand, was viewed as more characteristic of minority group members acquiring the language of the majority. Although it involves the development of proficiency in the second language, there is often a concomitant loss in first language skills and a loss in cultural identity as one comes to identify more and more with the second language (i.e., majority) group.

Many of the ideas and concepts introduced by Lambert are still influential in the research conducted today. Although there are some who question the role played by attitudes and motivation in second language learning (see, for example, Au, 1988; Oller & Perkins, 1978), the majority of studies demonstrate relationships between the two classes of variables (for a detailed review of many of these studies see Gardner, 1985). Others (see, for example, Burstall, 1975) agree that indices of attitudes and motivation are related to achievement in the second language but feel that perhaps heightened levels of attitudes and motivation are more dependent upon success in learning the language than vice versa.

There are currently a number of influential models of second language learning, many of which use concepts and propositions initially put forth by Lambert. An example of one such theoretical formulation is Krashen's (1982) monitor model which considers attitudinal variables as significant determinants of the "affective filter" which moderates language acquisition (as distinct from language learning). Other models that make explicit reference to attitudes and/or motivation influencing the development of second language proficiency and/or use other concepts proposed by Lambert are Schumann's (1978) acculturation model, Clément's (1980) social context model, and Giles and Byrne's (1982) intergroup model. Each of these theories emphasize somewhat different concepts, focus on different situations, and stress different processes as well, but they equally display the Lambert legacy.

SEARCHING FOR A CAUSE/EFFECT MODEL

Gardner and Smythe (1975) initially presented a theoretical model that attempted to extend the general theory proposed by Lambert, to formalize it by focussing on specific processes, and to suggest how these processes might operate to influence language proficiency. This model emphasized four classes of variables: the *social milieu* (reflected in cultural beliefs concerning the importance, relevance, assumed determinants of success, and expected results of second language learning); *individual differences* that could influence achievement (represented by intelligence, language aptitude, motivation, and situational anxiety); *second language acquisition contexts* where language material could be learned (distinguishing between formal language training situations like the language classroom and any other informal language experiences); and finally, *outcomes*. The model proposed that there were two classes of outcomes. Linguistic outcomes were those that involved any aspect of achievement in the language: the development of some particular linguistic skill, the acquisition of some linguistic knowledge, improved fluency, etc. Nonlinguistic outcomes, on the other hand, referred to any other consequences of the language learning experience. These could include an interest in using the language, an open appreciation of the other language community and/or other groups in general, increased motivation to learn more, etc. As conceived, the model was viewed as a dynamic one in which the individual difference variables were seen as influencing an individual's proficiency in the second language (i.e., linguistic outcomes) and the experience itself was seen as one that could influence at least some individual difference variables.

Although not referred to directly in early schematic representations of the model, attitudinal variables were viewed as potential determinants of motivation (cf. Lambert, 1963b), and were made explicit components in a later formalization (Gardner, 1983). The concept of the integrative motive, initially proposed by Gardner and Lambert (1972), was elaborated on as consisting of a constellation of attitudes and motivation. Three broad categories were hypothesized. One, *integrativeness,* was viewed as involving attitudes toward the second language community as well as other groups. In the context of English Canadians learning French, the concept of *integrativeness* was assessed in terms of three measures: Attitudes toward French Canadians, Degree of Integrative Orientation, and Interest in Foreign Languages. The second category involved *attitudes toward the learning situation* and was measured in terms of Evaluation of the French Course and Evaluation of the French Teacher. The final component involved *motivation*. It was assessed in terms of the effort expended in learning French (Motivational Intensity), Desire to Learn French, and Attitudes toward Learning French. In this representation, *integrativeness* and *attitudes toward the learning situation* were viewed as determinants of *motivation,* while *motivation* was considered to be the major determinant of second language achievement. (Language aptitude was also seen as an important determinant, of course.) Other measures were considered during the earlier research as potential means of assessing these and/or other motivational aspects, but the preceding eight measures were the ones that ultimately became the central ones (cf. Gardner, 1985).

It was during this time that Padric Smythe and I conducted a series of studies that had as their primary objective the development of measures to assess the major components of the integrative motive. We reasoned that, to the extent that valid and reliable measures were available, various tests of aspects of the model could be conducted, thus contributing to a greater understanding of the role of affective variables in second language learning. To this end, we conducted studies in London, Ontario, in order to pretest items for the measures, and later to validate them (Gardner & Smythe, 1975, 1981). We then tested the measures and their relationship to achievement in seven different cities across Canada using students of French as a second language in Grades 7 to 11 (Gardner, Smythe, Clément, & Gliksman, 1976; Gardner, Smythe, & Lalonde, 1984). Much of this research is described in detail by Gardner (1985); in essence, the same types of findings as reported by Gardner and Lambert (1972) were obtained. Although the factor structures tended to vary somewhat from city to city and from grade to grade (for details see Gardner et al., 1984), in all cases there were clear relationships between indices of achievement in French on the one hand and both language aptitude and attitudinal/motivational characteristics on the other. This project served another function, however, in that it produced a series of measures with high levels of reliability that could be adapted to many situations.

These results, as well as those from many other studies (for a review, see Gardner, 1985), indicate that there is a relationship between attitudes and motivation (and language aptitude) on the one hand and second language achievement on the other, but the process underlying the relationship is certainly open to question. One might argue that particular attitudinal/motivational characteristics facilitate the acquisition of a second language (which is the interpretation favoured by many researchers and by the theoretical models referred to above). Or it might be argued that success in learning a second language promotes particular attitudinal/motivational characteristics. This the view proposed by Burstall (1975) and which is recognized as a possibility in some theoretical models, such as the socio-educational model (see Gardner, 1985). A final position is that both achievement in a second language and various attitudinal and motivational characteristics share variance in common with some other factors (see, for example, Oller & Perkins, 1978).

These interpretative difficulties, of course, plague any attempt to explain relationships among individual differences and, in truth, no unequivocal interpretation is ever possible. This is reflected in the adage "correlation does not mean causation." Where one is interested in explaining individual differences, the best that can be done is to continually test implications of a particular interpretation by looking at the problem from different perspectives and by considering various relevant criteria.

This approach is being used in research concerned with the role of attitudes and motivation in second language learning. The socio-educational model of second language learning, for example, provides a description of a process by which attitudes and motivation can influence proficiency in the second language. One aspect of this process is the proposition that high levels of integrative motivation will be responsible for people choosing situations that will permit them to improve their second language. One place where such choice behaviour is demonstrated is in those situations where students are given the opportunity to visit the other language community. The many studies of "excursion programs" usually concentrate on the effects of these programs on attitudes (for a review of the effects of contact on attitudes, see Amir, 1976) but at least two studies have investigated the effects of such attitudes on the tendency to take part in excursions and to make contact with members of the other community. In both of these studies (Clément, Gardner, & Smythe, 1977; Desrochers, 1977) subjects who participated in an excursion to Quebec City scored higher, before actually going, on many of the measures used to assess integrative motivation than did those students who chose not to participate. Moreover, those participants who had more actual contact with French speakers scored higher on various pretest measures of attitudes and motivation than those with less contact.

A second instance where attitudes and motivation show meaningful relationships with such choice behaviour concerns the tendency to continue with language study once a course ends. Again, the available evidence suggests that attitudes and motivation are positively related to the tendency to pursue language study. In two ground-breaking studies, Bartley (1969, 1970) demonstrated that those with less positive attitudes toward the second language dropped out of further language study the following year, while those who continued language study had more favourable attitudes. Moreover, Bartley (1970) found that the dropouts had less positive attitudes at the end of the previous year than they did at its beginning, whereas those who continued language study evidenced more stable attitudes from the beginning to the end of the year. In a similar study, Gardner and Smythe (1975) also found that dropouts demonstrated less positive attitudes and lower motivation than students who continued with their language study the next year. The study also showed that the various attitudinal and motivational characteristics associated with integrative motivation were more predictive of who would continue (as opposed to those who would drop out) than was language aptitude.

A third situation that implicates attitudes and motivation in the language learning process has to do with classroom behaviour— another form of choice behaviour. To the extent that it can be shown that measures of attitudes and motivation taken early in the school year correlate with subsequent demonstrations of participation in the activities of the language class, interest in the material, and classroom performance, etc., it bolsters the argument that attitudes and motivation affect achievement. Moreover, it helps to clarify our understanding of the process of language learning because of the prediction that higher achievement occurs because of increased involvement in learning. Gliksman (1976) has, in fact, demonstrated this type of association. In two different studies, he showed that high school students who were classified as integratively motivated, on the basis of testing that took place early in the school term, tended to volunteer more answers in class and give more correct answers over a series of classes than students not so classified. In one study, these students also received more reinforcements from the teachers during these sessions, while in the other study they were rated by observers (who of course weren't aware of how the students were classified) as showing more interest in the class (the second of the two studies is reported in detail by Gliksman, Gardner, & Smythe, 1982). A study by Naiman, Fröhlich, Stern, and Todesco (1978) obtained similar results. They investigated attitudinal and motivational correlates of a large number of classroom activities, and though correlations involving many of the variables were not significant, many others were. By and large, the significant correlations suggested that there was an association between attitudes and motivation on the one hand and those behaviours that reflect individual differences in active involvement in the learning process.

The preceding results with respect to participation in excursion programs, persistence in language study, and classroom behaviour, are consistent with the notion that attitudes and motivation are predictive of choice behaviours reflecting an interest in developing more proficiency in the second language. It should be emphasized, however, that many of the criticisms concerning the inference of causality from correlational data are equally appropriate here. That is, this type of research still focuses on the relationship between two classes of individual difference variables, and one can ask whether such associations indicate that A causes B, or that B causes A, or that both A and B are caused by C, or that the measures of either A or B are faulty or confounded with some other variable. To the extent that the same causative link could explain all four sets of associations (i.e., the relationships between attitudes and motivation and (1) language achievement, (2) voluntary contact, (3) perseverance in language study, and (4) classroom behaviour), it helps to substantiate that explanation. It would appear that the most parsimonious one is that in fact attitudes and motivation do influence the behaviours concerned. Although alternative explanations can be provided for each type of association, it would seem to take a considerable amount of stretching to make the same alternative explanation fit each type of relationship. Thus, there is converging evidence in support of one particular causal sequence, namely, that attitudes and motivation (along with other variables, of course) influence second language achievement.

There are other approaches that can and have been used to support a particular cause-effect sequence. One that is gaining acceptance in this research area is that of causal modeling, and the current technique of choice in this regard is referred to as LISREL (*Li*near *S*tructural *Rel*ations; Jöreskog & Sörbom, 1984). This is a very powerful and sophisticated analytic procedure which, in essence, defines cause and effect in terms of regression parameters. The basic data, however, are still in the form of individual differences, and analysis is typically performed on either the covariance or the correlation matrix. As such, it, like any co-relational procedure, permits only a weak statement of causality. The best that can be said is that the obtained matrix of associations among the variables is consistent with the particular model under investigation. LISREL provides many indicators of goodness of fit of the data to a model, and there are numerous checks and balances in the application of the technique that can temper a researcher's enthusiasm for a particular model. One can use the technique to assess both the measurement and structural elements of the model of interest; however, it remains a co-relational procedure nonetheless.

Despite these qualifications, the technique has demonstrated its usefulness in the area of second language learning. Gardner (1985) summarizes three studies that have made use of the procedure to assess the applicability of the socio-educational model to data sets, and in all cases the model obtains strong support (see also Gardner, Lalonde, Moorcroft, & Evers, 1987; Lalonde & Gardner, 1984). Richard Clément has also made use of LISREL to test the adequacy of his social context model, and the results have been similarly supportive (see, for example, Clément & Kruidenier, 1985). Other researchers have also made use of the technique to assess other models or assumed causal connections (see, for example, Hall & Gudykunst, 1986; Nelson, Lomax, & Perlman, 1984).

It should not be surprising that different researchers using LISREL procedures to test the adequacy of supposedly different theoretical models obtain support for them. Each of the models invoke somewhat different parameters and variables and, since LISREL is a regression procedure, the model can prove to be a good fit— providing that the model is appropriate to the variables under investigation. The value in the LISREL procedure lies *not* in establishing that one theoretical model is better than another (unless the conflicting theoretical models are such that one is nested in the other), but rather in demonstrating the extent to which the relationships within a set of variables is consistent with the proposed model. This requires a clear link between the hypothesized latent variables and the various measures and thus forces the researchers concerned to be very explicit in their operationalization of key constructs, as well as in their hypothesized causal connections.

Another approach that can be used is a laboratory analogue to the language learning situation. Although such a setting is obviously highly artificial when compared to the language classroom, it permits a higher degree of control over the learning situation and language materials and thus eliminates considerable extraneous variation. We have begun to make use of this format more and more in an attempt to understand the language learning process. In our first study using this approach, Gardner, Lalonde, and Moorcroft (1985) investigated the role of attitudes and motivation, language aptitude, and mode of stimulus presentation/response (i.e., aural/oral vs. visual/written) on the learning of low frequency

English/French word pairs. The results demonstrated that the rate of learning over the six trials studied was steeper for high aptitude subjects than for low aptitude subjects, and also steeper for subjects with high levels of attitudes and motivation, as defined in terms of a median split on the Attitude/Motivation Index (AMI). In each case, the high and low groups were virtually identical on the first trial (with a mean near zero since the words were so rare) but by Trial 3, in both cases, the subjects classified as "high" had higher mean numbers of correct pairs than those classified as "low," and this effect was maintained over the subsequent trials.

Subjects were also asked to rate their motivation to learn the material and their interest at each trial; the results again indicated the validity of the initial assessment of attitudes and motivation. Subjects classified as "high" on the AMI evidenced higher levels of motivation and interest for all trials but one, though the pattern of results was affected by the mode of presentation/response; the differences were significant only for some trials, and primarily within the visual/written mode. Such results suggest that the general level of motivation assessed by the AMI is reflected in subjects' reported motivation and interest during the actual learning experience.

Although such results again support the notion that attitudes and motivation promote the actual learning of second language material, other interpretations are nonetheless possible. For example, because all of these students had studied French previously, and because it has been demonstrated that attitudes and motivation correlate with proficiency, it could easily be argued that the high AMI subjects in this study knew more French than those classified as low. Although these two groups were equivalent on Trial 1 in their lack of knowledge of the words used in this study, it could be argued that differential knowledge of other French vocabulary could be responsible for the different rates of learning. Such an interpretation is certainly plausible, though it is no more reasonable than postulating that the attitudes and motivation promote achievement. Nor, as indicated above, is it as consistent with the other findings in this research area.

Despite these limitations of the laboratory analogue procedure, we have found it to be an extremely useful one for investigating specific aspects of our theoretical formulation, and have recently developed a computer-based procedure for presenting stimulus materials and recording not only the subjects' responses, but also the amount of time taken to think about each response as well as the amount of time spent studying English/French pairs. The aforementioned study is the first, I believe, that actually examined the effects of aptitude and attitudes and motivation on the rate of learning of language material over time (in a relatively controlled situation), as opposed to the relation of these two classes of measures to performance on a one-shot assessment of proficiency. With the computer-based procedure that we have developed, we can now investigate directly the effects of prior attitudes and motivation on such variables as study time or viewing time or the relation of either of these to the number correct on each trial. Currently we are using this paradigm to study the role of attitudes and motivation in language learning in combination with monetary rewards for achievement and with various instructional sets. It is hoped that the results of these studies will further help to clarify the role played by attitudes and motivation in the language learning context.

THREE NEW DIRECTIONS IN THIS AREA OF RESEARCH

In our laboratory we are currently working on three different aspects of the language learning process that relate in one way or another to the role played by attitudes and motivation. One of these deals not with language learning itself but instead with the retention of language material once language training has terminated. This, in fact, is a common problem in the language learning context; one commonly hears statements to the effect that "I studied French (or any other language) for six (or some other number) years, but I can't remember any (or much, or some, etc.) of it." Even language teachers assume that language material can be forgotten after a period of disuse, and thus devote a period or so at the beginning of a new term reviewing material that had been covered during the previous session.

It is only comparatively recently (see, for example, Lambert & Freed, 1982) that attention has been devoted to the study of language loss following a period of disuse. One topic that seems very relevant in this regard is the role of attitudes and motivation in the retention of language material. Simply put, it seems reasonable to argue that if attitudes and motivation are important in determining the acquisition of second language material and skill, it seems equally likely to argue that they would influence language retention. The most obvious way to test this assumption would seem to be to assess attitudes and motivation at some point while students are in training, assess their proficiency at the end of training, allow some period of time (of disuse) to pass, and then assess proficiency again. To the extent that there is a correlation between attitudinal/motivational scores and the difference in achievement from Test 1 to Test 2, this would seem to demonstrate the hypothesized relation.

Although reasonable on the surface, this type of test, in fact, is not very meaningful, largely because it involves the use of a difference score. Many researchers have warned that the so-called "simple" difference score is itself very complex and have recommended that it not be used. Cronbach and Furby (1970, p. 78) state, for example: "There appears to be no need to use measures of change as dependent variables and no virtue in using them."

Linn and Slinde (1977, p. 147) echo the same sentiment when they caution that "problems in measuring change abound and the virtues in doing so are hard to find. Major disadvantages in the use of change scores are that they tend to conceal conceptual difficulties and that they can give misleading results."

In fact the correlation between a variable (e.g., A) and a difference score (i.e., Y-X) is a complex function of three correlations and the ratio of two standard deviations (Gardner & Neufeld, 1987). Thus, in the present type of situation, in order to obtain a high correlation between a variable (A) and the difference score (Y-X), one would require a large difference between the correlation between A and Y and that between A and X, provided that the standard deviation of Y is very similar to the standard deviation of X. (Because very little takes place between the assessments of X and Y in language loss studies, it is very meaningful to assume that these standard deviations would be similar.) But one generally would anticipate that the correlation between, for example, an index of motivation (i.e., A) and an assessment of achievement at one time (X) should be fairly similar to the correlation between that same measure of motivation (A) and a later measure of achievement (Y). That is, it is generally assumed that the correlations of various indices of attitudes and motivation with second language achievement are fairly consistent over time.

In point of fact, research into the relation of attitudes and motivation with the retention of second language skills suggests that attitudes and motivation are implicated in retention, even though many of the correlations with change are generally quite low, and often not significant. Gardner et al. (1987) show that aspects of the integrative motive are related to second language retention, and the reason seems to be that they tend to account for individual differences in attempts to use the second language once training ends. Whether language fluency, skill, or knowledge is retained would tend to depend upon such use of the language, and thus attitudes and motivation can be seen to have an indirect effect on retention through the mediator of use. We are currently completing other studies on this topic and, by and large, the results of these studies support this type of interpretation, thus again demonstrating the influential role of attitudes and motivation.

A second new direction in this area of research has to do with the measurement of attitudes and motivation and ways of improving their applicability. Although these measures have demonstrated considerable utility in research contexts, their use is somewhat limited in applied settings for the simple reason that it is relatively easy for respondents to see through the items and answer in what might seem to be the appropriate way. Thus, if an employer wished to use these tests to select employees for a language training program, their value would be limited because the tests are relatively transparent, and individuals might be able to fake their responses. In recent years, in our studies, we have tended to include measures of social desirability responding in our test battery to determine the extent to which scores on the various subtests relate to this response set. In one study, Gliksman (1981) found that the majority of the correlations were not significant, but nonetheless it is the case that individuals could fake positively on the tests if they so wished. That the correlations are low indicates only that, in research situations where anonymity is guaranteed, individuals tend to give honest responses.

For applied contexts, however, what is needed is some way of assessing the extent to which individuals are responding honestly to the various items. In our laboratory analogue studies, we have been experimenting with one procedure that could have great utility in applied settings. The instructions that accompany our measures of attitudes and motivation ask respondents to give their immediate reactions, and not to ponder over the individual items; thus we reasoned that individuals who respond slowly to the items might not be giving their immediate reactions. We are presently conducting three studies that are investigating the relationships among speed of responding to attitude items and level of attitude, the extent to which instructions to fake answers will influence either the attitudes themselves or the time to respond to the items, or whether individuals will respond to the attitude items differently if they have different feelings about how much they want to learn the language. We believe that this type of research represents a very useful first step in producing an Attitude/Motivation Test Battery that could be used in applied contexts. We are currently investigating this procedure more fully to explore the ramifications of this logic.

A third new direction in the investigation of the role of attitudes and motivation in second language learning deals not so much with attitudes and motivation but with a possible offshoot of them, namely language-related anxiety. The measures of French Classroom Anxiety or French Use Anxiety (or both) often have been included in various versions of the Attitude/Motivation Test Battery since its initial development (Gardner & Smythe, 1975) and, generally speaking, these measures tend to correlate negatively with attitude and motivation measures. Sometimes they load negatively on factors that primarily reflect attitudes and motivation and sometimes they define orthogonal factors, often with measures of self-ratings of proficiency, but, despite differences in factor composition, the negative relationships with attitudes and motivation on the one hand and second language achievement on the other are quite stable.

In his research, Richard Clément views indices of anxiety as a defining characteristic (albeit negatively) of factors involving self-confidence with another language (Clément, 1987; Clément & Kruidenier, 1985). He argues that in a multicultural context such self-confidence develops from positive experiences with the second language in interaction with members of the speech community. Clément (1980) argues that "it would be expected that self-confidence would be an interactive function of the frequency and quality of contact: a high frequency of pleasant contacts will have a more pleasant outcome than a low frequency. Conversely, much unpleasant contact will have a more negative effect than a little contact" (p. 151).

Our research has been conducted largely in a unilingual English-speaking community, and the opportunities to use the second language are rare. The primary source of second language experience is the language classroom, but it follows nonetheless that self-confidence with the second language could result from successful positive experiences in the classroom. Expressed in somewhat different terms, unsuccessful, unpleasant experiences with the second language in the classroom environment could give rise to the development of both French classroom and French use anxiety. There is some support for such conjecture. Using the analogue approach discussed above, MacIntyre and Gardner (1989) found that *Communicative Anxiety* (defined largely in terms of French Classroom and French Use Anxiety) interacted with trials in a paired associate learning task of French/English word pairs such that learning was slower for high anxious than for low anxious students. Such results suggest that anxiety interferes with the learning of the language material in ways suggested by Tobias (1986) in his model relating anxiety to learning. In the same study, measures of state anxiety (Spielberger, 1966) were taken after two of the learning trials. Cross-lagged panel analysis was used to differentiate between two conflicting hypotheses: (1) anxiety on one trial influences performance on a subsequent trial; (2) poor performance on one trial influences anxiety on a subsequent one. The results for both tests of these alternatives supported the second hypothesis. Thus, in this one study there is evidence to suggest that a general trait of communicative anxiety could have a deleterious effect on language learning; moreover, poor performance in the learning situation could give rise to increased feelings of anxiety.

MacIntyre and Gardner (1989) posit that the above scenario might, in fact, describe the process leading to the development of language-related anxiety. That is, students might initially enter the language-learning situation with optimism and enthusiasm. A series of unsuccessful experiences could, however, give rise to increases in state anxiety, but over time these anxieties in the classroom could lead to the development of a situationally specific anxiety (i.e., French classroom anxiety) which would lead to further unsuccessful experiences, etc. Such an analysis would suggest that French classroom and French use anxiety would be relatively independent of other forms of anxiety such as a general trait of anxiety, manifest anxiety, anxiety in other classes, etc., and this is generally what is found (see, for example, Clément, Gardner, & Smythe, 1980; Lalonde & Gardner, 1984; MacIntyre & Gardner, 1989).

This form of analysis would also suggest that measures like French Classroom and French Use Anxiety would relate negatively to measures of motivation to learn the language and various attitude measures. The dissatisfaction arising from the anxiety would be expected to decrease motivation and generalize to negative attitudes toward different factors associated with learning the language. Depending upon the context, one might even expect that French Classroom Anxiety might correlate more highly with measures of *attitudes toward the learning situation* (i.e., the French Class and French Teacher Evaluation) while French Use Anxiety might correlate higher with integrativeness attitudes (i.e., Attitudes Toward French Canadians, Degree of Integrative Orientation, and Interest in Foreign Languages). Both would be expected to correlate about evenly with the various aspects of *motivation* (i.e., Attitudes Toward Learning French, Motivational Intensity, and Desire to Learn French).

A CONCLUDING OVERVIEW

The intent of this chapter was to review some of the research dealing with the role of attitudes and motivation in second language learning and to show how this area has developed since the initial studies were conducted by Wally Lambert and his colleagues. I believe it is reasonable to conclude that there has been considerable development over the years, that issues are somewhat more focussed now, and that there is a greater appreciation for the processes underlying the link between attitudinal/motivational characteristics and second language acquisition. What started out as an interest in the simple correlation between attitudes and motivation on the one hand and proficiency in the second language on the other has blossomed into a search for links with other relevant behaviours and elaboration of particular cause/effect sequences.

In this chapter, attention was directed primarily to English-speaking students learning French, and French-speaking students learning English, but it would be incorrect to assume that research has been concerned only with these two types of settings. Similar studies have been conducted in many different contexts in many parts of the world with many different first and second languages; many of these studies have been summarized by Gardner (1985). By focussing attention on these two language contexts, however, I thought I could better illustrate the diversity of methods used and behaviours studied while using a fairly common attitude/motivation test battery. Nonetheless, there are other interesting issues that arise in this area of research when different investigators develop unique ways of measuring similar-named concepts (see, for example, Strong, 1984).

Other very real issues were also only briefly mentioned in this chapter. One extremely important one is the role of social context, which is central to Clément's (1980) model of second language learning, and is a core element in Lambert's (1974) distinction between additive and subtractive bilingualism. It was alluded to in the present chapter in the discussion of the role of the socio-cultural milieu in the socio-educational model of second language learning. Although some have argued that by postulating that the social context influences the role played by attitudes and motivation in language learning, researchers have a handy post hoc explanation for inconsistent relationships (cf. Au, 1988), the truth of the matter is that the context must play an important role. Not only does it influence the relative importance placed on language study itself, but it can determine the availability of the other language to individual users and set the stage for a host of dynamic interrelationships between individual difference characteristics, intergroup relations, and second language achievement. These have not been discussed in this chapter, but their role is clearly important as is demonstrated in a study by Genesee, Rogers, and Holobow (1983). They showed that perceived motivational support from the other-language community was an important determinant of second language achievement, often more so than individual motivation. Such findings do not diminish the importance of individual difference indices of attitudes and motivation, but rather simply highlight the very social nature of second language learning. This, of course, was a point made by Lambert (1963b) when he stressed the significance of a social psychological perspective of language learning.

In reviewing the literature, the one point that stands out, in my opinion, is how the early discussions by Lambert (1963b, 1967, 1974) are as applicable today as they were then. Various concepts such as the integrative/instrumental distinction in orientations, the linking of second language development with self-identification and feelings of anomie, the view that intergroup attitudes fostered motivation to learn the language, the notions of additive and subtractive bilingualism, etc., are still very influential today. I believe the area has grown and become more sophisticated with the presentation of somewhat different theoretical models, with more and diverse empirical investigations, and with greater attention to understanding underlying processes. But through it all, there is still a very great Lambert imprint on this area.

ACKNOWLEDGEMENT

This chapter is based, in part, on research funded by grant 410-88-0158 from the Social Sciences and Humanities Research Council.

REFERENCES

Amir, Y. (1976). The role of inter-group contact in change of prejudice and ethnic relations. In P. A. Katz (Ed.), *Towards the elimination of racism*. New York: Pergamon.

Anisfeld, M., & Lambert, W. E. (1961). Social and psychological variables in learning Hebrew. *Journal of Abnormal and Social Psychology, 63*, 524-529.

Arsenian, S. (1945). Bilingualism in the post-war world. *Psychological Bulletin, 42*, 65-86.

Au, S. (1988). A critical appraisal of Gardner's social psychological theory of second language (L2) learning. *Language Learning, 38*, 75-100.

Bartley, D. E. (1969). A pilot study of aptitude and attitude factors in language dropout. *California Journal of Educational Research, 20*, 48-55.

Bartley, D. E. (1970). The importance of the attitude factor in language dropout: A preliminary investigation of group and sex differences. *Foreign Language Annals, 3*, 383-393.

Burstall, C. (1975). French in the primary school: The British experiment. *Canadian Modern Language Review, 31*, 388-402.

Carroll, J. B., & Sapon, S. M. (1959). *Modern Language Aptitude Test, Manual*. New York: Psychological Corporation.

Clément, R. (1980). Ethnicity, contact and communicative competence in a second language. In H. Giles, W. P. Robinson, & P. M. Smith (Eds.), *Language: Social psychological perspectives*. Oxford: Pergamon.

Clément, R. (1987). Second language proficiency and acculturation: An investigation of the effects of language status and individual characteristics. *Journal of Language and Social Psychology, 5*, 271-290.

Clément, R., Gardner, R. C., & Smythe, P. C. (1977). Inter-ethnic contact: Attitudinal consequences. *Canadian Journal of Behavioural Science, 9*, 205-215.

Clément, R., Gardner, R. C., & Smythe, P. C. (1980). Social and individual factors in second language acquisition. *Canadian Journal of Behavioural Science, 12*, 293-302.

Clément, R., & Kruidenier, B. G. (1985). Aptitude, attitude and motivation in second language proficiency: A test of Clément's model. *Journal of Language and Social Psychology, 4*, 21-37.

Cronbach, L. J., & Furby, L. (1970). How we should measure "change"— Or should we? *Psychological Bulletin, 74*, 68-80.

Desrochers, A. (1977). *Bicultural excursion programs: Correlates and consequences*. Unpublished master's thesis, University of Western Ontario, London, Canada.

Dunkel, H. B. (1948). *Second-language learning*. Boston: Ginn.

Gardner, R. C. (1983). Learning another language: A true social psychological experiment. *Journal of Language and Social Psychology, 2*, 219-239.

Gardner, R. C. (1985). *Social psychology and second language learning: The role of attitudes and motivation*. London: Edward Arnold.

Gardner, R. C., Lalonde, R. N., & Moorcroft, R. (1985). The role of attitudes and motivation in second language learning: Correlational and experimental considerations. *Language Learning, 35*, 207-227.

Gardner, R. C., Lalonde, R. N., Moorcroft, R., & Evers, F. (1987). Second language attrition: The role of motivation and use. *Journal of Language and Social Psychology, 6*, 29-48.

Gardner, R. C., & Lambert, W. E. (1959). Motivational variables in second language acquisition. *Canadian Journal of Psychology, 13*, 266-272.

Gardner, R. C., & Lambert, W. E. (1972). *Attitudes and motivation in second language learning*. Rowley, MA: Newbury House.

Gardner, R. C., & Neufeld, R. W. J. (1987). Use of the simple change score in correlational analyses. *Educational and Psychological Measurement, 47,* 849-864.

Gardner, R. C., & Smythe, P. C. (1975). *Second language acquisition: A social psychological approach* (Research Bulletin No. 332). London, Canada: University of Western Ontario, Department of Psychology.

Gardner, R. C., & Smythe, P. C. (1981). On the development of the Attitude/Motivation Test Battery. *Canadian Modern Language Review, 37,* 510-525.

Gardner, R. C., Smythe, P. C., Clément, R., & Gliksman, L. (1976). Second-language learning: A social psychological perspective. *Canadian Modern Language Review, 32,* 198-213.

Gardner, R. C., Smythe, P. C., & Lalonde, R. N. (1984). *The nature and replicability of factors in second language acquisition* (Research Bulletin No. 605). London, Canada: University of Western Ontario, Department of Psychology. (ERIC Document Reproduction Service No. 248693)

Genesee, F., Rogers, P., & Holobow, N. (1983). The social psychology of second language learning: Another point of view. *Language Learning, 33,* 209-224.

Giles, H., & Byrne, J. L. (1982). An intergroup approach to second language acquisition. *Journal of Multilingual and Multicultural Development, 1,* 17-40.

Gliksman, L. (1976). *Second language acquisition: The effects of student attitudes on classroom behaviour.* Unpublished master's thesis, University of Western Ontario, London, Canada.

Gliksman, L. (1981). *Improving the prediction of behaviours associated with second language acquisition.* Unpublished doctoral dissertation, University of Western Ontario, London, Canada.

Gliksman, L., Gardner, R. C., & Smythe, P. C. (1982). The role of the integrative motive on students' participation in the French classroom. *Canadian Modern Language Review, 38,* 625-647.

Hall, B. J., & Gudykunst, W. B. (1986). The intergroup theory of second language ability. *Journal of Language and Social Psychology, 5,* 291-302.

Hebb, D. O. (1949). *The organization of behavior.* New York: Wiley.

Jones, W. R. (1950a). Attitude towards Welsh as a second language, a preliminary investigation. *British Journal of Educational Psychology, 19,* 44-52.

Jones, W. R. (1950b). Attitude towards Welsh as a second language, a further investigation. *British Journal of Educational Psychology, 20,* 117-132.

Jordan, D. (1941). The attitudes of central school pupils to certain school subjects and the correlation between attitude and attainment. *British Journal of Educational Psychology, 11,* 28-44.

Jöreskog, K. G., & Sörbom, D. (1984). *LISREL VI: Analysis of linear structural relationships by the method of maximum likelihood.* Mooresville, IN: Scientific Software Inc.

Krashen, S. D. (1982). *Principles and practices in second language acquisition.* New York: Pergamon.

Lalonde, R. N., & Gardner, R. C. (1984). Investigating a causal model of second language acquisition: Where does personality fit? *Canadian Journal of Behavioural Science, 16,* 224-237.

Lambert, R. D., & Freed, B. F. (1982). *The loss of language skills.* Rowley, MA: Newbury House.

Lambert, W. E. (1955). Measurement of the linguistic dominance of bilinguals. *Journal of Abnormal and Social Psychology, 50,* 197-200.

Lambert, W. E. (1956a). Developmental aspects of second-language acquisition: I. Associational fluency, stimulus provocativeness, and word-order influence. *Journal of Social Psychology, 43,* 83-89.

Lambert, W. E. (1956b). Developmental aspects of second-language acquisition. II. Associational stereotypy, associational form, vocabulary commonness, and pronunciation. *Journal of Social Psychology, 43,* 91-98.

Lambert, W. E. (1956c). Developmental aspects of second-language acquisition: A description of developmental changes. *Journal of Social Psychology, 43,* 99-104.

Lambert, W. E. (1963a). Psychological approaches to the study of language Part I: On learning, thinking and human abilities. *Modern Language Journal, 14,* 51-62.

Lambert, W. E. (1963b). Psychological approaches to the study of language Part II: On second language learning and bilingualism. *Modern Language Journal, 14,* 51-62.

Lambert, W. E. (1967). A social psychology of bilingualism. *Journal of Social Issues, 23,* 91-109.

Lambert, W. E. (1974). Culture and language as factors in learning and education. In F. E. Aboud & R. D. Meade (Eds.), *Cultural factors in learning and education.* Bellingham, WA: Western Washington State College.

Linn, R. L., & Slinde, J. A. (1977). The determination of the significance of change between pre- and post-testing periods. *Review of Educational Research, 47,* 121-150.

MacIntyre, P. D., & Gardner, R. C. (1989). Anxiety and second language learning: Toward a theoretical clarification. *Language Learning, 39,* 251-275.

Naiman, N., Fröhlich, M., Stern, H. H., & Todesco, A. (1978). *The good language learner* (Research in Education Series No. 7). Toronto: Ontario Institute for Studies in Education.

Nelson, F. H., Lomax, R. G., & Perlman, R. (1984). A structural equation model of second language acquisition for adult learners. *Journal of Experimental Education, 53,* 29-39.

Oller, J. W., & Perkins, K. (1978). Intelligence and language proficiency as sources of variance in self-reported affective variables. *Language Learning, 28,* 85-97.

Schumann, J. H. (1978). *The acculturation model for second-language acquisition and foreign language teaching.* Arlington, VA: Center for Applied Linguistics.

Skinner, B. F. (1957). *Verbal behavior.* New York: Appleton.

Spielberger, C. D. (1966). *Anxiety and behavior.* New York: Academic Press.

Strong, M. (1984). Integrative motivation: Cause or result of successful language acquisition? *Language Learning, 34,* 1-14.

Tobias, S. (1986). Anxiety and cognitive processing of instruction. In R. Schwarzer (Ed.), *Self-related cognition in anxiety and motivation.* Hillsdale, NJ: Lawrence Erlbaum Associates.

4 Developing a Language-Competent American Society: The Role of Language Planning

G. Richard Tucker
Center for Applied Linguistics

It is perhaps appropriate to begin by noting that there are today many more bilingual individuals in the world than there are monolingual; in addition, many more children throughout the world have been, and continue to be, educated via a second or a later-acquired language— at least for some portion of their formal education— than the number who are educated exclusively via their mother tongue. Thus, in many parts of the world, bilingualism and innovative approaches to education which involve the use of more than one language constitute the status quo, a way of life, a natural experience. In these settings, bilingualism and the use of several languages in education are not problematic, burdensome, or difficult.

Educators for at least five millennia have been faced with the necessity of developing innovative educational programs involving some form of bilingual instruction. For example, in 3000 B.C., in ancient Mesopotamia, Sumerian and Akkadian were the two languages used as media of instruction for training scribes. In more contemporary times bilingual education programs have arisen in diverse sociopolitical settings: for example, where a nonnative indigenous language of wider communication (e.g., Amharic in Ethiopia, Pilipino in the Philippines, Swahili in Tanzania) is used as a major language of instruction; in situations where large numbers of immigrant children with different native languages enter an otherwise monolingual school system (e.g., Mexican children in the United States); or even where speakers of a nonstandard language variety (e.g., Haitian or Cape Verdean Creole) attend schools where the teachers and texts use a standard, more prestigious form of the language. Programs of innovative language education have been developed in many countries for a variety of different reasons: a desire to provide universal, free, primary (and often secondary) education; to regionalize or nationalize educational systems which were previously controlled by, or modeled after, those of colonial powers; to foster a sense of self-esteem, ethnic awareness, or national unity. In some settings, bilingual education programs have been adopted to foster, or to maintain, equal facility in both languages with a concomitant development of appreciation for the values and traditions of both ethnolinguistic groups, while others use the development of early skills in the child's mother tongue as a bridge leading toward a more effective development of ability in some target language (and do not necessarily try to maintain children's proficiency in the first language). That is, the goals or the objectives of language education programs are noticeably different in different settings. (I find it to be an enduring paradox or dilemma of American education that bilingualism, becoming bilingual, and the encouragement of innovative language education programs as a part of the core or basic curriculum within public education, are so often viewed as problematic, difficult, and undesirable. Rather than viewing bilingual education as a form of cognitively enriching experience for children, it is too often viewed as compensatory education.)

In my work in different settings throughout the world during the past two decades, I have come to believe that the selection of a language or languages to be taught, or to be used for instruction, clearly constitutes an important aspect of educational and of national planning. Thus, when considering the establishment of innovative language education programs, there are two threads of literature to be examined: one dealing with language policy or language planning (e.g., Weinstein, 1983) and one dealing with the development and implementation of innovative language education (in many places, bilingual education) programs (e.g., Cziko & Troike, 1984; Genesee, 1987; Willig, 1985). A number of questions arise which should be addressed:

1. Does the country (or political unit) have an official language policy— either de jure or de facto? Does that policy govern the selection of language(s) of instruction in public education?

2. Does the country have complementary or conflicting federal and provincial language policies? (Here the example of the Canadian federal policy conflicting with that of the province of Quebec comes to mind.)

3. Is the population of the country relatively homogeneous in mother tongue and ethnic origin? If not, do there exist sizable ethnolinguistic groups who are cohesive and who have managed to achieve economic or political power? Have any or all of these diverse ethnolinguistic groups been recognized and accorded any special rights or treatment?

4. Does the country have a centrally controlled or administered system of public education? What is the role (obligatory vs. optional) of second

language teaching in formal education? Is there a national curriculum, or a set of nationally prescribed textbooks, or standardized examinations?

5. If responsibility for public education rests with the provincial government, does the federal government nonetheless influence educational policy by the way in which it allocates supplemental funding?

6. How specific are the curricular goals that have been established in the formal educational system? What standards of achievement in both content areas and in language proficiency have been set? What expectations exist concerning the roles that parents, peers, and other extracurricular societal resources will play in the lifelong education of the individual? What direct role, if any, do parents play in shaping educational policy? How is accomplishment or competency typically assessed?

7. What research evidence exists to support claims for the differential effectiveness of various pedagogical approaches? (Do remember, however, that language [education] policy is only rarely affected by the results of empirical research!)

THREE EDUCATION MODELS

These questions form a framework within which to examine language policy in disparate settings. By way of background, in many parts of the world renewed attention has been directed toward providing the soundest possible education for language minority *and* for language majority individuals. We find exciting, innovative programs in industrialized and in nonindustrialized countries; we find programs being implemented to improve the teaching of second or foreign languages for language majority individuals; and we find programs to enhance the teaching of the national or official language when it is not spoken as the mother tongue by language minority youngsters. Each represents an instance of language planning: needs assessment or information collection to establish goals and objectives, deliberation or discussion, policy implementation involving some demonstrable change, and evaluation or provision of formative feedback. In each setting, a major goal is the development of bilingual proficiency for some or for all students.

I believe it is often easier to bring a situation into sharper focus by means of comparison and contrast. Therefore I would like to present briefly information about the role of language in education from three settings— the People's Republic of China, Nigeria, and the Philippines. Each of these countries has adopted different policies and practices with regard to the role of language in education and I think it useful to consider the situation in our own area in the light of information about practices in these other settings. I have chosen these three examples purposefully. Each represents an instance of language planning, but each has a different emphasis. The first example, the People's Republic of China, represents a situation in which English is taught to many as a foreign language and then, intensively to a few through a "language for specific purposes" approach. In the second example, Nigeria, there is a transitional bilingual education program for all youngsters, with limited maintenance of the mother tongue; in the third example, the Philippines, there is a full integration of language and content instruction and provision for bilingual education during all phases of the formal education cycle. No single example is totally appropriate as a model for United States education. However, the general process by which each of these countries has arrived at a different program suited to its unique needs (needs assessment, information collection, deliberation, policy implementation, and both formative and summative evaluation with feedback leading to program revision) is directly applicable to the United States setting.

People's Republic of China (PRC)

The Mandarin "dialect" of Chinese is the official language of the PRC. Instruction for children at all educational levels (except in autonomous regions such as Uighur, Inner Mongolia, and Tibet) occurs via Chinese. Children are instructed using *Putonghua,* the so-called "common language." Furthermore, they are introduced to literacy training using *Pinyin* and then gradually bridged into reading with simplified Chinese characters. The country has a national curriculum for primary and middle (our secondary) schools with unified standard textbooks and a national examination system. There are bureaus of education and higher education in each of the provinces but their major task is to implement national educational policy. Under the Chinese constitution, the national autonomous regions are guaranteed certain language rights and are encouraged to use the indigenous languages for purposes of primary education (and local government). In effect, transitional bilingual education programs apparently exist in the various autonomous regions.

Foreign language study in the PRC is compulsory, beginning with the third grade of primary school; the goal is that by the end of middle school children will have acquired modest (receptive) proficiency in a foreign language. For the past ten years, English has been the most widely taught foreign language although it is not the only language available; previously Russian was the most commonly taught foreign language, but its popularity has rapidly declined over the last decade.

Several years ago, the Chinese party leaders decided, as a matter of public policy, that foreign language facility would be an indispensable tool in their pursuit of the "four modernizations." They decided not to rely upon the widespread translation of materials from other languages into Chinese but rather that the Chinese people should acquire the ability to work effectively in the necessary foreign language(s). This was a policy decision with immense consequences for educators because the party leaders could have decided to embark on a massive program of technical translation from foreign languages into Chinese. Rather, they concluded, for practical purposes, that their citizenry must develop proficiency in English for "access to science and technology." As mentioned previously, English is introduced in primary Grade 3, but students typically achieve only limited proficiency in English by the time that they graduate from middle school.

Thus, the Chinese have established national resource centers at, among other places, Jao Tung University in Shanghai, to facilitate the study and teaching of English for science and technology (EST)— an instance of language for specific purposes. They have recently approved a national EST curriculum for the tertiary level and are presently developing new texts and training teachers to implement the curriculum. It remains to be seen how successful the Chinese will be, but the notion of providing intensive English language training at higher levels of education to a restricted group— that is, only those with demonstrable need and high motivation— represents a carefully debated and principled policy decision.

One finds examples of this approach in many parts of the world (e.g., in Indonesia, Kuwait, and Saudi Arabia). In such instances there is a deliberate policy of introducing a broad spectrum of students to general study of a foreign language for a number of years as a part of the compulsory school curriculum, followed by the intensive teaching of that language at higher or tertiary levels to those with a demonstrable need. In addition, in these contexts, it is often the case that the teaching of language is "delinked" from the teaching of culture. This move to teach the language for a variety of technical, occupational, or other purposes (minus the culture represented by the host group) represents a controversial but interesting emerging trend. Let me turn now to quite a different example.

Nigeria

Nigeria is a large, multilingual country situated in central West Africa. English is the official language although a number of Nigerian languages have achieved prominence and are now used initially for primary instruction. Prior to Nigeria's independence from Great Britain, virtually all of the limited primary instruction available was provided in English. This was followed by a period in which the mother tongue, particularly if it happened to be one of the major Nigerian languages (such as Yoruba, Hausa, or Igbo), was used as the medium of instruction in the first three primary grades and was replaced by English at primary Grade 4. However, in 1970 an exciting and important educational innovation began, which has been referred to as the Yoruba Six-Year Primary Project (see *Language in Education in Africa,* 1985). In this project, Yoruba (the mother tongue of a majority of the children in what was once called the Western state of Nigeria) is used as the major medium of instruction during all six primary grades. In addition, English is taught as a second language (ESL) throughout each of the six years.

It is important to note that the Yoruba Six-Year Primary Project involved the development of: a new curriculum which was much more closely attuned to the content, values, and traditions of Nigerians than was the previous curriculum (the so-called "Oxbridge" model); a completely new textbook series written in Yoruba for Nigerian children; intensive and effective in-service as well as pre-service teacher training programs (at the University of Ife) to orient those who would use these materials in the project; and a new, more appropriate ESL program and materials for the primary levels. (It should be noted that project staff initially hoped that ESL would be taught entirely by specialist teachers, but they soon abandoned this innovation because of the exorbitant expense.) The aim of the project was to develop and implement an appropriate, integrated, and articulated curriculum which was responsive to the needs and interests of Nigerian children while simultaneously developing a set of tools and building blocks in English as a second language for these children so that those who would continue their formal schooling could effectively make a transition between primary Grade 6 and secondary Grade 1 from Yoruba to English as the medium of instruction.

The project involved the identification of carefully selected experimental and control groups of youngsters in both urban and rural areas. Formative and summative evaluations were carried out over a period of several years. At this point a word should be said about the longer-term goals of this educational option for Nigeria. As mentioned, at the secondary level, English becomes the medium of instruction and continues to be used throughout secondary as well as tertiary studies. In addition, of critical importance for educational planners is the fact that a robust Yoruba language arts program continues throughout the secondary level. This language arts program is viewed as an essential and integral part of the total educational offerings for the children. In many ways, this resembles what we refer to in the United States as a "maintenance" approach to bilingual education, albeit a limited one. As well, one of the other major Nigerian languages is introduced as a subject for study at the secondary level. Thus, children might add Hausa or Igbo or some other Nigerian language as a subject for study at secondary Grade 1 depending upon where in Yorubaland they happen to live.

Available results indicate that the children participating in this innovative educational program fare very well indeed. In fact, when the crucial comparison is made between experimental and control groups of children as they are about to enter secondary school, it has been found that a significantly higher proportion of children educated via the innovative Yoruba Six-Year Primary Project successfully pass their primary school leaving examinations than their carefully selected control counterparts. The experimental group youngsters also do extremely well on a variety of tests which were developed specifically for assessing the project. Furthermore, it has been reported that there is a much higher degree of parental involvement in the schooling of these innovatively educated youngsters than is the case for their control counterparts. By all accounts, the program seems to have been a pedagogical success since the participating children have been able to participate effectively in advanced study via English. Let us now move to an extremely different— and equally innovative— example from the Philippines.

Republic of the Philippines

The Philippines is an archipelago comprising some 7,000 islands and a multilingual country with approximately 150 mutually unintelligible languages. The country has a long history of thorough, longitudinal evaluation of various educational alternatives (see, for example, Sibayan, 1978; Tucker, 1977). After more than a decade of experimenting with diverse approaches to language education and as a result of a nationwide language policy survey undertaken during 1967 and 1968, policy makers in the Philippines adopted a novel approach to bilingual education in 1974 which involves language by subject matter specificity throughout the primary and secondary levels of education. This policy was adopted in an attempt to maintain the historically high level of English proficiency by Filipino students which helps to facilitate their access to tertiary study in English medium institutions at home and abroad, *and* to enhance the spread of Pilipino as a language of national unity.

It was decided after much deliberation involving educators and policy makers at the highest level that schooling at Grades 1 and 2 should be via the child's vernacular language(s) (if different from Tagalog, which is the basis for Pilipino) with English and Pilipino being taught as second languages for each of these two years. The purpose is to introduce the child to basic concepts and initial literacy training in a familiar language and to develop a set of solid "building blocks" in both English and Pilipino so that a transition can be made at Grade 3 to these two languages as dual media of instruction for the remainder of the child's formal education. Then, at primary Grade 3 a "double" transition is made for most children, with English being used to teach mathematics and various science subjects, and Pilipino being used to teach all remaining subjects (e.g., history, geography, etc.). In addition, of course, there continue to be courses in English language arts and Pilipino language arts. This program of language by subject matter specificity continues from Grade 3 through the end of the secondary cycle of education. Recently, the Linguistic Society of the Philippines (1986) conducted a summative evaluation of the impact of the bilingual education program (see also Tucker, 1987). They conducted a nation-wide quantitative and qualitative study to investigate English and Pilipino language proficiency and achievement in mathematics, science, and social studies of samples of approximately 7,500 Grade 4, 6, and 10 students and approximately 1,000 Grade 4, 6, and 10 teachers selected from 17 ethnolinguistic regions throughout the country. The results of this study were presented at a special seminar for key decision makers in the Ministry of Education in January 1987 and suggestions were made for "fine tuning" or modifying various aspects of policy and practice.

Findings, in brief, indicated a systematic downtrend in educational achievement from Grades 4 to 6 to 10; the teachers *were not*, in many instances, masters themselves of the content material which they were called upon to teach; many non-native-speaking Pilipino teachers were not proficient in Pilipino; there was a scarcity of materials, or poor distribution of existing materials, and there was little original scholarship in Pilipino which could lead to its further elaboration and cultivation. Participants at the special symposium reaffirmed the goal of developing a bilingual citizenry as being among one of the major tasks of Filipino education; they reaffirmed the desirability of a bilingual-by-subject-matter specialization; they emphasized once again the importance of teaching initial literacy skills and initial content material in the vernacular languages in non-Tagalog areas at Grades 1 and 2; they called attention to the special need to prepare teachers more effectively to teach Pilipino as a second language (an irony because such courses are virtually nonexistent in a country which prides itself on the level of preparation of its teachers of English as a Second Language); they called for additional sustained materials development, particularly for core and ancillary materials in Pilipino; they called for revitalized pre-service and in-service education for teachers, with language proficiency in either English or Tagalog being a prerequisite for entering the content strand; they called for the development of a country-wide examination system for students at Grades 4, 6, and 10; and they suggested that the present six-year cycle of primary education be expanded to seven years for children from non-Tagalog areas.

In February of 1987, Filipino legislators ratified a new constitution (which was endorsed in a public plebiscite) which asserted: "The state shall protect and promote the right of all citizens to quality education at all levels and shall take appropriate steps to make such education accessible to all." The implementing Department of Education Order in June 1987 continued: "The general goal . . . is to bring about competence in both Pilipino and English at the national level— the aspiration of the Filipino nation is to have its citizens possess skills in both languages equal to their functions and duties as citizens in Philippine society and equal to the needs of the country in the community of nations." Obviously, Filipinos view bilingual language proficiency as a natural and national resource to be developed to the highest possible degree. The approach which has been chosen by Filipinos to language education policy merits close scrutiny over the next several years to see whether such a program can facilitate the development of full and fluent bilinguality together with appropriate subject-matter achievement.

OVERVIEW OF THE THREE MODELS

My reason for drawing attention to these three very different approaches has been to indicate that systematic needs assessment/goals specification and policy implementation have occurred in many parts of the world. In the three examples that I have chosen, a number of critical attributes vary: the role and status of the languages in question, the presence or absence of a rich literary tradition in the language(s) in question, the availability of appropriate materials in the target language, the availability of trained teachers who are mother-tongue speakers or fluently bilingual speakers of a particular target language(s), parental and community expectations concerning the educational chances and choices available to the youngsters, etc.

On the basis of these three examples, and many other case studies, it is apparent that no single, simple recommendation concerning the choice or sequencing of languages as media for educational instruction can be made that will suffice for children in all settings. The available evidence indicates that a variety of factors— individual, social, and pedagogical— interact in unique ways in diverse settings to influence students' ultimate levels of language development and academic achievement. On the one hand, introducing children to education in their native language before exposing them to instruction via a second language appears to be successful and desirable in many countries. Bilingual education in such circumstances should include a carefully designed native language arts program integrated into a general curriculum which uses the children's native language for basic subject matter instruction and which adds a second language to the child's repertoire at some point, not only as a subject for study but, for at least some portion of the day, as a medium of instruction thereby leading to additive bilingualism (Lambert, 1980). On the other hand, educating children initially exclusively through a second language and subsequently through both the native and second languages is feasible and effective in settings where the native language of the children is the majority language of the society at large, where maintenance of the native language is desired, and where parents and educators actively encourage literacy in the native language. This type of bilingual education has been shown to lead to high levels of second language competence for children in these settings without loss of language proficiency or academic achievement. Because of the diverse models that characterize bilingual education, a systematic evaluation, both formative and summative, is an important, integral part of each program.

IMPLICATIONS FOR U.S. EDUCATORS

Despite the findings I've just discussed, bilingual education programs will not succeed unless they are also consistent with national policy— whether explicit or implicit— and with the clearly expressed goals of local education authorities. This is not surprising since the selection in a particular country, province, or city of the language(s) to be taught or to be used as a medium of instruction clearly constitutes an important aspect of educational and, therefore, national planning. What I have suggested is that innovative language education should be viewed as a special case of language planning. It is important to define goals or objectives as carefully as possible. There are various options or models available for consideration. If the goal in the United States is to develop the fullest possible degree of "language competence" among American students, then some form of bilingual education program would appear to be both feasible and desirable. In particular, programs now referred to as "two-way," "bilingual immersion," "interlocking bilingual," or "developmental bilingual education" programs may be extremely exciting. Whatever approach is chosen, there is a need for continuing formative feedback to help inform language policy and language practice. Such research has been noticeably lacking in many American school districts (but see Lindholm & Fairchild, 1988).

A Word about Demographics

A recent article in *The Washington Post* ("Children at Risk," 1987) cited demographic statistics which indicate that while the population of school-age children in public schools decreased by approximately eight million students between 1970 and 1985, the percentage of minority students increased from 24% in 1976 to 28.8% in 1984. In 1981, in California, New Mexico, and Texas, the percentage of minority students had exceeded 35%, and the percentage in Florida, Illinois, and New York was nearing 35%. Moreover, the national percentage is projected by the Department of Education to increase to 38.4% by the year 2000. Unfortunately, academic achievement and school completion rates for many minority students— particularly Hispanic students, who are the largest minority and the fastest growing sector of our population— are woefully low. In the Southwest, Rendon (1983) reports that 40% of the Hispanic students drop out by the 10th grade, and an additional 10% drop out before completing high school. Of those who do graduate from high school, only a small percentage attend college and the majority of those who do choose community colleges. Of those who attend four-year colleges, the majority study education, business, or social science. Less than 3% of the science, math, and technical majors are Hispanic. By the year 2000, the nation will have a smaller pool of potential workers and college students, and the people in this pool will be less prepared for work and college study due to circumstances such as poverty, unstable homes, and lack of English language skills.

While these statistics document a problem for all minority groups, particularly Hispanic and black children, language minorities (those for whom English is not the native language) are notably at risk. Due to a combination of migration patterns and family size, the fastest growing population in the United States is the language minority population. Almost one million refugees entered the United States between 1975 and 1985. The majority (650,000) arrived from Southeast Asia, but substantial numbers came from Eastern Europe, the Soviet Union, the Caribbean, Africa, and the Middle East. Added to these numbers are the several million undocumented aliens who arrived from Central America and the Caribbean. Moreover, both racial and ethnic minority families, particularly black and Hispanic, are characteristically larger than those of the American majority population. If current trends continue, we can expect that 53 of the major American cities will have minority language youngsters as a majority of the school population by the year 2000.

Educational Implications

What types of programs are available for language minority youngsters? Let me *greatly* oversimplify the situation by noting that:

1. Some enroll in bilingual education programs (particularly transitional bilingual programs) where they get some of their education in their native language while they are learning enough English to be mainstreamed;

2. Others take ESL or English tutorials while they are also taking some content classes taught in English;

3. Finally, still others are submerged in an entirely English-speaking classroom, with the hope that they will finally somehow make sense of both the English and the academic content being taught.

Transitional bilingual education (TBE) programs, in principle, involve the use of the mother tongue for initial literacy training and content instruction together with an ESL component that would lead to a gradual transition to instruction entirely in English. In academic year 1986-1987, approximately 170,000 children with limited English proficiency were served by Title VII funds, 725,000 with state funds, 390,000 with other funds, and 690,000 with local funds. The General Accounting Office, in a recent review, reported that there was little available information on the amount of native language instruction within TBE programs, but they did document that English was the predominant classroom language in two programs evaluated by carefully conducted case studies to which they had access (the Significant Bilingual Instructional Features study and the study recently conducted by Development Associates). In fact, it was concluded that many so-called exemplary/demonstration bilingual programs really do not provide bilingual education at all.

There is a growing consensus concerning the desirable characteristics of an exemplary program. Let me give the example of a hypothetical group of youngsters homogeneous in mother tongue (e.g., Spanish) who might begin their education in a school in which there would be a native language arts component, a native language literacy component, and teaching of content material via the native language. In addition, from the beginning, there would be an ESL strand, and ideally one in which the curriculum model for the ESL strand was content-based. This plan would continue for from four to six years with the content-based language instruction gradually increasing so that over the course of four to six years, while the native language would continue to be used as a principle medium of instruction, the amount of English language instruction would also increase. This is, of course, almost never the case at present.

We might also note that teachers should be proficient speakers of the target language(s), that they should be well trained, that support services (such as counselling and remediation) should be offered, that library and other resources should be available, and that there should be active parental involvement. There should, thus, be an attempt to facilitate additive bilingualism. What might one expect the results of such a program to be? Willig (1985), in her careful review of available evidence, concluded: "Participation in bilingual education programs consistently produced small to moderate differences *favoring* [italics added] bilingual education for tests of reading, language skills, math, and total achievement— even when the tests were in English."

What are some of the problems which I see at the moment? There still exists a scarcity of trained teachers, too few years are devoted to bilingual education, there is a lack of material in many languages other than Spanish, etc. There is also a notable lack of communication among mainstream teachers, bilingual education teachers, special education teachers, and resource people.

Increasingly, I have become interested in programs intended to improve language and subject matter achievement opportunities for both language minority and language majority youngsters. Such programs are developing in many parts of the country and have come to be referred to as interlocking, two-way, or bilingual immersion programs (Lindholm, 1987). Some characteristics of such a program might be as follows: Imagine a situation in which, at Grade 1, there were 15 Anglo youngsters and 15 Hispanic youngsters. They would be grouped in a class with some portion of the school day devoted to Spanish language arts (for the Hispanics), Spanish as a second language (for the Anglos), English language arts (for the Anglos), English as a second language (for the Hispanics), and teaching of some of the content material in English and some in Spanish with the opportunity for cooperative learning, peer group tutoring, modeling, etc. The idea is to develop a bilingual ambience in which representatives of both of the major ethnolinguistic groups have an opportunity to develop and hone their literacy skills while acquiring the fullest possible proficiency in a second language. Such programs are now actively underway in the states of California, Maryland, Virginia, and New York, to name but a few places, and the results are very positive (see Tucker & Crandall, 1989). All too often, in any type of educational program involving language innovation, the amount of time devoted to the task of developing children's cognitive academic language skills is seriously underestimated. From my perspective, it is sobering to note that it can take from five to seven years for children to learn the academic language skills which will enable them to solve math problems, conduct science experiments, analyze the causes or effects of a particular historical event, or write a comparative essay (Collier, 1987). The task of educating youngsters in their own language, let alone another, is not a trivial one. Clearly one must devote additional resources to doing so when a second language is involved.

CONCLUSION

Why should we be concerned with improving the quality of language education programs for all American youngsters? Domestically, our country is rapidly and drastically changing in terms of demography. The composition and needs of our workforce are changing, and the demands on our children and young adults to develop problem-solving and decision-making skills are growing rapidly. Isn't it interesting that we find (Hakuta, 1986) that those who develop bilingual proficiency consistently outperform their monolingual counterparts in terms of creativity and problem-solving? Internationally if we are to compete effectively, we must communicate more effectively in English as well as in the languages of our clients, our trading partners, and our allies.

It is my opinion that we must take steps immediately, rapidly, and increasingly to broaden the base of additive bilingualism in our society because there are cognitive, personal, social, and economic benefits that will accrue when we do so. It should be viewed as unacceptable that so few youngsters and so few young adults in the United States develop bilingual language proficiency or have an opportunity to do so, as is now the case. It is not acceptable that fewer than 1% of our youngsters or young adults study or master foreign languages which are spoken by 99% of the world's population. It is not acceptable that the development of a language competent American society should be accorded such a low priority. One of the ways to do this is to examine critically our social needs and objectives and to use the tools of language education planning to implement a language education program that will benefit all American youngsters.

REFERENCES

Children at risk (1987, October 11). *The Washington Post*, p. 16.

Collier, V. P. (1987). Age and rate of acquisition of second language for academic purposes. *TESOL Quarterly, 21*, 617-641.

Cziko, G. A., & Troike, R. C. (1984). Contexts of bilingual education: International perspectives and issues. *AILA Review, 1*, 7-33.

Genesee, F. (1987). *Learning through two languages: Studies of immersion and bilingual education*. Cambridge, MA: Newbury House.

Hakuta, K. (1986). *Mirror of language. The debate on bilingualism*. New York: Basic Books.

Lambert, W. E. (1980). The two faces of bilingual education. *NCBE Forum, 3*.

Language education in Africa. (1985). Edinburgh: Center of African Studies.

Lindholm, K. (1987). *Directory of bilingual immersion programs: Two-way bilingual education for language minority and language majority students* (Educ. Rep. No. 9). Los Angeles: University of California, Center for Language Education and Research.

Lindholm, K., & Fairchild, H. H. (1988). *Evaluation of an "exemplary" bilingual immersion program* (Tech. Rep. No. 13). Los Angeles: University of California, Center for Language Education and Research.

Linguistic Society of the Philippines (1986, September). *Eleven years of bilingual schooling in the Philippines (1974-1985): A summative evaluation*. Unpublished manuscript.

Rendon, L. I. (1983). *Mathematics education for Hispanic students in the Border College Consortium. Report on the Math Intervention Project*. Laredo, TX: The Border College Consortium.

Sibayan, B. P. (1978). Bilingual education in the Philippines: Strategy and structure. In J. E. Alatis (Ed.), *International dimensions of bilingual education*. Georgetown University Round Table on Languages and Linguistics 1978. Washington, DC: Georgetown University Press.

Tucker, G. R. (1977). Some observations concerning bilingualism and second-language teaching in developing countries and in North America. In P. A. Hornby (Ed.), *Bilingualism: Psychological, social and educational implications*. New York: Academic Press.

Tucker, G. R. (1987). Educational language policy in the Philippines: A case study. In P. Lowenberg (Ed.), *Language spread and language policy: Issues, implications and case studies*. Georgetown University Round Table on Languages and Linguistics 1987. Washington, DC: Georgetown University Press.

Tucker, G. R., & Crandall, J. A. (1989). The integration of language and content instruction for language minority and language majority youngsters. In J. E. Alatis (Ed.), *Language teaching, testing, and technology: Lessons from the past with a view toward the future*. Georgetown University Round Table on Languages and Linguistics 1989. Washington, DC: Georgetown University Press.

Weinstein, B. (1983). *The civic tongue: Political consequences of language choices*. New York: Longman.

Willig, A. C. (1985). A meta-analysis of selected studies on the effectiveness of bilingual education. *Review of Educational Research, 55*, 269-317.

5 Neuropsychological Perspectives on Bilingualism: Right, Left, and Center

Jyotsna Vaid
Texas A & M University
D. Geoffrey Hall
Harvard University

Although it is often difficult to separate fact from artifact in the field of neuropsychology, one finding that has survived a century of investigation is that, in the vast majority of right-handed adults and to a lesser extent in left-handers, the left cerebral hemisphere is dominant for language functioning. The question we would like to consider in this chapter is whether this pattern of cerebral lateralization for language differs in users of more than one language. It is perhaps an accident of history that neuropsychological research, including research on language lateralization, has been conducted in predominantly monolingual societies. An implicit monolingual bias in research outlook could explain why systematic study of the "bilingual brain," and cross-linguistic approaches to aphasiology in general (e.g., Bates & Wulfeck, 1989; Menn & Obler, 1988), have been fairly recent.

Laterality studies using brain-intact individuals date back to the 1950s and 1960s when paradigms such as dichotic listening (e.g., Kimura, 1967) and tachistoscopic viewing (e.g., Bryden, 1965) began to be used to infer hemispheric involvement in higher cognitive functions. Although some of the earliest tachistoscopic studies of bilinguals also date back to this period (e.g., Mishkin & Forgays, 1952), these studies focused primarily on perceptual issues, for example the influence of directional scanning biases related to reading habits on visual field asymmetries in word recognition. It was not until the late 1970s that researchers began to use the available noninvasive techniques for assessing brain functional asymmetry to investigate

81

neuropsychological aspects of being or becoming bilingual. By now there are at least 80 studies comprising this literature.

In the present review we will first provide a historical/theoretical context for this body of work by identifying three separate lines of inquiry that motivated research on language lateralization in bilinguals. Because our intent here is simply to describe the intellectual *Zeitgeist* that may have led researchers to examine the neuropsychology of bilingualism in the way they did, our discussion of these areas is neither comprehensive nor evaluative. In contrast, our discussion of the bilingual lateralization literature, to which we next turn, *is* evaluative and based on a comprehensive meta-analytic assessment of five hypotheses pertaining to lateralization in bilinguals or second language learners (for a detailed presentation, see Hall & Vaid, 1990).

INTELLECTUAL ANTECEDENTS OF BILINGUAL LATERALIZATION RESEARCH

The different lines of inquiry that have shaped the particular questions and methodologies used in the study of brain functioning in brain-intact bilinguals include: 1) developments in research and theory in the mainstream laterality literature (i.e., studies based on monolinguals); 2) cognitive investigations of concept formation and reasoning in bilinguals as opposed to monolinguals, and of bilingual lexical organization; and 3) clinical neuropsychological studies of brain-damaged bilingual or polyglot patients and, specifically, reports of aphasia in such individuals. We summarize in the following the contributions of each of these areas to theories of cerebral lateralization in bilinguals.

Developments in Lateralization Research and Theory

A clinically derived view of cerebral functional asymmetry, prevalent in the 1960s, was rooted in stimulus-based differences, with the left hemisphere (in most right-handers) considered to be specialized for verbal stimuli and the right for nonverbal stimuli. This view underwent several modifications as more and more laterality studies with brain-intact individuals drawn from a variety of monolingual populations (e.g., musicians, dyslexics) indicated the existence of subject, task, and methodological influences on patterns of hemispheric asymmetry (see Hellige, 1990, for a recent review of this literature). The original, stimulus-based characterization of hemispheric differences was replaced by an information processing-based account (e.g., Moscovitch, 1979), although researchers rarely articulated precisely differences in processing mode, beyond referring to such general distinctions as "analytic/sequential" versus "holistic/simultaneous" (see Bradshaw & Nettleton, 1981). Despite problems (both theoretical and methodological) in documenting consistent differences using the standard noninvasive measures of hemispheric asymmetry in brain-intact individuals, there was considerable interest among psychologists in investigating neuropsychological repercussions of a variety of individual differences. For researchers in bilingualism, the contribution of the mainstream laterality literature was simply the possibility that individual differences in language experience or skill could be reflected in different patterns of hemispheric asymmetry.

Cognitive Investigations of Bilingualism

Investigations of cognitive aspects of bilingualism have been conducted in two domains, both of which have inspired neuropsychological investigations. One line of research has compared monolingual and bilingual children on various measures of intelligence and metalinguistic ability (e.g., Peal & Lambert, 1962; see Hamers & Blanc, 1989, for a review). The other domain of research has focused on individual differences among bilinguals (e.g., their age of acquisition of their languages or their proficiency in their languages) as factors influencing the extent to which the lexicons of the two languages are functionally separate (e.g., Lambert, 1981; Segalowitz, 1986). Although it is unclear when cognitive repercussions can be causally attributed to bilinguality (see, for example, Reynolds, this volume), investigations of bilingualism led psychologists to speculate about possible differences between bilinguals and monolinguals, or among bilinguals, related to the bilingual experience.

Clinical Neuropsychological Investigations of Bilingualism

Independent of both the cognitive literature on bilingualism and the lateralization literature on monolinguals, there developed a body of research on language impairment and recovery in brain-damaged bilinguals or polyglots. These studies were of three types: 1) clinical descriptions of aphasia in bilinguals or polyglots (there are over 300 published cases) from unilateral brain injury caused by stroke, trauma, or disease (see Paradis, 1983); 2) studies of cortical mapping of speech functions in a small group of bilinguals who underwent elective surgery for removal of epileptic foci (e.g., Ojemann & Whitaker, 1978; Rapport, Tan, & Whitaker, 1983); and 3) studies of a small group of bilinguals injected unilaterally with sodium amytal, a drug that experimentally induces temporary aphasia (Rapport et al., 1983). There also exist isolated cases of hemispherectomized bilinguals and split-brain individuals who are bilingual; however, researchers have not actually tested these individuals in both their languages. Because the polyglot aphasia literature constitutes the largest clinical source (there being less than a dozen cases studied in the other two sources), we will focus primarily on it in our discussion of the clinical literature. Furthermore, because the conclusions of the bilingual aphasia literature may have the most direct bearing on questions pertaining to bilingual lateralization, our discussion of this field is more detailed than that of the two previously discussed intellectual precursors.

Reports of aphasia in speakers of more than one language date back to the late 1800s (see Paradis, 1983, 1989a, for reviews of this literature). Two phenomena reported in this literature have implications for language lateralization: differential language loss or recovery from aphasia and the occurrence of aphasia following damage to the right hemisphere. Let us first consider the phenomenon of differential language impairment and/or recovery.

Selective impairment and/or recovery in bilingual aphasia. When bilingual individuals become aphasic as a result of brain injury, they may be impaired in their two languages either differentially or in proportion to their premorbid usage of those languages. Paradis (1989a) has described six different patterns of impairment and/or recovery of language in bilingual aphasia. However, because two-thirds of the reported cases of polyglot aphasia are single case studies (Vaid, 1984a), which may or may not be representative of the bilingual population at large, it is difficult to establish definitively the relative incidence of the different patterns of impairment and/or recovery reported. Nonetheless, the lack of a reliable estimate of the incidence of nonparallel forms of language recovery has not prevented speculation about possible causes of differential recovery patterns, when these do occur.

A variety of psychosocial variables related to language acquisition and/or use have been invoked to explain particular patterns of language recovery. These factors include: primacy of acquisition, according to which the first learned language will be the more resistant to impairment and/or the first to recover (Ribot, 1882); familiarity or practice with the language (Pitres, 1895); recency of acquisition or use (such that the more recently used language will be the first to recover); affect (the language associated with positive affect will recover first [Minkowski, 1963]); modality of acquisition (such that languages learned in a primarily written mode will recover better than those used primarily auditorily [Luria, 1960]); age and context of acquisition (such that languages learned in the same context and/or at the same time should be similarly impaired while those learned at different times should show differential impairment [Lambert & Fillenbaum, 1959; Vildomec, 1960]); and structural distance between languages (two languages that are more similar structurally should show more similar patterns of impairment and/or recovery [Ovcharova, Raichev, & Geleva, 1968]).

In addition to the preceding factors, neuropsychological factors influencing selective recovery in bilinguals also have been proposed. One suggestion has been that the right hemisphere plays an important role in language recovery, whether of the first or second language. In addition, it has been suggested that there is a differential premorbid pattern of hemispheric involvement in bilingual language organization. Albert and Obler (1978) commented, for example, that the recovering language might be less severely impaired than the nonrecovering language because it might be "more bilaterally represented than the nonrecovering language" (p. 240). Other researchers have directly entertained the possibility that one or both languages of bilinguals might be premorbidly organized in the nondominant, right hemisphere (Ovcharova et al., 1968; Vildomec, 1960).

Incidence of crossed aphasia in bilinguals. It was not until the 1970s that the notion of greater right hemisphere involvement in bilingual language processing was examined empirically, through an assessment of the relative incidence of crossed aphasia (aphasia arising from damage to the right hemisphere) in bilinguals and monolinguals (see Solin, 1989, for a review). In a comprehensive study of the published cases of polyglot aphasia, Galloway (1981) was able to extract sufficient information about side of lesion and handedness from 88 cases to allow an estimate of the incidence of crossed aphasia. She compared this with a sample of some 340 cases of aphasia in monolinguals and came up with a startling observation: In contrast to the low incidence of crossed aphasia found in right-handed monolinguals (around 4%), the incidence in polyglots was three times as high (14.6%).

While this finding would appear to support the notion of greater right hemisphere involvement in bilingual language processing, it was based on a population that may not have been representative of bilinguals in general given, as previously noted, that the majority of the clinical reports represented selected case studies. A better estimate of the incidence of crossed aphasia in bilinguals would require a comparison between randomly selected groups of bilingual and monolingual aphasics. It was not until fairly recently that this requirement was met. Chary (1986), describing a sample of nearly 100 patients in her clinic in Madras, South India, reported that the incidence of crossed aphasia in right-handed bilinguals was 13.6%. While this would appear to corroborate Galloway's claim, Chary also found an equally high incidence of crossed aphasia in her right-handed monolingual sample (12.9%). An additional Indian study, on aphasic patients randomly drawn from the population of patients presenting at a neurological institute in Bangalore, reported a similar finding of a high incidence of crossed aphasia in bilinguals and monolinguals (Karanth & Rangamani, 1988). Rather than suggest that there is something peculiar about Indic languages that makes them more right-lateralized, Karanth and Rangamani proposed that the high overall incidence of crossed aphasia probably reflects a cultural suppression of left-handedness in India, particularly among the older generation. Thus, the presence of even a few forced right-handers in the Indian samples could have inflated the estimate of crossed aphasia.

The claim of differential involvement of the right hemisphere in bilinguals thus remains controversial within the clinical literature. However, even with a reliable and valid estimate of crossed aphasia in the bilingual population at large, knowledge of the characteristics of the bilinguals' language acquisition histories would still be relevant to establishing which, if any, might be associated with greater right hemisphere involvement. A systematic approach to the study of aphasia in bilinguals would also provide needed information on cross-linguistic differences and similarities in patterns of aphasic impairments and on possible interactions of language-specific variables with language-acquisitional ones. It may not be too long before these issues can be systematically addressed, because a comprehensive and standardized bilingual aphasia test battery for over 60 different language pairs is currently being administered in different parts of the world (Paradis, 1987). For the present, the primary contribution of the clinical literature with brain-damaged bilinguals has been heuristic; that is, individual case studies have highlighted the potential importance of specific language-structural or language-acquisitional variables mediating language representation in the brain. These variables have in turn been studied under more controlled laboratory settings using brain-intact bilinguals, in the bilingual lateralization literature, to which we next turn.

CEREBRAL LATERALIZATION IN BRAIN-INTACT BILINGUALS

Over the last two decades, a number of laterality studies of brain-intact bilinguals have been conducted, using the standard methods of inferring hemispheric involvement (e.g., dichotic listening, tachistoscopic viewing, electrophysiological monitoring, and dual task performance).

Although differing widely in method and outcome, studies of lateralization in bilinguals have tended to address two general questions: 1) whether there are differences in cerebral lateralization between bilinguals and monolinguals; and 2) whether there are differences in cerebral lateralization among bilinguals in either or both of their languages. Answers to these two questions have been varied and often contradictory; some studies have found group and/or language differences while others have reported no differences, and still others have reported differences only on certain tasks. In view of the diversity of outcomes, the bilingual laterality literature would appear to be inconclusive at best and contradictory at worst, leading some researchers (e.g., Paradis, 1989b; Sussman & Simon, 1988) to advocate an end to further studies of this type.

The variability in outcomes of lateralization patterns should come as no surprise to those familiar with laterality studies in general, in that even subtle differences in method, task, and stimulus characteristics have been shown to affect patterns of asymmetries (see Hellige, Bloch, & Taylor, 1988; Sergent & Hellige, 1986). The additional variable of individual differences associated with bilingual language experience can only complicate the situation.

Sensitivity to methodological considerations has prompted some researchers (e.g., Bergh, 1989; Green & Vaid, 1986; Mendelsohn, 1988; Obler, Zatorre, Galloway, & Vaid, 1982; Zatorre, 1989) to identify variables that need to be controlled or systematically investigated in bilingual laterality studies. Among these are subject and procedural variables shared by bilinguals and monolinguals (e.g., age, handedness, and sex; stimulus and task characteristics; and modes of data reduction and analysis) and variables that are unique to bilinguals (e.g., differences associated with when, how, and how well the bilinguals acquired their languages, as well as the specific combinations of languages used by subjects).

Aside from the methodological diversity characterizing the bilingual laterality studies, there also has been considerable variation in the theoretical orientation of different studies. As a result, perhaps, of differing theoretical assumptions, some researchers have included monolingual and bilingual comparison groups in their studies while others have used only bilinguals. In the latter category, some researchers have looked at a single bilingual group's performance on the first versus second language while others have looked at the performance of more than one bilingual subgroup on one or both of their languages. Finally, some researchers have used bilinguals to investigate language-specific variables without controlling for language acquisitional differences, while others have investigated language acquisitional variables without controlling for language-specific differences. These facts make the task of comparing studies even more difficult. Aside from differences in method, then, differences in subject screening and classification need to be considered.

HYPOTHESES ABOUT BILINGUALISM AND BRAIN LATERALIZATION

From the laterality literature it is possible to distinguish at least five different hypotheses about bilingualism and brain lateralization (see, for example, Vaid & Genesee, 1980; Galloway, 1983). Two of these consider bilinguals as a single group while the remaining three classify bilinguals into various subgroups. In the following section we present the rationales provided, either explicitly or implicitly, for each of these theoretical positions before presenting a quantitative assessment of them.

The Balanced Bilingual Hypothesis:
Bilinguals versus Monolinguals

According to this hypothesis, becoming a skilled user of two languages, or a so-called "balanced bilingual," involves a cognitive "restructuring" which may have distinct neuropsychological implications for how language is processed in bilinguals. Specifically, it is suggested that proficient bilinguals may call on the right hemisphere to a greater degree (relative to monolinguals), whether in second or first language processing (Galloway, 1983).

The Second Language Hypothesis:
Bilinguals' First versus Second Language

Unlike the balanced bilingual hypothesis, the second language hypothesis posits a difference in lateralization between the two languages of bilinguals. Specifically, right hemisphere involvement, according to this view, is thought to be greater in the acquisition of the second language than in that of the first (Galloway, 1983).

Three additional hypotheses in the literature have attempted to specify the role of the right hemisphere in language processing in particular subgroups of bilinguals.

The Stage of L₂ Acquisition Hypothesis

Obler (1981) argued that left hemisphere involvement in the bilingual's second language will increase with increasing proficiency in that language. This claim came to be known as the stage hypothesis, according to which laterality differences between the two languages of bilinguals should decrease with increasing second language proficiency; also, individuals in the beginning stages of acquiring a language should show greater right hemisphere involvement than that characterizing more advanced users of that language.

Although directed at second language acquisition, the stage hypothesis is applicable to first language acquisition as well, to the extent that the task of acquiring a first or a second language involves the same processing requirements. The assumptions underlying the stage hypothesis are threefold: 1) that the linguistically mature native speaker processes a given linguistic unit differently than someone acquiring that language; 2) that the left hemisphere, given its analytic processing mode, is better suited to processing language in the linguistically mature user; and 3) that the right hemisphere, given its holistic processing mode, better meets the processing requirements of the beginning language learner. Schneiderman (1986) has discussed the theoretical and empirical bases for these assumptions.

From the perspective of the stage hypothesis, the right hemisphere is thought to subserve the acquisition of novel, unsegmented utterances that convey affective and/or pragmatic information. These types of utterances are thought to be especially important in the beginning learner's perception and production of language. The core aspects of language processing by the mature user are thought to involve phonetic and syntactic analysis (see McLaughlin, Rossman, & McLeod, 1984) which are considered to be more under the control of the left hemisphere.

The Manner of L₂ Acquisition Hypothesis

The motivation for the manner hypothesis came in part from clinical findings suggesting a differential influence of modality of learning (e.g., visual vs. auditory) on patterns of language recovery from aphasia (Luria, 1960). In addition, results from the second language acquisition literature led some researchers to suggest that informal language acquisition may involve different processes than formal language learning (Krashen, 1981) and that greater right hemisphere participation should therefore characterize only those individuals acquiring the language in an informal, naturalistic context, in which communicative needs are emphasized (Galloway & Krashen, 1980). A corollary to this hypothesis is that when a language is acquired in settings that emphasize structural aspects (e.g., rules of grammar, spelling, etc.), greater left hemisphere involvement would be expected (Carroll, 1980).

According to the manner hypothesis, then, right hemisphere involvement will be greater when the second language is acquired in an informal, naturalistic acquisition context; in a more formal and primarily written mode of L₂ learning, greater left hemisphere involvement in language processing would be expected.

The Age of L₂ Acquisition Hypothesis

Whereas the preceding two hypotheses focused on the language acquisition process, the age hypothesis considers hemispheric correlates of early as opposed to late acquisition of the second language. The impetus for considering age-related differences in brain lateralization of language in bilinguals came from two sources: neurological evidence that the cerebral cortex continues to develop until at least the age of five years, and possibly until puberty, and psychological evidence for differences in language processing strategies between early and late bilinguals. On neurological grounds alone, it might be plausible to expect a different pattern of hemispheric involvement in late bilinguals (especially in their second language) than that in either language of early bilinguals. Whitaker (1978) suggested, for example, that "research on maturational correlates of language acquisition would lead one to conclude that the earlier a second language is introduced, the more likely the neural substrate for it will parallel that of the native or first language" (p. 30).

Psychological studies on verbal learning and memory in bilinguals have reported differences between early and late bilinguals on a variety of behavioral tasks including Stroop interference, free recall, and concept formation (see Lambert, 1981, and Hamers & Blanc, 1989, for reviews). Taken together, the pattern of group differences suggests that early bilinguals are more influenced by the semantic content of verbal stimuli than late bilinguals who, in turn, are more readily attuned to surface (e.g., acoustic) features of input (see McLaughlin et al., 1984; Vaid & Lambert, 1979; Vaid, 1984b).

On the basis of these findings and their own observation of a right hemisphere superiority in late bilinguals, Genesee et al. (1978) hypothesized that differences between early and late bilinguals in language processing strategy might be translated on the cerebral level into a predominance of a left hemisphere "semantic-type" strategy in early bilinguals and for a right hemisphere "acoustic-type" strategy in late bilinguals. Vaid and Genesee (1980), in referring to the age hypothesis, further predicted that "the pattern of hemispheric involvement of balanced bilinguals will more closely resemble that of monolinguals of the same age the earlier second language acquisition takes place and will differ from that of monolinguals the later the second language is acquired" (p. 435).

ASSESSING THE LATERALITY LITERATURE

Previous reviews of laterality research on bilinguals (e.g., Galloway, 1983; Vaid, 1983; Vaid & Genesee, 1980) have used a traditional qualitative approach to assessing the outcomes of the studies. While no doubt useful in isolating potentially relevant variables, this approach has offered neither a way to evaluate the exact magnitude of the effects of these variables nor a method of combining and comparing these effects. To accomplish these goals, it is necessary to use meta-analytic procedures (e.g., Rosenthal, 1984). In order to add a new level of precision and clarity to an understanding of the laterality literature, we undertook a meta-analysis of this body of work (Hall & Vaid, 1990). In the following section we summarize the results of this meta-analysis.[1]

---

[1] For further details on the meta-analysis, refer to Hall and Vaid (1990).

THE META-ANALYSIS

Criteria for Study Inclusion

Given the methodological diversity across the studies and previous criticisms of the laterality literature for inadequacies in experimental design or analysis, we first faced the difficult decision of which studies to include in the meta-analysis. We decided to include all relevant studies, published or unpublished, so long as they allowed us to assess hemispheric involvement on a linguistic task through a comparison of either: 1) two or more groups, one of which had knowledge of more than one language; or 2) two languages spoken by one or more groups. Our corpus thereby is more complete than that used in the most recently published reviews of this literature (e.g., Mendelsohn, 1988; Zatorre, 1989), and allows a thorough treatment of the results from the studies included.[2]

Types of Comparisons

From the results of each study that passed the initial screening, we sought four kinds of comparisons. These were cases that involved:

1. L_1 versus L_2 — one or more bilingual group(s) tested in their first language (L_1) and one or more bilingual group(s) tested in their second language (L_2);
2. L_1 — one or more bilingual group(s) tested in L_1 and (optionally) a monolingual group;
3. L_2 — one or more bilingual group(s) tested in L_2 and (optionally) a monolingual group;
4. L_1/L_2 — one or more bilingual group(s) tested in L_1 and/or L_2 and (optionally) a monolingual group. Comparisons of type 4 included bilingual groups that were tested in one language that was the L_1 for some members and the L_2 for other members.

We coded each comparison for a variety of independent variables including the type of groups involved (e.g., bilingual vs. monolingual), the

---

[2]A number of studies were not included in the meta-analysis, because they had been conducted or analyzed after we completed the meta-analysis or because we were unaware of their existence at the time of our study. They include: Corina and Vaid (1990), Endo, Shimizu, and Nakamura (1981a, 1981b), Hoosain and Shiu (1989), Jinn (1988), Judd (1988), Kang (1984), Kutas and Bates (1988), Mägiste (1989), McClung (1981), Neville and Corina (1990), Obrzut, Conrad, Bryden, and Boliek (1988), and Green, Schweda Nicholson, Vaid, White, and Steiner (1990).

sample size of the groups, the paradigm and response measure(s) used, the year of publication or completion (for unpublished studies) of the study, the handedness and sex composition of the sample, and the age of the subjects in the sample. Where sufficient L_2 acquisitional information was available, we abstracted it with regard to the three factors of age, stage, and manner of L_2 acquisition. We classified a given group along each of these acquisitional dimensions relative to the other groups within a particular study.

Once we had obtained a comparison, we tried to determine whether it supported or refuted one of the five hypotheses. We thus looked for scores on two dependent measures. The first was the overall hemisphere main effect, which indicated the direction and extent of difference between the two hemispheres on performance on the task. We assigned a positive sign to all effects showing greater left hemisphere involvement. The second was the interaction effect of hemisphere (left or right) with group or the interaction effect of hemisphere with language. We gave a positive sign to the hemisphere by group interaction effect whenever it supported the particular acquisitional hypothesis under investigation (as summarized earlier). Similarly, we assigned a positive sign to the hemisphere by language interaction effect whenever it supported the hypothesis that there will be more right hemisphere involvement for L_2 than for L_1.

Estimation of Effect Size

The effect size estimates we used in this meta-analysis were simply Pearson product-moment correlations (r) (see Rosenthal & Rosnow, 1985; Rosenthal & Rubin, 1982). These correlations indicate the direction in which, and the extent to which, scores on a laterality task varied with involvement of a particular hemisphere or in a particular combination of hemisphere and group or hemisphere and language. To estimate these effect sizes for each comparison, we relied whenever possible on the results of t tests or analyses of variance, from which we computed r and its significance level Z. Whenever more than two groups were involved in a comparison, we computed contrasts (single degree of freedom tests) in order to obtain the r testing the hypothesis in question. Where results from the significance tests based on raw scores were not available, we estimated the rs using other means, as described in further detail in Hall and Vaid (1990). The five hypotheses discussed earlier were then evaluated in the meta-analysis.

The Balanced Bilingual Hypothesis:
Bilinguals versus Monolinguals

According to this hypothesis, there should be more right hemisphere involvement in one or both languages of bilinguals relative to that in monolingual controls. Seventeen studies in our corpus included monolingual controls;[3] in the majority of the studies English was the second language of the bilinguals and the language spoken by the monolingual controls. The key below explains the abbreviations used in Tables 5-1 through 5-5; Table 5-1 summarizes 11 studies (representing 15 comparisons) that bear on the balanced bilingual hypothesis (6 other studies in Table 5-1 that utilized unusual stimuli were analyzed separately; see below).

Key to Abbreviations in Tables

Paradigm

DL = Dichotic listening
T = Tachistoscopic viewing
Dual = Dual task performance
EEG = Electroencephalogram
ERP = Event-related brain potentials

Measurement

acc = accuracy
rt = reaction time

Groups

b = bilingual group
m = monolingual group
t = trilingual group
beg = beginning stage/level of L_2 acquisition
int = intermediate stage/level of L_2 acquisition
adv = advanced stage/level of L_2 acquisition
soc = "social" bilinguals
pro = interpreters
ear = early age of L_2 acquisition
bab = infant age of L_2 acquisition
chi = childhood age of L_2 acquisition
ado = adolescent age of L_2 acquisition
lat = late age of L_2 acquisition
for = formal manner/context of L_2 acquisition
inf = informal manner/context of L_2 acquisition

(These classifications are all assigned within a study, according to the study's own criteria.)

Languages

Ara = Arabic; ASL = American Sign Language; Chi = Chinese; Cro = Crow; Dut = Dutch; Eng = English; Est = Estonian; Fin = Finnish; Fre = French; Fri = Friulian; Ger = German; Heb = Hebrew; Hop = Hopi; Ita = Italian; Nav = Navajo; Pol = Polish; Por = Portuguese; Rus = Russian; Spa = Spanish; Swe = Swedish; Tha = Thai; Var = Various languages; Vie = Vietnamese; Yid = Yiddish.

---

[3] Some studies that used bilinguals with monolingual controls were excluded from the bilingual/monolingual comparison in the meta-analysis because they contained information in a form that was not amenable to the meta-analysis; these were: Hall and Lambert (1988), Vaid (1981, 1982, 1984b, 1987), and Vaid and Lambert (1979).

TABLE 5-1

Laterality Studies Comparing Bilinguals and Monolinguals

Paradigm	Author(s)	Year	Groups	L_1	L_2
DL-acc, ord	Bellisle & Lambert	1975	b1:	Eng/Fre	Fre/Eng
			m1:	Eng	-
			m2:	Fre	-
DL-acc, ord	Starck, Genesee, Lambert, & Seitz	1977	t1:	Eng	Fre/Heb
			m:	Eng	-
DL-acc	Galloway & Scarcella	1982	b1:	Spa	Eng
			m1:	Spa	-
			m2:	Eng	-
DL-rt	Soares	1982	b1: lat	Por	Eng
			b2: lat	Por	Eng
			m1:	Eng	-
DL-acc (CVs)	Scott, Hynd, Hunt, & Weed	1979	b1:	Nav	Eng
			m1:	Eng	-
DL-acc (CVs)	Hynd & Scott	1980	b1:	Nav	Eng
			m1:	Eng	-
DL-acc (CVs)	Hynd, Teeter, & Stewart	1980	b1:	Nav	Eng
			m1:	Eng	-
DL-acc (CVs)	McKeever & Hunt	1984	b1:	Nav	Eng
			m1:	Eng	-
DL-acc (CVs)	Vocate	1984	b1:	Cro	Eng
			m1:	Eng	-
DL-acc (CVs)	McKeever, Hunt, Wells, & Yazzie	in press	b1:	Nav	Eng
			m1:	Eng	-
T-acc	Barton, Goodglass, & Shai	1965	b1:	Heb	Eng
			m1:	Eng	-
T-rt	McKeever	1981	b1:	Nav	Eng
			m1:	Eng	-
T-rt	Soares & Grosjean	1. 1981	b1:	Por	Eng
			m1:	Eng	-
		2. 1981	b1:	Por	Eng
			m1:	Eng	-
T-acc	Sewell & Panou	1983	b1:	Eng	Ger
			b2:	Eng	Ger
			m1:	Eng	-
T-acc	Mägiste	2. 1987	b1:	Pol	Swe
			m1:	Pol	-
Dual	Sussman, Franklin, & Simon	1982	b1:	Var	Var
			m1:	Eng	-
	Soares	1984	b1: lat	Por	Eng
			b2: lat	Por	Eng
			m1:	Eng	

We found a nonsignificant and small mean effect size for comparisons of lateralization between monolinguals and bilinguals tested in either their L_1 or in their L_1 and/or L_2. Significant support for the hypothesis that bilinguals are less lateralized than monolinguals was obtained, however, for studies in which bilinguals were tested in their second language only. In this subset of eight comparisons, the combined effect size indicated that bilinguals were significantly more right-lateralized in their second language (English in all but one case) relative to monolingual users of that language (English in all but two cases). However, closer examination of the studies contributing to this finding revealed that only two of the eight contributing comparisons (Mägiste, 1987, and Sussman, Franklin, & Simon, 1982) showed effect sizes that were of any appreciable magnitude; for the remaining studies, the effect sizes either bordered on zero or had negative values. Thus, while the balanced bilingual hypothesis was supported in a subset of comparisons (i.e., those involving the bilinguals' second language), the mean effect size was small and the group difference was negligible in most of the studies contributing to the comparison.

We analyzed an additional set of six studies separately (see Table 5-1) because these studies used pairs of consonant-vowel (CV) syllables as stimuli in a dichotic listening task. Because these stimuli do not constitute actual words in either L_1 or L_2, we decided not to include them in the overall analysis. All six studies involved speakers of native American languages (typically Navajo) and monolingual English speakers. The analysis of this subset of studies revealed a significant hemisphere by group interaction whereby the bilinguals were found to be more right-lateralized than the monolinguals. Because it is unclear what the linguistic status of these CV syllables is for native speakers of either English or Navajo, it is uncertain whether the reliable mean effect size should be interpreted in terms of the balanced bilingual hypothesis.

The Second Language Hypothesis: First versus Second Language

Forty-five comparisons from 39 studies contributed to testing the second language hypothesis (see Table 5-2).

There was no significant support for the hypothesis that the second language is more right-lateralized than the first; in fact, the mean effect size was near zero. However, we discovered several variables that moderated the size of the effect. Specifically, the hypothesis was more likely to be supported under the following conditions: 1) the samples consisted exclusively of right handers; 2) subjects were L_2 users of a right-to-left script; 3) subjects received a visual task (typically tachistoscopic) rather than an auditory task (typically dichotic); and 4) subjects' response latency, rather than accuracy, was recorded. Other variables we considered did not reliably moderate the magnitude of the effect sizes. These variables were sex (whether only males

TABLE 5-2
Laterality Studies Comparing L_1 and L_2 of Bilinguals

Paradigm	Author(s)	Year	Groups	L_1	L_2
DL-acc	Maitre	1974	b1: int/for	Eng	Spa
			b2: int/inf	Eng	Spa
			b3: adv/for	Eng	Spa
			b4: adv/inf	Eng	Spa
DL-acc	Kotik	1975	b1:	Rus	Est
			b2:	Est	Rus
			b3:	Est	Rus
			b4:	Est	Rus
DL-acc	Schonle	1978	b1:	Rus	Ger
			b2:	Ger	Rus
DL-acc	Albert & Obler	1978	b1: adv	Heb/Eng	Eng/Heb
			b2: int/inf	Eng	Heb
			b3: int/for	Heb	Eng
DL-acc	Carroll	1. 1980	b1:	Nav	Eng
		2. 1980	b1: beg	Eng	Spa
			b2: int	Eng	Spa
			b3: adv	Eng	Spa
		3. 1980	b1: ear/inf	Eng	Spa
			b2: ado/for	Eng	Spa
			b3: lat/for	Eng	Spa
			b4: lat/inf	Eng	Spa
		4. 1980	b1:	Eng	Spa
DL-acc	Gordon	1980	b1:	Heb	Eng
DL-acc	Rupp	1980	b1:	Vie	Eng
DL-acc (and dual task)	Winfield aka Carroll	1981	b1:	Spa	Eng
DL-acc	Gordon & Zatorre	1981	b1: int	Spa	Eng
			b2: adv	Spa	Eng
DL-acc	Kotik & Kiroy	1. 1982	b1:	Spa	Rus
			b2:	Spa	Rus
			b3:	Spa	Rus
		2. 1982	b1:	Vie	Rus
			b2:	Vie	Rus
			b3:	Vie	Rus
		3. 1982	b1:	Fre	Rus
			b2:	Fre	Rus
			b2:	Fre	Rus
DL-rt	Soares	1982	b1: lat	Por	Eng
			b2: lat	Por	Eng
DL-acc	Wesche & Schneiderman	1982	b1:	Eng	Fre
			b2:	Fre	Eng
DL-acc	Albanese	1985	b1: beg	Eng	Fre
			b2: adv	Eng	Fre
DL-acc	Mohr & Costa	1985	b1: beg	Eng	Fre
			b2: adv	Eng	Fre
DL-acc	Bergh	1986	b1: beg	Swe	Eng
			b2: int	Swe	Eng
			b3: adv	Swe	Eng
DL-acc	Fabbro, Gran, & Bava	1987	b1: beg	Ita	Eng
			b2: int	Ita	Eng
			b3: adv	Ita	Eng

TABLE 5-2 cont'd.

T-acc	Mishkin & Forgays	1952	b1:	Eng	Yid
T-acc	Orbach	1952	b1:	Eng	Yid
			b2:	Yid	Eng
T-acc	Barton, Goodglass, & Shai	1965	b1:	Heb	Eng
T-acc	Orbach	1967	b1:	Heb	Eng
			b2:	Heb	Eng
T-acc	Kershner & Jeng	1972	b1:	Chi	Eng
T-rt	Hamers & Lambert	1977	b1:	Fre	Eng
T-rt	Gaziel, Obler, & Albert	1978	b1: adv	Eng/Heb	Heb/Eng
			b2: int/inf	Eng	Heb
			b3: int/inf	Eng	Heb
			b4: int/inf	Eng	Heb
			b5: int/for	Heb	Eng
			b6: int/for	Heb	Eng
T-rt	Hardyck, Tzeng, & Wang	1978	b1:	Eng/Chi	Chi/Eng
			b2:	Eng/Chi	Chi/Eng
T-rt	Silverberg, Bentin, Gaziel, Obler, & Albert	1979	b1: beg	Heb	Eng
			b2: int	Heb	Eng
			b3: adv	Heb	Eng
T-rt	Bentin	1981	b1:	Heb	Eng
T-rt	Soares & Grosjean	1. 1981	b1:	Por	Eng
		2. 1981	b1:	Por	Eng
T-acc, rt	Shanon	1982	b1: lat	Eng	Heb
			b2: lat	Heb	Eng
			b3: ear	Eng/Heb	Heb/Eng
T-acc	Garnham & Jones	1983	b1:	Eng	Fre
T-acc	Sewell & Panou	1983	b1:	Eng	Ger
			b2:	Eng	Ger
Dual (and DL)	Winfield	1981	b1:	Spa	Eng
Dual	Sussman, Franklin, & Simon	1982	b1:	Var	Var
Dual	Soares	1984	b1:	Por	Eng
Dual	Sanchez, Manga, Babecki, & de Tembleque	1987	b1: beg	Spa	Eng
			b2: adv	Spa	Eng
Dual	Fabbro	1988	b1: beg	Fri	Ita
			b2: adv	Fri	Ita
Dual	Hall & Lambert	1988	b1: ear	Eng	Fre
			b2: lat	Eng	Fre
Dual	Vaid, Green, Schweda Nicholson, & White	1989	b1: ear1	Spa	Eng
			b2: ear2	Spa	Eng
EEG	Rogers, TenHouten, Kaplan, & Gardner	1977	b1:	Hop	Eng
ERP	Genesee et al.	1978	b1: ear	Fre	Eng
			b2: chi	Fre	Eng
			b3: ado	Fre	Eng
EEG	TenHouten	1980	b1:	Chi	Eng

were tested), year of study completion or publication, and age of subjects (below or above 16 years of age).

In testing the three remaining hypotheses, we combined results separately for comparisons in the first language, those in the second language, and those in the L_1 and/or L_2.

The Stage of L_2 Acquisition Hypothesis

According to this hypothesis, there should be more right hemisphere involvement in beginning, rather than in advanced, stages of second language acquisition. Twenty-two comparisons drawn from 17 studies focused on the variable of stage of second language acquisition. The studies are listed in Table 5-3.

TABLE 5-3
Laterality Studies on the Stage Variable

Paradigm	Author(s)	Year	Groups	L_1	L_2
DL-acc	Maitre	1974	b1: int/for	Eng	Spa
			b2: int/inf	Eng	Spa
			b3: adv/for	Eng	Spa
			b4: adv/inf	Eng	Spa
DL-acc	Albert & Obler	1978	b1: adv	Heb/Eng	Eng/Heb
			b2: int/inf	Eng	Heb
			b3: int/for	Heb	Eng
DL-acc	Carroll	2. 1980	b1: beg	Eng	Spa
			b2: int	Eng	Spa
			b3: adv	Eng	Spa
DL-acc	Gordon	1. 1980	b1: beg	Eng/Heb	Heb/Eng
			b2: int	Eng/Heb	Heb/Eng
			b3: adv	Eng/Heb	Heb/Eng
		2. 1980	b1: beg	Eng/Heb	Heb/Eng
			b2: int	Eng/Heb	Heb/Eng
DL-acc	Gordon & Zatorre	1981	b1: int	Spa	Eng
			b2: adv	Eng	Spa
DL-acc	Albanese	1985	b1: beg	Eng	Fre
			b2: adv	Eng	Fre
DL-acc	Mohr & Costa	1985	b1: beg	Eng	Fre
			b2: adv	Eng	Fre
DL-acc	Schouten, van Dalen, & Klein	1. 1985	b1: int	Dut	Eng
			b2: adv	Dut	Eng
		2. 1985	b1: int	Dut	Eng
			b2: adv	Dut	Eng
DL-acc	Bergh	1986	b1: beg	Swe	Eng
			b2: int	Swe	Eng
			b3: adv	Swe	Eng
DL-acc	Fabbro, Gran, & Bava	1987	b1: beg	Ita	Eng
			b2: int	Ita	Eng
			b3: adv	Ita	Eng
DL-acc	Mägiste	1. 1987	b1: beg	Ger	Swe
			b2: int	Ger	Swe
			b3: adv	Ger	Swe

TABLE 5-3 cont'd.

T-rt	Gaziel, Obler, & Albert	1978	b1: adv	Eng/Heb	Heb/Eng
			b2: int/inf	Eng	Heb
			b3: int/inf	Eng	Heb
			b4: int/inf	Eng	Heb
			b5: int/for	Heb	Eng
			b6: int/for	Heb	Eng
T-rt	Silverberg, Bentin, Gaziel, Obler, & Albert	1979	b1: beg	Heb	Eng
			b2: int	Heb	Eng
			b3: adv	Heb	Eng
T-rt	Coulter	1982	b1: ear/adv	Ara/Eng	Eng/Ara
			b2: lat/int	Ara	Eng
			b3: lat/int	Eng	Ara
Dual	Green	1986	b1: beg	Eng	Spa
			b2: int	Eng	Spa
			b3: adv	Eng	Spa
Dual	Sanchez, Manga, Babecki, & de Tembleque	1987	b1: beg	Spa	Eng
			b2: adv	Spa	Eng
Dual	Fabbro	1988	b1: beg	Fri	Ita
			b2: adv	Fri	Ita

The results of the contrasts performed on the studies offered no significant support for the hypothesis of greater left hemisphere involvement with increasing language proficiency. Of the 22 comparisons, 9 were drawn from studies that lacked information that would have provided a precise estimate of effect size (i.e., they offered only an indication of whether the result was significant or nonsignificant, without specifying the exact level of significance). Of the remainder, 5 effects were in a positive direction, consistent with the hypothesis, but 8 were in a negative direction. In fact, overall negative support of the stage hypothesis was close to reliable for both the L_1 and the L_1/L_2 comparisons, although the mean effect sizes were again small.

The Manner of L_2 Acquisition Hypothesis

According to this hypothesis, there should be more right hemisphere involvement when a language is acquired in a primarily informal mode of instruction rather than a formal mode. The manner of acquisition hypothesis was tested in a total of six comparisons, based on five studies (see Table 5-4).

We found no reliable difference in the lateralization pattern of formally versus informally learned languages. However, we noted that five of the six comparisons showed effect sizes that were positive, although quite small, in the direction predicted by the hypothesis.

TABLE 5-4
Laterality Studies on Manner
of Second Language Acquisition

Paradigm	Author(s)	Year	Groups	L_1	L_2
DL-acc	Maitre	1974	b1: int/for	Eng	Spa
			b2: int/inf	Eng	Spa
			b3: adv/for	Eng	Spa
			b4: adv/inf	Eng	Spa
DL-acc	Albert & Obler	1978	b1: int/inf	Eng	Heb
			b2: int/for	Heb	Eng
DL-acc	Walters & Zatorre	1978	b1: for	Eng	Spa
			b2: inf	Spa	Eng
DL-acc	Carroll	3. 1980	b1: ear/inf	Eng	Spa
			b2: ado/for	Eng	Spa
			b3: lat/for	Eng	Spa
			b4: lat/inf	Eng	Spa
T-rt	Gaziel, Obler,	1978	b1: int/inf	Eng	Heb
	& Albert		b2: int/inf	Eng	Heb
			b3: int/inf	Eng	Heb
			b4: int/for	Heb	Eng
			b5: int/for	Heb	Eng

The Age of L₂ Acquisition Hypothesis

According to this hypothesis, there should be more right hemisphere involvement in late than in early fluent bilinguals. A total of 16 comparisons based on 12 studies focused on differences between early and late fluent bilinguals. The criteria for classifying bilinguals as early or late were defined within each study; typically, "early" onset of bilingualism referred to mastery of both languages prior to the age of 6 years and "late" bilingualism to mastery of the second language after the age of 10 years. The studies are summarized in Table 5-5.

TABLE 5-5
Laterality Studies on Age of Second Language Acquisition

Paradigm	Author(s)	Year	Groups	L_1	L_2
DL-acc	Carroll	3. 1980	b1: ear/inf	Eng	Spa
			b2: ado/for	Eng	Spa
			b3: lat/for	Eng	Spa
			b4: lat/inf	Eng	Spa
DL-acc	Gordon	1. 1980	b1: ear	Eng/Heb	Heb/Eng
			b2: chi	Eng/Heb	Heb/Eng
			b3: lat	Eng/Heb	Heb/Eng
DL-acc	Mägiste	1. 1987	b1: ear	Ger	Swe
			b2: lat	Ger	Swe

TABLE 5-5 cont'd.

T-rt	Vaid	1981	b1: ear	Eng/Fre	Fre/Eng
			b2: lat	Eng/Fre	Fre/Eng
T-rt	Coulter	1982	b1: ear/adv	Ara/Eng	Eng/Ara
			b2: lat/int	Ara	Eng
			b3: lat/int	Eng	Ara
T-rt	Vaid	1. 1984	b1: ear	Eng/Fre	Fre/Eng
			b2: lat	Eng/Fre	Fre/Eng
		2. 1984	b1: ear	Eng/Fre	Fre/Eng
			b2: lat	Eng/Fre	Fre/Eng
		3. 1984	b1: ear	Eng/Fre	Fre/Eng
			b2: lat	Eng/Fre	Fre/Eng
T-rt	Vaid	1987	b1: ear	Eng/Fre	Fre/Eng
			b2: lat	Eng/Fre	Fre/Eng
Dual	Hall & Lambert	1988	b1: ear	Eng	Fre
			b2: lat	Eng	Fre
Dual	Furtado & Webster	1988	b1: ear	Eng/Fre	Fre/Eng
			b2: lat	Eng	Fre
			b3: lat	Fre	Eng
Dual	Vaid, Green, Schweda Nicholson, & White	1989	b1: ear-pro	Spa	Eng
			b2: ear-soc	Spa	Eng
			b3: lat-pro	Spa/Eng	Eng/Spa
Dual	Corina & Vaid	in press	b1: ear-pro	Eng/ASL	ASL/Eng
			b2: lat-pro	Eng	ASL
ERP	Genesee et al.	1978	b1: ear-bab	Fre/Eng	Eng/Fre
			b2: ear-chi	Fre	Eng
			b3: lat-ado	Fre	Eng

We uncovered no reliable support for the hypothesis on any of the three types of comparisons. However, for the L_2 and the L_1/L_2 comparisons, we found reliably *negative* results. That is, early rather than late bilinguals were the more right-lateralized subgroup.

DISCUSSION

In general, the hemisphere main effects were large and highly significant, indicating strongly dominant left hemisphere processing of language across groups and languages. However, the mean effect sizes testing differences in lateralization among bilingual groups or between bilinguals and monolinguals were small, indicating minimal support for the hypotheses. In some cases the mean effect sizes were even negative in direction. We first discuss the meta-analytic results in greater detail with reference to each of the hypotheses before assessing the implications of our analysis.

Hypotheses Regarding Lateralization in Bilinguals

The hypothesis that bilinguals are more right-lateralized than monolinguals received partial support in that reliable group differences were not uncovered for the L_1 or the L_1/L_2 comparisons but *were* found for studies in which bilinguals were tested in their second language. However, a closer examination of the individual effect sizes contributing to the significant result obtained in the L_2 comparison makes it apparent that the bilingual/monolingual difference is the exception rather than the rule because six of the eight studies contributing to the significant effect showed near-zero values or values that were opposite in direction to the hypothesized effect. The effect sizes of the remaining two studies were large and positive, which resulted in the significant positive overall effect obtained. The hypothesis that bilinguals are more right-lateralized than monolinguals has, thus, been supported by only limited evidence. It is interesting to note that, whereas studies involving bilinguals tested in their L_2 constituted slightly more than half of the total number of studies in which monolingual controls were included, the latter in turn constitute less than a fourth of the total corpus of bilingual laterality studies. In other words, relatively few studies have actually used monolingual controls. Moreover, even when monolinguals have been tested, the comparison has rarely involved the use of monolingual speakers of each of the languages spoken by the bilinguals (only two studies — Bellisle & Lambert, 1975, and Galloway & Scarcella, 1982 — tested monolinguals who were speakers of each of the languages of the bilinguals).

In contrast to the paucity of studies that have compared bilinguals and monolinguals, a large number of laterality studies have compared bilinguals on their L_1 and L_2. Given the methodological and linguistic diversity characterizing this corpus of studies (see Table 5-2), it is perhaps not surprising that no significant effects were obtained in the meta-analysis of the L_1/L_2 variable and that the effect sizes contributing to this question were significantly heterogeneous. Interestingly, however, differences in lateralization between L_1 and L_2 were more likely under certain conditions than others: where left-handers were excluded from the comparisons; where the users' L_2 was a language read from right-to-left (suggesting the operation of scanning effects; Obler, 1989); where visual rather than auditory paradigms were used; and where the dependent measure was reaction time rather than accuracy.

The three remaining hypotheses examined in the meta-analysis focused on parameters of bilingual language acquisition history. Of the three acquisitional variables examined in the literature, that of stage of L_2 acquisition has been studied the most. The overall absence of a significant positive effect in general suggests that there is little support for the hypothesis of increased left hemisphere involvement with increasing proficiency in the second language.

Although modality effects have been effectively demonstrated in clinical studies of bilingual aphasia, the variable of manner of language instruction has not received as much attention in the laterality literature as the other acquisitional hypotheses. Only five studies directly addressed this variable, but together the results provided no evidence in support of the hypothesis.

Whereas the variables of stage and manner of second language acquisition have been investigated in diverse languages and settings, age of onset of bilingualism has been studied in a more homogeneous setting— primarily at McGill University. This has resulted in a greater homogeneity in subject characteristics (e.g., most studies have used early and late fluent speakers of French and English drawn from Montreal and/or Ottawa), subject screening criteria, and other methodological characteristics (e.g., many studies used a tachistoscopic, reaction time procedure). It may not come as a surprise, therefore, that of the four individual difference variables studied, the age variable yielded the largest and most reliable results in the meta-analysis with some of the largest effect sizes for the group by hemisphere effect (although the mean effect sizes were again small compared to the magnitude of the main effect of hemisphere). What *may* come as somewhat of a surprise is the direction of the age effect: Contrary to expectation, late bilinguals were not more right-lateralized than early bilinguals; rather, early bilinguals were the more right-lateralized subgroup.

It is interesting to speculate about the nature of this difference. If one looks closely at the studies comparing early and late bilinguals, it can be seen that, on tasks calling for phonetic or syntactic judgments (e.g., Vaid, 1984b, 1987), no group differences were obtained; both early and late bilinguals showed a left hemisphere superiority. However, group differences *were* obtained on tasks requiring semantic decisions, such as in a synonym judgment task (Vaid, 1984b, Expt. 3), or on tasks which allow, but do not require, processing for meaning, such as language classification tasks (Genesee et al., 1978) or shadowing tasks (Vaid, Green, Schweda Nicholson, & White, 1989). In studies using such tasks, early bilinguals showed either no asymmetry or greater right hemisphere involvement relative to late bilinguals.

Summarizing studies where differences between early and late bilinguals had been observed, Genesee et al. (1978) noted that "these studies suggest that those who develop their bilinguality early are more inclined to process the deeper meaning of linguistic information, especially those aspects of meaning that cut across language demarcations, than are those who become bilingual at some later developmental period" (pp. 2-3). It was argued that this difference in language processing strategy results in a differential deployment of the specialized information processing strategies of the two hemispheres. At the time that the age hypothesis was formulated (in the late 1970s), it was thought that the processing of semantic judgments is handled primarily by the left hemisphere, hence the expectation by Genesee et al. (1978) that early bilinguals might be more prone than late bilinguals to adopt a "left hemisphere biased semantic-type strategy." However, recent studies with monolingual split-brain patients, aphasics, and right-brain-damaged patients (see the review by Joanette, Goulet, & Hannequin, 1990) and with monolingual brain-intact subjects (e.g., Chiarello, 1988; Vaid, 1981, Expt. 5) indicate that tasks calling for semantic judgments may be more likely to involve the right hemisphere than tasks calling on other linguistic judgments (e.g., phonetic or syntactic). Because few studies have directly examined hemisphere differences in different groups and on different tasks, the finding from our meta-analysis of an apparently greater reliance on the right hemisphere among early bilinguals may really be an oversimplification of a more complex group and task-related difference in hemispheric involvement.

Caveats in an Assessment of the Bilingual Laterality Literature

The largely negative findings from the meta-analysis must be taken seriously as reflecting a general lack of support for the five hypotheses as they have been addressed in the literature to date. However, it is important to consider two caveats before accepting this assessment.

First, the operationalization of several of the hypotheses was in many studies less than ideal. For example, no test of the stage hypothesis employed a longitudinal design, using child and adult second language learners, to permit comparisons within the same individual at different stages of second language competence. Moreover, the contention of the stage hypothesis that beginning second language learners are more attuned to semantic and pragmatic aspects of language input and become more competent in phonetic or syntactic processing only in more advanced stages would necessitate systematically testing second language learners on laterality tasks varying in these different components of language; this has not, however, been undertaken. Similarly, with the exception of one study (Gordon, 1980), no test of the age hypothesis separately examined age of onset of bilingualism and recency of second language acquisition (as has been done in a different context by Johnson & Newport, 1989).

Second, and crucially, as the results from testing the age hypothesis led us to speculate, few studies included a relevant task manipulation. The critical importance of considering task variables is underscored further by findings from the mainstream lateralization research that demonstrate that different kinds of linguistic judgments may be differentially lateralized, with semantic judgments being the most right-lateralized (Chiarello, 1988). It is becoming increasingly apparent that language, whether in monolinguals or bilinguals, should not be studied as though it were a monolithic entity. Rather, different linguistic capabilities may be differentially inhibited as a result of brain damage and, depending on the level of processing demanded by the task, different patterns of hemispheric involvement may be observed in brain-intact individuals.

Conclusion

The bulk of the evidence to date, from both clinical and normative populations, appears to converge on there being no clear differential neuropsychological implications of the bilingual experience. The imprecise tests of some of the hypotheses and the failure to manipulate or control for certain potentially relevant subject and task-related variables mitigate somewhat the strength of this conclusion. However, the generally null findings obtained from the meta-analysis suggest that lateralization of language is indeed similar in bilinguals and monolinguals. It remains to be seen if newer theoretical and methodological approaches to the study of the brain (e.g., Scheibel & Wechsler, 1990) might offer a different perspective on the workings of the bilingual brain than that suggested by the laterality-dominated perspective of the research to date.

ACKNOWLEDGMENT

Preparation of this manuscript was supported by a Faculty Summer Research Award given to the first author by the College of Liberal Arts, Texas A & M University.

REFERENCES

Albert, M., & Obler, L. (1978). *The bilingual brain*. New York: Academic Press.

Bates, E., & Wulfeck, B. (1989). Comparative aphasiology: A cross-linguistic approach to linguistic breakdown. *Aphasiology, 3,* 111-142.

Bellisle, F., & Lambert, W. E. (1975). *Early bilingualism and cerebral dominance*. Unpublished manuscript, McGill University, Department of Psychology, Montreal.

Bergh, G. (1989). Bilingual lateralization: A methodological evaluation. *Investigaciones Psicologicas, 7,* 79-94.

Bradshaw, J. L., & Nettleton, N. C. (1981). The nature of hemispheric specialization in man. *Behavioral and Brain Sciences, 4,* 51-63.

Bryden, P. (1965). Tachistoscopic recognition, handedness, and cerebral dominance. *Neuropsychologia, 3,* 1-8.

Carroll, F. (1980). Neurolinguistic processing of a second language: Experimental evidence. In R. Scarcella & S. Krashen (Eds.), *Research in second language acquisition*. Rowley, MA: Newbury House.

Chary, P. (1986). Aphasia in a multilingual society: A preliminary study. In J. Vaid (Ed.), *Language processing in bilinguals: Psycholinguistic and neuropsychological perspectives.* Hillsdale, NJ: Lawrence Erlbaum Associates.

Chiarello, C. (Ed.). (1988). *Right hemisphere contributions to lexical semantics.* Berlin: Springer Verlag.

Corina, D. P., & Vaid, J. (1990). *Hemispheric specialization for linguistic and nonlinguistic hand movements in deaf and hearing users of ASL.* Unpublished manuscript, University of California, San Diego.

Endo, M., Shimizu, A., & Nakamura, I. (1981a). Laterality differences in recognition of Japanese and Hangul words by monolinguals and bilinguals. *Cortex, 17,* 1-9.

Endo, M., Shimizu, A., & Nakamura, I. (1981b). The influence of Hangul learning upon laterality difference in Hangul word recognition by native Japanese subjects. *Brain and Language, 14,* 114-119.

Galloway, L. (1981). *Contributions of the right cerebral hemisphere to language and communication: Issues in cerebral dominance with special emphasis on bilingualism, second language acquisition, sex differences and certain ethnic groups.* Unpublished doctoral dissertation, University of California, Los Angeles.

Galloway, L. (1983). Etudes cliniques et expérimentales sur la répartition hémisphèrique du traitement cérébral du language chez les bilingues: Modèles théoriques. *Langages, 72,* 79-113.

Galloway, L., & Krashen, S. (1980). Cerebral organization in bilingualism and second language. In R. Scarcella & S. Krashen (Eds.), *Research in second language acquisition.* Rowley, MA: Newbury House.

Galloway, L., & Scarcella, R. (1982). Cerebral organization in adult second language acquisition: Is the right hemisphere more involved? *Brain and Language, 16,* 56-60.

Genesee, F., Hamers, J. F., Lambert, W. E., Mononen, L., Seitz, M., & Starck, R. (1978). Language processing in bilinguals. *Brain and Language, 5,* 1-12.

Gordon, H. W. (1980). Cerebral organization in bilinguals: I. Lateralization. *Brain and Language, 9,* 255-268.

Green, A., Schweda Nicholson, N., Vaid, J., White, N., & Steiner, R. (1990). Hemispheric involvement in shadowing versus interpretation: A time sharing study of simultaneous interpreters with matched bilingual and monolingual controls. *Brain and Language, 39,* 107-133.

Green, A., & Vaid, J. (1986). Methodological issues in the use of the concurrent activities paradigm. *Brain and Cognition, 5,* 465-476.

Hall, D. G., & Lambert, W. E. (1988). French immersion and cerebral language processing: A dual-task study. *Canadian Journal of Behavioural Science, 20*(1), 1-14.

Hall, D. G., & Vaid, J. (1990). *Cerebral lateralization of language in bilinguals and second language learners: A meta-analysis.* Manuscript submitted for publication.

Hamers, J., & Blanc, M. (1989). *Bilinguality and bilingualism.* New York: Cambridge University Press.

Hellige, J. (1990). Hemispheric asymmetry. *Annual Review of Psychology.* Palo Alto, CA: Annual Reviews.

Hellige, J., Bloch, M., & Taylor, A. K. (1988). Multi-task investigation of individual differences in hemispheric asymmetry. *Journal of Experimental Psychology: Human Perception and Performance, 14,* 176-187.

Hoosain, R., & Shiu, L.-P. (1989). Cerebral lateralization of Chinese-English bilingual functions. *Neuropsychologia, 27,* 705-712.

Jinn, Y. (1988). *Effects of word orthography and concreteness on cerebral hemispheric asymmetry in Korean bilinguals.* Unpublished doctoral dissertation, University of Florida, Gainesville.

Joanette, Y., Goulet, P., & Hannequin, D. (1990). *Right hemisphere and verbal communication.* New York: Springer Verlag.

Johnson, E., & Newport, E. (1989). Critical period effects in second language learning: Influence of maturational state on acquisition of English as a second language. *Cognitive Psychology, 21,* 60-99.

Judd, J. (1988). *The effects of learning environment and task difficulty on the processing of verbal input as measured by the dichotic listening task.* Unpublished master's thesis, University of Illinois, Urbana.

Kang, M. J. (1984). *The function of hemispheric lateralization in second language processing.* Unpublished doctoral dissertation, Indiana University, Bloomington.

Karanth, P., & Rangamani, G. N. (1988). Crossed aphasia in multilinguals. *Brain and Language, 34*(1), 169-180.

Kimura, D. (1967). Functional asymmetry of the brain in dichotic listening. *Cortex, 3,* 163-178.

Krashen, S. (1981). *Language acquisition and second language learning.* Oxford: Pergamon Press.

Kutas, M., & Bates, E. (1988). *ERP to grammatical and semantic anomalies in bilinguals* (Tech. Rep. No. 9009). San Diego: University of California.

Lambert, W. E. (1981). Bilingualism and language acquisition. In H. Winitz (Ed.), *Native language and foreign language acquisition.* New York: The New York Academy of Sciences.

Lambert, W. E., & Fillenbaum, S. (1959). A pilot study of aphasia among bilinguals. *Canadian Journal of Psychology, 13*(1), 28-34.

Luria, A. (1960). Differences between disturbances of speech and writing in Russian and in French. *International Journal of Slavic Linguistics and Poetics, 3,* 13-22.

Mägiste, E. (1987). Changes in the lateralization pattern of two immigrant groups in Sweden. In *International and Intercultural Communication Annual: Vol. 11. Cross-cultural adaptation: Current theory and research.* Beverly Hills, CA: Sage.

Mägiste, E. (1989). Conjugate lateral eye movements in response to verbal, spatial and emotional tasks. *Investigaciones Psicologicas, 7,* 69-78.

McClung, B. (1981). *Lateralization of a second language in monolingual and bilingual subjects as determined by dichotic listening.* Unpublished doctoral dissertation, Wayne State University, Detroit.

McLaughlin, B., Rossman, T., & McLeod, B. (1984). Second language learning: An information-processing perspective. *Language Learning, 33*(2), 135-158.

Mendelsohn, S. (1988). Language lateralization in bilinguals: Facts and fantasy. *Journal of Neurolinguistics, 3*(2), 261-292.

Menn, L., & Obler, L. (1988). *Agrammatic aphasia.* Amsterdam: John Benjamin.

Minkowski, M. (1963). On aphasia in polyglots. In L. Halpern (Ed.), *Problems of dynamic neurology.* Jerusalem: Hebrew University.

Mishkin, M., & Forgays, D. (1952). Word recognition as a function of retinal locus. *Journal of Experimental Psychology, 43,* 43-48.

Moscovitch, M. (1979). Information processing and the cerebral hemispheres. In M. Gazzaniga (Ed.), *Handbook of behavioral neurobiology. Vol. 2.* New York: Plenum.

Neville, H., & Corina, D. P. (1990). *ERP studies of brain lateralization for ASL and English in deaf and hearing bilinguals.* Unpublished manuscript, University of California, San Diego.

Obler, L. (1981). Right hemisphere participation in second language acquisition. In K. Diller (Ed.), *Individual differences and universals in language learning aptitude*. Rowley, MA: Newbury House.

Obler, L. (1989). The boustrophedal brain: Laterality and dyslexia in bi-directional readers. In K. Hyltenstam & L. Obler (Eds.), *Bilingualism across the lifespan: Aspects of acquisition, maturity, and loss*. Cambridge: Cambridge University Press.

Obler, L., Zatorre, R. J., Galloway, L., & Vaid, J. (1982). Cerebral lateralization in bilinguals: Methodological issues. *Brain and Language, 15*, 40-54.

Obrzut, J., Conrad, P., Bryden, P., & Boliek, C. (1988). Cued dichotic listening with right-handed, left-handed, bilingual, and learning-disabled children. *Neuropsychologia, 26*, 119-131.

Ojemann, G., & Whitaker, H. A. (1978). The bilingual brain. *Archives of Neurology, 35*, 409-412.

Ovcharova, P., Raichev, R., & Geleva, T. (1968). Afaziia u Poligloti. *Nevrologiia, Psikhiatriia i Nevrokhirurgiia, 7*, 183-190.

Paradis, M. (1983). *Readings on aphasia in bilinguals and polyglots*. Montreal: Didier.

Paradis, M. (1987). *The assessment of bilingual aphasia*. Hillsdale, NJ: Lawrence Erlbaum Associates.

Paradis, M. (1989a). Bilingual and polyglot aphasia. In F. Boller and J. Grafman (Eds.), *Handbook of neuropsychology: Vol. 2*. Amsterdam: Elsevier Science.

Paradis, M. (1989b). La lateralizacion cerebral diferencial en los bilingues: ¡Basta, por favor! *Investigaciones Psicologicas, 7*, 95-106.

Peal, E., & Lambert, W. E. (1962). The relation of bilingualism to intelligence. *Psychological Monographs, 76*, 1-23.

Pitres, A. (1895). Etude sur l'aphasie chez les polyglottes. *Revue de Médecine, 15*, 873-899.

Rapport, R., Tan, C. T., & Whitaker, H. A. (1983). Language function and dysfunction among Chinese- and English- speaking polyglots: Cortical stimulation, Wada testing, and clinical studies. *Brain and Language, 18*, 342-366.

Ribot, T. (1882). *Diseases of memory: An essay in the positive psychology*. London: Paul.

Rosenthal, R. (1984). *Meta-analytic procedures for social research*. Beverly Hills, CA: Sage Publications.

Rosenthal, R., & Rosnow, R. (1985). *Contrasts: Focused comparisons in the analysis of variance*. New York: Cambridge University Press.

Rosenthal, R., & Rubin, D. (1982). Comparing effect sizes of independent studies. *Psychological Bulletin, 92*, 500-504.

Scheibel, A., & Wechsler, A. (Eds.). (1990). *Neurobiology of higher cognitive function*. New York: Guilford.

Schneiderman, E. (1986). Leaning to the right: Thoughts on lateralization and second language acquisition. In J. Vaid, (Ed.), *Language processing in bilinguals: Psycholinguistic and neuropsychological perspectives*. Hillsdale, NJ: Lawrence Erlbaum Associates.

Segalowitz, N. (1986). Skilled reading in the second language. In J. Vaid (Ed.), *Language processing in bilinguals: Psycholinguistic and neuropsychological perspectives*. Hillsdale, NJ: Lawrence Erlbaum Associates.

Sergent, J., & Hellige, J. (1986). Role of input factors in visual-field asymmetries. *Brain and Cognition, 5*, 174-199.

Solin, D. (1989). The systematic misrepresentation of bilingual crossed aphasia data and its consequences. *Brain and Language, 36*, 92-116.

Sussman, H., Franklin, P., & Simon, T. (1982). Bilingual speech: Bilateral control? *Brain and Language, 15*, 125-142.

Sussman, H., & Simon, T. (1988). The effects of gender, handedness, L1/L2 and baseline tapping rate on language lateralization: An assessment of the time-sharing paradigm. *Journal of Clinical and Experimental Neuropsychology, 10,* 69.

Vaid, J. (1981). *Hemisphere differences in bilingual language processing: A task analysis.* Unpublished doctoral dissertation, McGill University, Montreal.

Vaid, J. (1982). *Visual field asymmetries in rhyme judgments by early and late bilinguals: Further data.* Unpublished manuscript, McGill University, Montreal.

Vaid, J. (1983). Bilingualism and brain lateralization. In S. Segalowitz (Ed.), *Language functions and brain organization.* New York: Academic Press.

Vaid, J. (1984a). A review of Readings on aphasia in bilinguals and polyglots. *Journal of the History of the Behavioral Sciences,* October, 372-374.

Vaid, J. (1984b). Visual, phonetic, and semantic processing in early and late bilinguals. In M. Paradis & Y. Lebrun (Eds.), *Early bilingualism and child development.* Lisse: Swets & Zeitlinger.

Vaid, J. (1987). Visual field asymmetries for rhyme and syntactic category judgements in monolinguals and fluent early and late bilinguals. *Brain and Language, 30,* 263-277.

Vaid, J., & Genesee, F. (1980). Neuropsychological approaches to bilingualism: A critical review. *Canadian Journal of Psychology, 34,* 417-445.

Vaid, J., Green, A., Schweda Nicholson, N., & White, N. (1989). Hemispheric specialization for shadowing versus interpretation: A dual task study of simultaneous interpreters and matched unilingual controls. *Investigaciones Psicologicas, 7,* 43-54.

Vaid, J., & Lambert, W. E. (1979). Differential cerebral involvement in the cognitive functioning of bilinguals. *Brain and Language, 8,* 92-110.

Vildomec, V. (1960). *Multilingualism.* Leyden: A. W. Sythoff.

Whitaker, H. A. (1978). Bilingualism: A neurolinguistics perspective. In W. Ritchie (Ed.), *Second language acquisition and research: Issues and implications.* New York: Academic Press.

Zatorre, R. (1989). On the representation of multiple languages in the brain: Old problems and new directions. *Brain and Language, 36,* 127-147.

APPENDIX
PAPERS INCLUDED IN THE META-ANALYSIS

Albanese, J. F. (1985). Language lateralization in English-French bilinguals. *Brain and Language, 24,* 284-296.

Albert, M., & Obler, L. (1978). *The bilingual brain.* New York: Academic Press.

Barton, M. J., Goodglass, H., & Shai, A. (1965). Differential recognition of tachistoscopically presented English and Hebrew words in right and left visual fields. *Perceptual and Motor Skills, 21,* 431-437.

Bellisle, F., & Lambert, W. E. (1975). *Early bilingualism and cerebral dominance.* Unpublished manuscript, McGill University, Department of Psychology, Montreal.

Bentin, S. (1981). On the representation of a second language in the cerebral hemispheres of right-handed people. *Neuropsychologia, 19,* 599-603.

Bergh, G. (1986). *The neuropsychological status of Swedish-English subsidiary bilinguals.* Goteburg, Sweden: Acta Universitatis Gothoburgensis.

Carroll, F. (1980). Neurolinguistic processing of a second language: Experimental evidence. In R. Scarcella & S. Krashen (Eds.), *Research in second language acquisition*. Rowley, MA: Newbury House.

Corina, D. P., & Vaid, J. (in press). Shadowing words vs. signs: A dual-task laterality study with A.S.L.-English interpreters. *Investigaciones Psicologicas*.

Coulter, L. C. (1982, March). *Brain lateralization for reading in Arabic-English bilinguals*. Paper presented at the BABBLE conference, Niagara Falls, Ontario.

Fabbro, F. (1988). Cerebral lateralization in early learning of a second language. *Proceedings of the 6th National Symposium of Primatology*, Trieste, Italy.

Fabbro, F., Gran, L., & Bava, A. (1987). *Modifications in cerebral lateralization during the acquisition of a second language (English) in adult Italian-speaking females*. Unpublished manuscript, Istituto per l'Infanzia "Burlo Garofalo,"Trieste, Italy.

Furtado, J., & Webster, W. (1988). *Language-specific lateralization in bilinguals*. Unpublished manuscript, Carleton University, Ottawa.

Galloway, L., & Scarcella, R. (1982). Cerebral organization in adult second language acquisition: Is the right hemisphere more involved? *Brain and Language, 16,* 56-60.

Garnham, A., & Jones, C. (1983). *Is a second language lateralized in the same way as a first?* Unpublished manuscript.

Gaziel, T., Obler, L., & Albert, M. (1978). A tachistoscopic study of Hebrew-English bilinguals. In M. Albert & L. Obler (Eds.), *The bilingual brain*. New York: Academic Press.

Genesee, F., Hamers, J. F., Lambert, W. E., Mononen, L., Seitz, M., & Starck, R. (1978). Language processing in bilinguals. *Brain and Language, 5,* 1-12.

Gordon, D. P., & Zatorre, R. J. (1981). A right-ear advantage for dichotic listening in bilingual children. *Brain and Language, 13,* 389-396.

Gordon, H. W. (1980). Cerebral organization in bilinguals: I. Lateralization. *Brain and Language, 9,* 255-268.

Green, A. (1986). A time-sharing cross-sectional study of monolinguals and bilinguals at different levels of second language acquisition. *Brain and Cognition, 5,* 477-497.

Hall, D. G., & Lambert, W. E. (1988). French immersion and cerebral language processing: A dual-task study. *Canadian Journal of Behavioural Science, 20*(1), 1-14.

Hamers, J., & Lambert, W. E. (1977). Visual field and cerebral hemisphere preferences in bilinguals. In S. J. Segalowitz & F. A. Gruber (Eds.), *Language development and neurological theory*. New York: Academic Press.

Hardyck, C., Tzeng, O., & Wang, W. S.-Y. (1978). Cerebral lateralization of function and bilingual decision processes: Is thinking lateralized? *Brain and Language, 5,* 56-71.

Hynd, G., & Scott, S. (1980). Propositional and appositional modes of thought and differential speech lateralization in Navajo Indian and Anglo children. *Child Development, 51,* 909-911.

Hynd, G., Teeter, A., & Stewart, A. (1980). Acculturation and the lateralization of speech in the bilingual native American. *International Journal of Neuroscience, 11,* 1-7.

Kershner, J. R., & Jeng, A. G.-R. (1972). Dual functional hemispheric asymmetry in visual perception: Effects of ocular dominance and post-exposure processes. *Neuropsychologia, 10,* 437-445.

Kotik, B. (1975). *Investigation of speech lateralization in multilinguals*. Unpublished doctoral dissertation, Moscow State University, Moscow.

Kotik, B., & Kiroy, V. (1982). *On the role of right brain hemisphere in the speech of bilinguals*. Unpublished manuscript, Rostov State University, USSR.

Mägiste, E. (1987). Changes in the lateralization pattern of two immigrant groups in Sweden. In *International and Intercultural Communication Annual: Vol. 11. Cross-cultural adaptation: Current theory and research*. Beverly Hills, CA: Sage.

Maitre, S. (1974). *On the representation of second languages in the brain.* Unpublished master's thesis, University of California, Los Angeles.

McKeever, W. F. (1981). Evidence against the hypothesis of right hemisphere language dominance in the native American Navajo. *Neuropsychologia, 19,* 595-598.

McKeever, W. F., & Hunt, L. J. (1984). Failure to replicate the Scott et al. finding of reversed ear dominance in the native American Navajo. *Neuropsychologia, 22*(4), 539-541.

McKeever, W. F., Hunt, L. J., Wells, S., & Yazzie, C. (in press). Language laterality in Navajo reservation children: Dichotic test results depend on the language context of the testing. *Brain and Language.*

Mishkin, M., & Forgays, D. (1952). Word recognition as a function of retinal locus. *Journal of Experimental Psychology, 43,* 43-48.

Mohr, E., & Costa, L. (1985). Ear asymmetries in dichotic listening tasks which increase in difficulty. *Brain and Language, 24,* 233-245.

Orbach, J. (1952). Retinal locus as a factor in the recognition of visually perceived words. *American Journal of Psychology, 65,* 555-562.

Orbach, J. (1967). Differential recognition of Hebrew and English words in right and left visual fields as a function of cerebral dominance and reading habits. *Neuropsychologia, 50,* 127-134.

Rogers, L., TenHouten, W., Kaplan, C., & Gardner, M. (1977). Hemispheric specialization of language: An EEG study of bilingual Hopi children. *International Journal of Neuroscience, 8,* 1-6.

Rupp, J. (1980). *Cerebral language dominance in Vietnamese-English bilingual children.* Unpublished doctoral dissertation, University of New Mexico, Albuquerque.

Sanchez, P., Manga, D., Babecki, P., & de Tembleque, R. (1987). *Language lateralization in bilingual speakers.* Unpublished manuscript, Universidad Complutense, Madrid.

Schonle, P. (1978). *Otitat versus lingualitat: Dichotische Untersuchungenzur Pravalenzder Ohrigkeit und Sprachigkeit bei deutschen und russischen Studenten.* Unpublished doctoral dissertation, University of Tubingen, Germany.

Schouten, M. E. H., van Dalen, T. E., & Klein, A. J. J. (1985). Right ear advantage and second language proficiency. *Journal of Phonetics, 13,* 53-60.

Scott, S., Hynd, G., Hunt, L., & Weed, W. (1979). Cerebral speech lateralization in the native American Navajo. *Neuropsychologia, 17,* 89-92.

Sewell, D. F., & Panou, L. (1983). Visual field asymmetries for verbal and dot localization tasks in monolingual and bilingual subjects. *Brain and Language, 18,* 28-34.

Shanon, B. (1982). Lateralization effects in the perception of Hebrew and English words. *Brain and Language, 17,* 107-123.

Silverberg, R., Bentin, S., Gaziel, T., Obler, L., & Albert, M. (1979). Shift of visual field preference for English words in native Hebrew speakers. *Brain and Language, 8,* 184-190.

Soares, C. (1982). Converging evidence for left hemisphere language lateralization in bilinguals. *Neuropsychologia, 20,* 653-659.

Soares, C. (1984). Left-hemisphere language lateralization in bilinguals: Use of the concurrent activities paradigm. *Brain and Language, 23,* 86-96.

Soares, C., & Grosjean, F. (1981). Left hemisphere language lateralization in bilinguals and monolinguals. *Perception and Psychophysics, 29,* 599-604.

Starck, R., Genesee, F., Lambert, W. E., & Seitz, M. (1977). Multiple language experience and the development of cerebral dominance. In S. J. Segalowitz & F. A. Gruber (Eds.), *Language development and neurological theory.* New York: Academic Press.

Sussman, H., Franklin, P., & Simon, T. (1982). Bilingual speech: Bilateral control? *Brain and Language, 15,* 125-142.

TenHouten, W. D. (1980). *Lateralized and generalized EEG alpha effects of semantically and socially varied narratives heard in Mandarin Chinese and in English.* Unpublished manuscript.

Vaid, J. (1981). *Hemisphere differences in bilingual language processing: A task analysis.* Unpublished doctoral dissertation, McGill University, Montreal.

Vaid, J. (1984). Visual, phonetic, and semantic processing in early and late bilinguals. In M. Paradis & Y. Lebrun (Eds.), *Early bilingualism and child development.* Lisse: Swets & Zeitlinger.

Vaid, J. (1987). Visual field asymmetries for rhyme and syntactic category judgements in monolinguals and fluent early and late bilinguals. *Brain and Language, 30,* 263-277.

Vaid, J., Green, A., Schweda Nicholson, N., & White, N. (1989). Hemispheric specialization for shadowing versus interpretation: A dual task study of simultaneous interpreters and matched unilingual controls. *Investigaciones Psicologicas, 7,* 43-54.

Vocate, D. R. (1984). Differential cerebral speech lateralization in Crow Indian and Anglo children. *Neuropsychologia, 22*(4), 487-494.

Walters, J., & Zatorre, R. (1978). Laterality differences for word identification in bilinguals. *Brain and Language, 6,* 158-167.

Wesche, M. B., & Schneiderman, E. (1982). Language lateralization in adult bilinguals. *Studies in Second Language Acquisition, 4*(2), 153-169.

Winfield, F. E. (1981, October). *Cerebral dominance and cognitive-academic function: A study of Mexican immigrant children.* Paper presented at the Sixth Boston University Conference on Language Development, Boston, MA.

6 Mental Representation in Bilinguals

Allan Paivio
University of Western Ontario

My title refers to the cognitive structures and processes that underlie the functional capacities of the bilingual. The functional capacities have priority in the research described in this chapter because they define what needs to be explained by representational constructs. For example, we would like to answer the following question in representational terms: "How is it that the bilingual is able to 'gate out' or, in some fashion, set aside a whole integrated linguistic system while functioning in a second one, and a moment later, if the situation calls for it, switch the process, activating the previously inactive system and setting aside the previously active one?" The question was posed by Wally Lambert (1969, p. 99) in a chapter entitled "Psychological studies of the interdependencies of the bilingual's two languages."

The degree to which the two languages function independently or interdependently in a variety of tasks is the functional theme of this chapter. A parallel theme concerns the mental structures and processes that are postulated in theories of bilingual mental representation to explain why the bilingual's languages sometimes appear to be independent and at other times, interdependent. Such functional variability implies that the underlying cognitive systems must be both structurally separate and yet interconnected. The goal of structurally oriented bilingual research is to specify what separate but interconnected means in the context of different theories.

This chapter reviews the theoretical and empirical developments since the 1950s, when Wally Lambert began his studies of bilingualism and pioneered in taking specific research approaches to both the functional and representational problems. I cover the topic under three headings that correspond to different periods of conceptual and methodological emphases that have been in favour in psychological science during the last three and a half decades. The first period emphasized the language learning history of the bilingual and the compound-coordinate distinction. The second period focussed on memory storage systems of bilinguals. The third is the current period, which emphasizes general theories of cognition that can also accommodate bilingual phenomena.

LANGUAGE-LEARNING CONTEXTS AND THE COMPOUND-COORDINATE DISTINCTION

Weinreich (1953) and Ervin and Osgood (1954) introduced the hypothesis that bilinguals could be divided into compound and coordinate types on the basis of the degree to which translation equivalents in the two languages have the same or different meanings: same for compounds, different for coordinates. This hypothesis implies that the two languages can function more independently in the case of coordinate than compound bilinguals. Moreover, it was suggested that these differences depended on similarities or differences in acquisition contexts. Lambert and his collaborators refined and operationalized the hypothesis in various behavioral and neuropsychological studies. For example, Lambert, Havelka, and Crosby (1958) used questionnaires and other sources of information to classify French-English bilinguals as compound or coordinate according to differences in acquisition contexts. They found that French-English bilinguals classified as having learned their two languages in separate contexts, as compared to those who had learned them in what they called "fused" contexts, showed greater differences in semantic differential ratings and more associative independence for translation-equivalent words. This was the first evidence that two languages could be more or less separate and functionally independent, depending on how they were learned.

At about the same time, Lambert and Fillenbaum (1959) proposed a representational substrate for the compound-coordinate distinction in neuropsychological terms. They suggested "that coordinate bilinguals should have more functionally separate neural structures underlying their languages than should compound bilinguals. Thus, the concepts 'house' and 'maison' which are more functionally independent for co-ordinate than for compound bilinguals would be 'stored' in neural elements which have some sort of greater functional discreteness for the co-ordinate bilinguals" (p. 29). They tested their hypothesis using data from polyglot aphasics reported in the literature and from cases of such aphasics obtained from several hospitals and rehabilitation centres in Montreal. Their study revealed selective patterns of loss and recovery of one or both languages depending on whether the languages had been learned in the same or different time periods and contexts, and how well each had been learned prior to the aphasic insult. Lambert and Fillenbaum concluded tentatively that the data were generally consistent with the compound-coordinate distinction. The neuropsychological implications were followed up more systematically in later studies using more direct methods. Those studies are reviewed thoroughly by Vaid and Hall (this volume), and I mention this one study only to illustrate Wally's early involvement in research on mental representation in bilinguals and the more specific idea that the representational systems could be functionally independent or interdependent. His involvement continued in the next phase.

SEPARATE VERSUS SHARED MEMORY STORES

Kolers (1963) recast the functional independence-interdependence issue in terms of bilingual memory stores. The independence position, which he favored, was that bilingual memory is represented by two functionally independent storage and retrieval systems that interact only through translation processes (the separate stores hypothesis). The interdependence alternative was that all information exists in a single memory store that has access to different input and output language systems (the shared-store hypothesis). The interdependence view generally implies that performance on a given task would be comparable whether a relevant variable is varied between or within languages, whereas independence implies different effects in the two conditions. The considerable research generated by this debate has been reviewed elsewhere (e.g., McCormack, 1974, 1977; Paivio, 1986, chap. 11; Paivio & Desrochers, 1980), so I will only sample the kinds of findings that were taken as support for one or the other position.

Kolers originally favored the independence view because of his own findings on transfer of practice and associative performance. Kolers (1964) reported that bilingual subjects who practiced saying the alphabet backwards in one language showed no transfer of this learning experience to the other language. His interpretation was that encoding and storage of information occur within two linguistic systems that are insulated from each other. In another study, Kolers (1963) had subjects associate to words in one language and their translation equivalents in the other language. The shared-store hypothesis predicts a high level of common associations to L_1 and L_2 translation equivalents; the separate stores hypothesis, on the other hand, implies a low level of common associations across languages. Kolers found that the proportion of shared responses to translation equivalents was generally low (cf. Dalrymple-Alford & Aamiry, 1969) but varied somewhat with word class. Thus, the proportions were .23 for concrete nouns (e.g., *lamb*), .14 for abstract nouns (e.g., *freedom*), and .10 for emotion words (e.g., *pain*). Kolers interpreted his results as support for the independence position, although he later qualified this by suggesting that concrete information is stored partly in a common form because of the similar ways of manipulating referents of concrete nouns in different countries, whereas abstract information is more closely bound to the language by which it was stored in the mind. Note that Kolers' reliance on word referents in his analysis parallels Lambert, Havelka, and Crosby's use of similarities and differences in referential experience in their analysis of compound and coordinate bilingualism. The role of concrete referents becomes especially important in the bilingual dual coding model that I describe in a later section.

Next, I sample relevant memory experiments, beginning with those that seem to support functional independence and the separate storage hypothesis. Lambert, Ignatow, and Krauthamer (1968) presented English-French and English-Russian subjects with word lists in one or the other, or both, of their languages. The lists either contained words from two distinct semantic categories or else they were uncategorized. Free recall tests permitted measurement of amount recalled, the degree to which recalled items were clustered by semantic category and by language (in the case of bilingual lists), and the relation between organization and recall. Lambert et al. concluded generally that recall performance benefitted more from semantic than language organization. However, the notable finding in the present context was that, overall, subjects categorized recalled items as much by language as by semantic category. This suggests some functional independence of the storage or retrieval systems for the two languages, consistent with the separate stores view of bilingual memory. Of course, we would also have to conclude that categorical groupings within languages are functionally independent as well. I consider such possibilities in more detail later on.

Goggin and Wickens (1971; replicated by Dillon, McCormack, Petrusic, Cook, & LaFleur, 1973) capitalized on the phenomenon of release from proactive interference (PI) to test the separate stores hypothesis. Studies of release from PI typically use the Brown-Peterson paradigm in which a subject is shown three or four words followed by an interval up to 18 sec in duration, during which the subject engages in some rehearsal-interfering task before attempting to recall the words. This is repeated for a series of trials with different sets of words. The typical result is that performance declines over three or four trials (word sets), indicating PI. Release from PI occurs if the nature of the items is changed; for example, words are changed to digits. The release is manifested as a sharp increase in recall for the new set of items; this is taken as evidence that the stimulus dimensions or attributes involved are psychologically distinct from each other. Using Spanish-English bilinguals as subjects, Goggin and Wickens shifted either (a) the semantic category (from foods to body parts or vice versa), or (b) the language (from Spanish to

English or English to Spanish), or (c) they shifted both dimensions simultaneously. The relevant result was strong release from PI with a shift in language, especially with bilinguals who were highly fluent in both languages. Goggin and Wickens concluded conservatively that their data could be interpreted as supporting the hypothesis of separate memory stores for each language.

The separate stores hypothesis has also been supported by an experiment that used a repetition-lag procedure. The typical lag effect is that recall of repeated items improves up to a point the more the repetitions are spaced in the list. Glanzer and Duarte (1971) investigated repetition lag effects using Spanish-English word lists and Spanish-English bilingual subjects. Items were repeated at different lags in the same language or in different languages. The important result was that the lag effect was attenuated so that repetition of Spanish-English translation equivalents produced higher recall than same-language repetitions at shorter lags but not at long lags. Because recall at longer lags tends to be additive, asymptoting at a level that would be expected for independent events, the attenuated lag effect for bilingual repetitions means that their recall at zero lag more closely approximated additivity and independence of the two events than did within-language repetitions.

I turn next to some findings that have been taken as evidence for the shared-store view of bilingual memory. The rationale for one set of experiments was that any positive transfer from learning and recalling words in L_1 to the same concepts in L_2 would be evidence that the two languages are functionally interdependent and presumably stored in a common system of some kind. Using Spanish-English bilinguals, Young and Saegert (1966) found highly significant positive transfer from serial learning of a list of words in L_1 to lists in L_2. Lopez and Young (1974) extended the finding by prefamiliarizing bilingual subjects with items in one language and then giving them free recall trials with the same or control items in the other language. Positive transfer occurred across languages. MacLeod (1976) used a savings variant of the transfer paradigm. French-English bilinguals learned a list of 10 number-noun pairs in one language to a criterion of one perfect trial. Five weeks later they were retested on the same pairs and then relearned the pairs in the other language. The results showed positive transfer in that the translated pairs were learned in fewer trials than were comparable but different control pairs.

A bilingual transfer experiment by Lambert et al. (1958) antedates the transfer studies I have described but I mention it last because the results qualify the conclusion from the more recent ones. Bilinguals learned a list of words in one language followed by a list of translation equivalents in the other language, and then were tested for recall of the first list. As compared to a control task, the interpolated list of translation equivalents generally facilitated recall of the original list, thereby suggesting that the two languages are functionally interdependent. However, the positive transfer was less for coordinate than for compound bilinguals, suggesting that the degree of linguistic interdependence can vary, depending on the language acquisition history of the bilingual. This finding is problematic for the memory storage theories because it simultaneously supports both the separate stores and shared-store models. I show later how this paradox can be resolved by dual coding theory.

GENERAL REPRESENTATIONAL THEORIES APPLIED TO BILINGUALS

Up to this point, I have considered specific models of bilingual mental representation that were applied to the findings on functional independence-interdependence. Recall that Lambert and Fillenbaum (1959) proposed the neuropsychological hypothesis that languages could be represented in neural structures that are separate and independent to the degree that the language acquisition contexts have been separated. However, it is unclear whether these neural structures pertain to languages as lexical-syntactic systems or to the semantic systems associated with those linguistic units or structures. Kolers (1963) contrasted a common conceptual or semantic store connected to two languages with two separate stores for each of the languages, presumably including their meanings as represented in some form. In addition, Paradis (1980) proposed a model in which both of a bilingual's languages are differentially connected to the same conceptual-experiential store. I will now discuss more general cognitive theories that differ in their representational assumptions and which have been applied to the bilingual case. I emphasize bilingual dual coding theory in particular and contrast it with single-code representational models.

The bilingual dual coding model (Paivio & Desrochers, 1980) is similar to the models proposed by Kolers and Paradis, with the important difference that it assumes direct connections between L_1 and L_2 as well as a nonverbal imagery system capable of functioning as a shared conceptual system for the two languages. The assumptions concerning structural interconnections and processes are also more specific than those in the storage models. These assumptions are easiest to describe with reference to the visual model shown in Figure 6-1.

The model shows separate verbal systems corresponding to each of the bilingual's two languages and a third, nonverbal, imagery system. The three systems are assumed to be functionally independent but also interconnected in ways that would produce effects consistent with functional interdependence under appropriate conditions. Representations in the imagery system, called "imagens" (image generators) for descriptive convenience, are connected to representations ("logogens") in both verbal

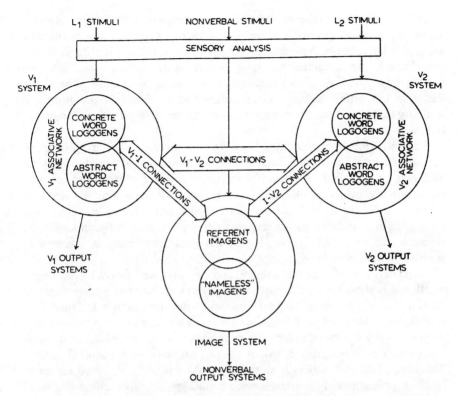

Fig. 6-1. Schematization of the bilingual version of dual coding showing the verbal symbolic systems (V₁ and V₂) corresponding to the bilingual's two languages (L₁ and L₂) and the nonverbal image system (I), along with their functional interconnections. (Reprinted from Paivio & Desrochers, 1980. Copyright 1980. Canadian Psychological Association. Reprinted with permission)

systems (V_1 and V_2) in a one-to-many fashion in both directions. Logogens corresponding to translation equivalents in L_1 and L_2 could be connected to the same imagens or to imagens corresponding to different referents of the same class, depending on the acquisition history of the bilingual, much as in the compound-coordinate distinction.

The relations between L_1 and L_2 are assumed to involve direct associations between V_1 and V_2 logogens corresponding to translation equivalents in the two languages. Logogens within languages are also interconnected, but the between- and within-language connections differ in the following ways: V_1-V_2 associations are assumed to be strong between translation equivalents (e.g., *boy-garçon*) and weak between nonequivalent terms (e.g., *boy-fille*). Functionally, this implies that conditional uncertainty is lower between translation equivalents than between nontranslations. Thus, there is a steep associative hierarchy between languages, so that translations are highly probable cross-language responses to words and nontranslations are highly improbable. Associations between words within a language, on the other hand, are assumed to be generally more diffuse than between translation equivalents in two languages. That is, the associative hierarchy is flatter in the within-language case. Kolers and Gonzalez (1980) proposed similarly that the bonds between words tend to be stronger across languages than within.

The structural assumptions require a parallel set of processing assumptions. Activation of connections between referentially related imagens and logogens is called *referential processing*. Naming objects and imaging to words are prototypical examples. Activation of associative connections between logogens is called *associative processing*. However, given the difference in associative structures, associative processing between languages is much like referential processing in that less uncertainty is involved in translating than in within-language associative processing.

Another class of representational theories assumes that all knowledge, whether it is about the nonlinguistic world or about one or more languages, is represented in a common, amodal, abstract form rather than in the modality-specific form assumed in dual coding theory. This common representational form is usually described in terms of propositions or propositional structures, but sometimes it is simply called an abstract semantic or conceptual system. This class of theories differs from the single-store models described earlier in that the propositional theories assume explicitly that representational units and structures in the common system are abstract and amodal. Some researchers have applied this general theory to the performance of bilinguals in relevant tasks (e.g., Potter, So, Von Eckardt, & Feldman, 1984; Rosenberg & Simon, 1977). The general implication is that bilingual performance should uniformly show strong functional interdependence of the two languages.

The direct tests of the bilingual dual coding model to date have focused on the independence of representations in the two verbal systems because a good deal is already known about functional relations between imagery and language. Nonetheless, imagery has also been implicated in the bilingual studies.

The most direct way to test the hypothesis that associative connections are more diffuse within than between languages would be to have bilinguals generate associations to words in the same language or in the other language under relevant instructions. This was done by Harbluk, Paivio, and Clark (1987) using free association and same-meaning (synonym or translation) instructions. Consistent with the hypothesis, we found that the number of different free or same-meaning associations was greater within languages than between languages.

Wally Lambert collaborated on the two major memory studies that I describe next. One of these (Paivio & Lambert, 1981) involved two experiments in which bilinguals were required to encode words in different ways prior to a recall test. In one experiment, the subjects saw a mixed list of pictures, French words, and English words to which they responded by writing the English name of each picture, translating the French words into English, and simply copying the English words. They were then asked unexpectedly to recall the list of English words they had written down. The second experiment reversed the encoding and recall tasks in that the subjects were shown only English words and, in response to encoding cues, they imaged and quickly sketched the referents of one-third of the words, translated one-third into French, and copied the remaining third. Then they were asked to recall the English stimulus words they had been shown. In both experiments, therefore, the subjects recalled English response words they had generated by different encoding processes or stimulus words they had encoded in different ways. The results of both experiments showed an identical pattern, with recall increasing sharply from the copy condition, to translation, to the verbal-nonverbal coding condition. Recall was about twice as high for translated as for copied items, suggesting that the bilingual verbal encodings were at least additive in their effect. The further large increase from the bilingual to the verbal-nonverbal encoding condition is consistent with the dual coding assumption (supported by prior monolingual studies; see references cited in Paivio & Lambert, 1981) that verbal and nonverbal episodic trace components are independent and that the nonverbal (imaginal) component is mnemonically stronger than the verbal one. In brief, the results were entirely consistent with the bilingual version of dual coding theory. We considered alternative interpretations in terms of processing levels and versions of the common coding theories and found each of these wanting for logical and empirical reasons. Vaid (1988) arrived at a similar conclusion on the basis of the results from her extension of our coding experiment.

In our second study (Paivio, Clark, & Lambert, 1988), we extended Glanzer and Duarte's (1971) bilingual repetition lag experiment by adding variation in word concreteness and within-language synonym repetitions to the design. I will mention only the more pertinent findings from this multifaceted study. First, we generally replicated the Glanzer and Duarte findings in that the lag effect was attenuated for bilingual repetitions. In addition, several new findings supported specific predictions from bilingual dual coding theory. First, in the case of abstract as well as concrete words, bilingual repetitions had additive (statistically independent) effects on recall at zero lag. This observation not only supports the independence hypothesis of bilingual memory but also allows us to assign the independence specifically to the two lexical systems rather than to some unspecified semantic systems.

Second, synonym repetitions also showed the attenuated lag effect but the effect of repetition was generally weaker than in the case of bilingual repetitions, as expected from the assumption that between-language associative relations are more constrained or less diffuse than within language relations. Finally, semantic repetitions (bilingual and synonym) were more effective with concrete words than with abstract words, presumably because recall was augmented by the availability of shared images for concrete semantic equivalents.

The remainder of this chapter reconsiders some key issues from the bilingualism literature reviewed earlier. First, dual coding theory could account for findings that had been taken as support for shared-store or abstract conceptual views of bilingual mental representation. Positive cross-language transfer and savings in learning tasks could be mediated by common images elicited by translation equivalents or by a direct translation tactic. The role of imagery is plausible because the transfer experiments generally used concrete nouns. The direct translation hypothesis also is plausible because the rate of item presentation was slow enough to permit subjects to translate on the second list.

The translation hypothesis was, in fact, considered by MacLeod (1976) and anticipated earlier, though not tested, by Lambert et al. (1958) in the context of the compound-coordinate distinction (see further below). MacLeod compared savings across languages on the relearning test for items that had or had not been reinstated (remembered) on a second retention test for originally learned items after the relearning trials. Both reinstated and forgotten items showed significant savings in the relearning test in the other language, but the variance accounted for was much greater for reinstated items than for the forgotten ones. Thus, item reinstatement in the original language was associated with facilitated learning in the second language, perhaps because translation could be used in the case of the reinstated words.

I now come around full circle to the issue with which we started, the compound-coordinate distinction. The original classification system was difficult to operationalize and received only mixed empirical support. Mindful of such criticisms, Lambert (1969) proposed a modified definition in terms of early versus late bilingualism, but its behavioral implications also have been inconsistently supported. Nonetheless, as we have already seen, the general compound-coordinate idea has had enough predictive successes that it should not be completely dismissed. For example, translation equivalents were found to differ more in meaning and show more associative independence in a learning task (Lambert et al., 1958) and show less interference in a bilingual Stroop task (Lambert, 1969) among bilinguals classified as coordinates than those classified as compounds.

Desrochers and I (Paivio & Desrochers, 1980) proposed a dual coding interpretation that could accommodate the variable findings and lead to novel predictions. We began with the general view that we should think of the compound-coordinate distinction as a matter of degree rather than extreme types. In dual coding terms, bilingual verbal systems have multiple connections to the nonverbal imagery system, some converging on a common set of imagens (reflecting a "compound" aspect of bilingual mental representation) and others accessing different imagens (reflecting a "coordinate" aspect). For some bilinguals and some concepts, the converging connections might predominate, so that *church* and *église,* for example, might elicit images of the same kind of building, whereas for others, the separate connections might predominate, resulting in images of different kinds of churches. This is essentially a cognitive reinterpretation of the suggestion made by Lambert et al. (1958) that *church* and *église* might have different referents for coordinate bilinguals but not for compound bilinguals. In addition, bilinguals could differ in the strength and variety of direct associations between verbal representations corresponding to translation equivalents. For example, compound bilinguals who learned both languages in the same setting might have had more experience with direct translation and thereby develop more and stronger between-language connections than coordinate bilinguals who learned their two languages at different times and in different settings. This hypothesis is consistent with the suggestion made by Lambert et al. (1958, p. 243) that compound ("fused") bilinguals apparently made use of the interpolated translations in the associative learning task I described earlier and accordingly improved in their retention scores, perhaps because they were "more set to translate" than were the coordinates.

Such possibilities are testable in principle but actual tests are likely to run into the same operational complexities that plagued the original research on the compound-coordinate distinction. Two anecdotal examples illustrate the potential impediments. Bugelski (1977) described a personal observation that he also confirmed with other bilinguals. He had spoken Polish as a child in Europe before moving to the United States. Thus, he qualifies as a coordinate bilingual for whom the later acquired language is dominant. He noticed that stimulus words in his two languages elicited quite different imagery. Polish words evoked images of objects and scenes from his childhood, whereas English words learned in the North American setting did not. These observations are consistent with the dual coding hypothesis of separate verbal-imaginal connections. Now consider my own case. My parents immigrated from Finland to the United States and then to Canada. They spoke only Finnish, so I learned Finnish as my first language in Thunder Bay, where I was born. However, my older brothers and sisters often spoke English to each other in the home and after age 4 I began to play with English-speaking friends outside the home, so I quickly learned English. Thus, I would have to be defined as a compound English-Finnish bilingual on the basis of fused acquisition contexts and only subtly coordinate on the basis of the early-late criterion. Nonetheless, I have noticed the same imagery differences as Bugelski. For me, the word *church* elicits an image of one or another Canadian Protestant or Catholic church. The Finnish equivalent *kirkko* elicits a vague image of the white, wood-frame, Finnish Lutheran church in the region of Sudbury where I lived between the ages of 4 and 8 years. These contrasts suggest that the antecedent conditions and resulting images and behaviors can differ in more subtle and probabilistic ways than was implied by the original compound-coordinate distinction.

Despite such problems, the implications of the dual coding approach could be directly tested using extensions of past procedures. For example, imagery reaction times to concrete and abstract translation equivalents could be obtained from bilinguals who differ on traditional measures of the compound-coordinate dimension. Such bilinguals could also be asked to sketch or describe their images to the words as they go along. Relative differences in coordinateness might correlate with differences in imagery reaction time and imagery content for translation equivalents, at least for some words, reflecting differences in the referential experiences that are the basis of word-evoked imagery. Similarly, data on latency and content of translations and word associations would allow us to evaluate possible differences in verbal associative networks between and within languages for both types of bilinguals. The Lambert et al. (1958) semantic differential study could be replicated and extended by questioning subjects about any imagery or verbal thoughts that they experience while rating the words. Bilingual dual coding theory generates such studies readily, and the trick is to come up with ones that are most likely to inform us about unresolved but tantalizing issues, such as the compound-coordinate distinction, that survive as a legacy from Wally Lambert's pioneering research on the bilingual mind.

ACKNOWLEDGEMENT

The author's research reported in this chapter was supported by grant A0087 from the Natural Sciences and Engineering Research Council of Canada.

REFERENCES

Bugelski, B. R. (1977). The association of images. In J. M. Nicholas (Ed.), *Images, perception, and knowledge*. Boston: D. Reidel.

Dalrymple-Alford, E., & Aamiry, A. (1969). Language and category clustering in bilingual free recall. *Journal of Verbal Learning and Verbal Behavior, 8*, 763-768.

Dillon, R. F., McCormack, P. D., Petrusic, W. M., Cook, M., & LaFleur, L. (1973). Release from proactive interference in compound and coordinate bilinguals. *Bulletin of the Psychonomic Society, 2*, 293-294.

Ervin, S. M., & Osgood, C. E. (1954). Second language learning and bilingualism. In C. E. Osgood & F. Sebeok (Eds.), Psycholinguistics. *Journal of Abnormal and Social Psychology, 49*, 139-146.

Glanzer, M., & Duarte, A. (1971). Repetition between and within languages in free recall. *Journal of Verbal Learning and Verbal Behavior, 10*, 625-630.

Goggin, J., & Wickens, D. D. (1971). Proactive interference and language change in short-term memory. *Journal of Verbal Learning and Verbal Behavior, 10*, 453-458.

Harbluk, J., Paivio, A., & Clark, J. (1987, June). *Representation in bilingual memory: Differences between translations and synonyms*. Paper presented at the meeting of the Canadian Psychological Association, Vancouver.

Kolers, P. A. (1963). Interlingual word association. *Journal of Verbal Learning and Verbal Behavior, 2*, 291-300.

Kolers, P. A. (1964). Specificity of a cognitive operation. *Journal of Verbal Learning and Verbal Behavior, 3*, 244-248.

Kolers, P. A., & Gonzalez, E. (1980). Memory for words, synonyms, and translations. *Journal of Experimental Psychology: Human Learning and Memory, 6*, 53-65.

Lambert, W. E. (1969). Psychological studies of the interdependencies of the bilingual's two languages. In J. Puhvel (Ed.), *Substance and structure of language*. Los Angeles: University of California Press.

Lambert, W. E., & Fillenbaum, S. (1959). A pilot study of aphasia among bilinguals. *Canadian Journal of Psychology, 13*(1), 28-34.

Lambert, W. E., Havelka, J., & Crosby, C. (1958). The influence of language acquisition contexts on bilingualism. *Journal of Abnormal and Social Psychology, 56*, 239-244.

Lambert, W. E., Ignatow, M., & Krauthamer, M. (1968). Bilingual organization in free recall. *Journal of Verbal Learning and Verbal Behavior, 7*, 207-214.

Lopez, M., & Young, R. K. (1974). The linguistic interdependence of bilinguals. *Journal of Experimental Psychology, 102*, 981-983.

MacLeod, C. M. (1976). Bilingual episodic memory: Acquisition and forgetting. *Journal of Verbal Learning and Verbal Behavior, 15*, 347-364.

McCormack, P. D. (1974). Bilingual linguistic memory: Independence or interdependence: Two stores or one? In S. T. Carey (Ed.), *Bilingualism, biculturalism and education*. Edmonton: University of Alberta Printing Department.

McCormack, P. D. (1977). Bilingual linguistic memory: The independence-interdependence issue revisited. In P. A. Hornby (Ed.), *Bilingualism: Psychological, social, and educational implications*. New York: Academic Press.

Paivio, A. (1986). *Mental representations: A dual coding approach*. New York: Oxford University Press.

Paivio, A., Clark, J. M., & Lambert, W. E. (1988). Bilingual dual-coding theory and semantic repetition effects on recall. *Journal of Experimental Psychology: Learning, Memory, and Cognition, 14*, 163-172.

Paivio, A., & Desrochers, A. (1980). A dual-coding approach to bilingual memory. *Canadian Journal of Psychology, 34*, 390-401.

Paivio, A., & Lambert, W. (1981). Dual coding and bilingual memory. *Journal of Verbal Learning and Verbal Behavior, 20*, 532-539.

Paradis, M. (1980). Language and thought in bilinguals. In H. J. Izzo & W. E. McCormack (Eds.), *The sixth LACUS forum*. Columbia, SC: Hornbeam Press.

Potter, M. C., So, K., Von Eckardt, B., & Feldman, L. B. (1984). Lexical and conceptual representation in beginning and proficient bilinguals. *Journal of Verbal Learning and Verbal Behavior, 23*, 23-38.

Rosenberg, S., & Simon, H. A. (1977). Modelling semantic memory: Effects of presenting semantic information in different modalities. *Cognitive Psychology, 9,* 293-325.

Vaid, J. (1988). Bilingual memory representation: A further test of dual coding theory. *Canadian Journal of Psychology, 42,* 84-90.

Weinreich, U. (1953). *Languages in contact.* New York: Linguistic Circle of New York.

Young, R. K., & Saegert, J. (1966). Transfer with bilinguals. *Psychonomic Science, 6,* 161-162.

7 L'ontogénèse de la bilingualité: Dimensions sociales et trans-culturelles

Josiane F. Hamers
Université Laval

Si la majorité des recherches de Lambert n'ont pas porté directement sur les aspects développementaux de la bilingualité, l'influence de sa pensée a cependant eu un impact énorme dans ce domaine. En effet, en étant le premier à attirer l'attention sur le fait que différentes formes de bilingualité se développent en fonction du contexte socio-culturel dans lequel l'expérience bilingue a lieu, il a produit un travail de pionnier qui a permis de nouvelles vues sur la relation entre le bilinguisme et le développement social et cognitif précoce. Avant que Lambert ne propose un modèle théorique reliant l'expérience bilingue précoce et ses conséquences cognitives au contexte socioculturelle et aux mécanismes socio-psychologiques à travers desquels le contexte influence le développement de l'enfant, les connaissances dans le domaine se limitaient à une accumulation de données empiriques qui semblaient contradictoires.

La première moitié du siècle fut surtout marquée par deux types d'études, soit (a) d'une part, l'élaboration minutieuse de biographies d'enfants bilingues, dont celles de Ronjat (1913) et de Leopold (1939-1949) et (b) d'autre part, des études comparatives entre les comportements scolaires des enfants monolingues et bilingues. Alors que les biographies semblent de façon générale indiquer un développement harmonieux de l'enfant bilingue, le deuxième type d'approche, comme, par exemple, les études de Pintner et Keller (1922) et de Saer (1923) démontrent l'existence d'un retard développemental de l'enfant bilingue par rapport à l'enfant monolingue. La contradiction apparente entre, d'une part, les avantages de l'enfant bilingue, telle, par exemple, une plus grande sensibilité à la relation entre le mot et son sens mentionnée par Ronjat et, d'autre part, les soi-disant conséquences négatives du bilinguisme, mentionnées dans les études psycho-métriques, n'a pas été relevée par les chercheurs de l'époque, sans doute parce que les deux courants de recherche s'ignoraient. Même dans les années cinquante Darcy (1953), se basant sur les données psychométriques et ignorant la plupart des études de cas, en vient à la conclusion que le bilinguisme est néfaste pour le développement de l'enfant.

L'effet de l'expérience bilingue précoce sur le développement cognitif est une préoccupation des différentes disciplines qui s'intéressent à l'étude du contact des langues. Un problème majeur consiste notamment a trouvé une explication pour la différence entre les résultats mentionnés lorsqu'il s'agit d'un bilinguisme "d'élite," tels ceux décrits dans les biographies ou obtenus dans les écoles internationales et ceux décrits dans le cas d'un bilinguisme populaire.

LE MODELE D'ADDITIVITE-SOUSTRACTIVITE

Lambert (1974, 1977) a suggéré qu'il faut chercher les racines de la bilingualité dans les aspects socio-psychologiques du comportement langagier, plus particulièrement dans le rôle qui joue le statut social relatif des deux langues en question et la perception de ce statut par l'individu. En effet, il fut le premier à mentionner de façon explicite qu'il faut distinguer deux formes de bilingualité, soit une forme additive et une forme soustractive qui se développent chacune en fonction du milieu socio-culturel dans lequel a lieu l'expérience bilingue. Dans la forme additive de bilingualité, le développement est tel, que les deux langues et les deux cultures vont apporter des éléments positifs complémentaires au développement de l'enfant; cette situation se retrouve lorsque la communauté et la famille attribuent des valeurs positives aux deux langues. Dans ce cas l'apprentissage d'une L_2 ne menace pas de remplacer la L_1.

A l'opposé, la forme soustractive de la bilingualité se développera lorsque les deux langues sont concurrentes plutôt que complémentaires; cette forme se développera lorsqu'une communauté rejette ses propres valeurs socioculturelles au profit de celles d'une langue culturellement et économiquement plus prestigieuse. Dans ce cas, la langue la plus prestigieuse qui sera apportée à l'enfant aura tendance à remplacer la langue maternelle qui se détériorera. Cette situation se retrouve notamment lorsqu'un enfant d'une minorité ethnolinguistique reçoit sa scolarisation dans une langue nationale plus prestigieuse que la sienne. Le degré de bilingualité reflête alors une étape dans la soustraction de la compétence dans les deux langues (Lambert, 1977, p. 19). Cette soustraction se manifeste à différents niveaux et influence le développement intellectuel et la personnalité; la compétence langagière d'abord développée en langue maternelle est affectée de façon négative.

Deux questions importantes peuvent être posées à propos de cette approche théorique. D'abord, quels sont les données empiriques et modèles qui ont amené la formulation de ce construit? Ensuite, quelle a été l'impact de ce modèle sur la recherche et les développements théoriques ultérieurs? Ce construit théorique est fondée sur un ensemble de travaux portant tant sur le comportement bilingue, sur les relations entre la bilingualité et le développement cognitif, sur l'évaluation des programmes bilingues pour les enfants de la majorité et des minorités ainsi que sur les dimensions affectives du bilinguisme. Cette diversité d'approches a permis la formulation théorique actuelle.

Dès les premiers travaux de Lambert portant sur la définition du bilinguisme (Lambert, 1987) et sur la vérification empirique de typologies de bilingues (e.g., les travaux de Lambert, Havelka, & Crosby, 1958, sur les différences de comportement des bilingues coordonnés et composés ou encore ceux de Lambert & Fillenbaum, 1959, sur la différence des troubles aphasiques en fonction de l'histoire d'acquisition des deux langues) il est apparu que l'histoire d'acquisition des deux langues, donc le développement de la bilingualité joue un rôle important dans le comportement bilingue tant sur le plan cognitif qu'affectif.

LES DIMENSIONS COGNITIVES DU DEVELOPPEMENT BILINGUE

Les premiers travaux de Lambert qui réfèrent au développement bilingue ont tenté de vérifier la croyance qu'une expérience bilingue précoce était la cause de déficits et de retard dans le développement cognitif de l'enfant. Afin de vérifier cette idée, Peal et Lambert (1962) ont comparé les résultats à des tests d'intelligence verbale et non verbale d'enfants monolingues et bilingues français-anglais, âgés de 10 ans, et ont constaté la supériorité intellectuelle des bilingues. Cette recherche était la première à répondre à une rigueur méthodologique permettant une comparaison valable entre monolingues et bilingues: les échantillons avaient été soigneusement appariés pour l'âge, le sexe et l'origine socio-économique. Une précision quantitative était apportée à la définition de bilinguisme, puisque pour faire partie de l'échantillon bilingue le sujet était identifié au moyen d'une mesure d'un indice d'équilibre, calculé sur la base de tests de vocabulaire et d'association ainsi que d'une échelle d'auto-évaluation de compétence linguistique dans les deux langues. De même, le groupe monolingue était identifié par des scores relativement bas dans ces deux mesures en langue seconde. Ces contrôles assurés, les résultats ont démontré non seulement que les bilingues ne subissaient aucune forme de retard, mais qu'ils accusaient un avantage significatif dans la majorité des tests utilisés. Les auteurs ont conclu que le meilleur rendement intellectuel des bilingues était l'expression d'une plus grande "flexibilité cognitive" résultant de l'habitude de passer d'un système de symbole à l'autre. Cette flexibilité cognitive permettrait au bilingue de faire, en outre, une analyse plus détaillée des traits sémantiques sous-adjacents au mot.

Depuis cette étude de Peal et Lambert on a vu se développer un nombre considérable de recherches empiriques qui tentent de mieux cerner les différents paramètres impliqués dans l'avantage cognitif du bilingue. Citons à titre d'exemple: l'étude de Balkan (1970) en Suisse, dans laquelle une plus grande habileté à reconstruire une situation perceptuelle a été démontrée chez des enfants bilingues français-anglais, comparés à des monolingues; celle de Cummins et Gulutsan (1974) qui signalent une plus grande habileté verbale et non verbale chez des enfants bilingues ukrainien-anglais que chez des monolingues; celle de Liedtke et Nelson (1968) qui ont observé une meilleure performance dans des tâches piagétiennes de formation de concepts et celle de Bain (1975) rapportant l'avantage des bilingues dans des tâches de découverte de règles tant chez des enfants bilingues français-anglais dans l'ouest canadien que chez des bilingues français-alsatien et allemand-anglais (Bain & Yu, 1978).

Un nombre considérable de recherches indiquent que c'est l'aspect créatif du développement cognitif qui semble avantagé par l'expérience bilingue. Les bilingues semblent davantage utiliser la pensée divergente, tel que démontré par Scott (1973) pour des bilingues français-anglais et par Carringer (1974) pour des bilingues anglais-espagnol. De même, par rapport à des monolingues, des enfants bilingues chinois-anglais démontrent une supériorité à des tests d'originalité et d'élaboration (Torrance, Gowan, Wu, & Aliotti, 1970); des bilingues anglais-espagnol et vietnamien-espagnol sont supérieurs à des tests psychometriques traditionnels (*WISC-R Block Design* [Gorrell, Bregman, McAllistair, & Lipscombe, 1982]); des bilingues suédois-finnois sont supérieurs à des tâches de transformation verbale et de substitution symbolique (Ekstrand, 1981). Les bilingues sont également supérieurs dans des tâches de solution de problèmes; Kessler et Quinn (1982) interprètent ces résultats comme une preuve d'une plus grande compétence métalinguistique et de processus cognitifs plus développés. Pour résumer, les avantages cognitifs liés à l'expérience bilingue ont trait à une plus grande créativité et une meilleure capacité de réorganiser de l'information. Cet avantage peut s'étendre à des tâches non verbales telle la coordination motrice (Powers & Lopez, 1985).

Au cours des dernières années ces observations ont reçu une confirmation provenant d'études utilisant diverses combinaison de langues indo- et non-indo-européennes, tant dans des pays industrialisés que dans des pays en voie de développement. S'il existe certaines indications que la différence de créativité entre bilingues et monolingues est universelle et peut être attribuée à l'expérience bilingue précoce de l'enfant, certains aspects de cette créativité semblent cependant influencés par des particularités culturelles (Hamers & Blanc, 1989). Okoh (1980) a, par exemple, démontré que des bilingues yoruba-anglais au Nigéria et des bilingues gallois-anglais au pays de Galles obtiennent des scores supérieurs en pensée divergente et en créativité verbale que ne le font les monolingues dans leur pays respectifs mais que bilingues nigérians et gallois diffèrent entre eux sur des mesures de créativité non verbale. Des variations culturelles dans le type de tâche créative avantagée chez le bilingue ont également été observée entre des bilingues espagnol-anglais et des bilingues vietnamien-anglais (Gorrell et al., 1982).

Le plus grand potentiel créatif des bilingues est aussi ressorti dans une série d'expériences avec des enfants de différentes tribus en Inde: par exemple, les enfants de la tribu Kond, bilingues en Kui (une langue tribale dravidienne) et en Orya (une langue indo-européenne qui est la langue officielle de l'état d'Orissa) obtiennent des résultats supérieurs à des mesures métalinguistiques, au test de matrices de Raven, à des tests piagétiens de conservation et à des mesures de détection d'ambiguité syntaxique que ne le font leur pairs monolingues en Orya (Babu, 1984; Mohanty & Babu, 1983; Pattnaik & Mohanty, 1984). Ces résultats seraient la preuve d'une plus grande habileté métalinguistique, d'une flexibilité cognitive plus développée ainsi que d'une plus grande capacité de réflexion sur le langage, développés suite à l'expérience précoce avec deux langues. Dans un contexte africain, Da Silveira (1988) a démontré que plus l'enfant béninois, bilingue en fon et en français, a développé une forme équilibrée de bilingualité dans les deux langues, plus il fait preuve de pensée divergente.

LA NATURE DU DEVELOPPEMENT COGNITIF DU BILINGUE

Il semble donc qu'à l'heure actuelle nous possédons une quantité imposante d'évidence empirique qui démontre l'avantage cognitif lié à une expérience bilingue précoce, quelles que soient les combinaisons de langues et de cultures impliquées. Il y a suffisamment d'indications transculturelles pour conclure au caractère universel d'un avantage cognitif lié à l'expérience bilingue précoce, même si la forme de créativité peut varier d'une culture à l'autre. Pour résumer, cet avantage a trait aux aspects créatifs du fonctionnement cognitif; il inclut une plus grande capacité d'abstraction, une meilleure perception d'indices conceptuelles, une plus grande pensée divergente, une plus grande compétence métalinguistique, et davantage de flexibilité cognitive. Being able to express the same thought in different languages will enable the child "to see his language as one particular system among many, to view its phenomena under more general categories, and this leads to an awareness of his linguistic operations" (Vygotsky, 1934/1962, p. 110).

La recherche empirique qui s'est développée à la suite de l'étude de Peal et Lambert a non seulement confirmé les propos de Vygotsky, mais a également permis de nouveaux développements théoriques. Par exemple, approchant le problème de la bilingualité sous l'angle de la conscience métalinguistique, Segalowitz (1977) a suggéré que l'intériorisation de deux langues amène l'enfant à développer un mécanisme permettant l'alternance entre deux systèmes de règles dans la manipulation de symboles. Dans le même ordre d'idées Lambert (1987) a lui aussi suggéré que le bilingue peut développer une perception "tri-dimensionnelle" du langage, un point de vue "stéréoscopique" qui ne serait pas accessible au monolingue.

Quelle est la nature de ce mécanisme? Dans leur analyse de la nature cognitive de la conscience métalinguistique Bialystok et Ryan (1985a, 1985b) suggèrent que la compétence métalinguistique est le résultat du développement de deux compétences cognitives indépendantes, soit (a) la capacité d'analyser des connaissances qui donne accès à la structure et à la manipulation des représentations et (b) la capacité d'exercer un contrôle cognitif, c.à.d. de sélectionner, coordonner, et hiérarchiser les connaissances dans le temps et dans l'espace. Plus l'enfant est capable de développer ses deux compétences, plus il est en mesure de passer du langage contextualisé vers le langage décontextualisé et les actes métalinguistiques, c.à.d. des actes de réflexion sur le langage. Pour Bialystok et Ryan l'expérience bilingue permettrait d'abord à l'enfant d'exercer un plus grand contrôle sur le traitement de l'information; ceci lui permettrait à son tour de développer davantage sa compétence métalinguistique. Ce que l'enfant bilingue développerait seraient des mécanismes cognitifs généraux de traitement de l'information; une fois ces mécanismes mis en action, l'enfant serait capable de les utiliser pour toute tâche de traitement de l'information, linguistique ou non.

L'EVIDENCE EMPIRIQUE DES PROGRAMMES D'IMMERSION ET D'EDUCATION D'ENFANTS DE MINORITES ETHNIQUES

Le développement d'une théorisation sur la nature de l'avantage cognitif de l'enfant bilingue n'est pas la seule influence de la pensée de Lambert. Celle-ci a eu également un impact en pédagogie, et notamment sur le développement de programmes d'éducation bilingue, qu'ils soient destinés aux enfants de la majorité ou de minorités ethnolinguistiques.

Ce n'est pas un hasard si les programmes d'immersion se sont développés d'abord au Québec durant les années 60 alors que la communauté anglophone du Québec était à la recherche d'un programme pédagogique qui permettait aux enfants anglophones de développer une connaissance fonctionnelle du français, suffisante pour être en mesure de l'utiliser comme langue de travail. Ces programmes sont discutés ailleurs dans le présent colloque et je ne m'attarderai pas sur ceux-ci sauf pour mentionner leur apport à nos connaissances sur le développement bilingue. Basée sur deux hypothèses, soit (1) que la L_2 est apprise de façon similaire à la L_1; et (2) que la langue est la mieux apprise dans un contexte stimulant qui met l'accent sur les fonctions du langage et expose l'enfant aux formes naturelles du langage (Lambert & Tucker, 1972), l'immersion a-t-elle donné les résultats escomptés?

Dans les vingt ans qui se sont écoulés depuis sa création de nombreuses variantes ont été expérimentées, et les résultats des évaluations vont toujours dans le même sens. Les programmes d'immersion sont supérieurs à la didactique des langues secondes traditionnelle: un haut niveau de compétence est atteint dans les habiletés réceptives sans que l'élève atteigne la compétence du locuteur natif dans les habiletés expressives; ni la compétence en langue maternelle ni les résultats académiques ne souffrent de retard; et, enfin, il existe certaines indications que l'immersion précoce favorise le développement cognitif de l'enfant, donc la forme additive de la bilingualité. Au cours des années les attentes des résultats ont cependant beaucoup diminuées et l'on est loin de l'objectif initial de bilingualité équilibrée exprimé par les parents du projet St-Lambert.

Les élèves en immersion entrent rarement en contact avec les membres de la communauté francophone (Cziko, Lambert, Sidoti, & Tucker, 1978). Si les attitudes envers la communauté de L_2 sont modifiées (Lambert & Tucker, 1972), l'immersion ne semble cependant pas favoriser le contact social nécessaire à l'apprentissage de la L_2; or, les contacts sociaux semblent indispensables pour développer la maîtrise des compétences orales (Chun, 1979). Des résultats très semblables à ceux de l'immersion peuvent être obtenus avec moins d'heures d'exposition à la langue lorsque le contexte social d'apprentissage est présent, notamment dans les écoles internationales (Baetens Beardsmore & Swain, 1985). Les résultats des programmes d'immersion nous semblent révélateurs quant au rôle joué par le contexte social dans le développement bilingue.

En même temps que l'on obtenait les premiers résultats sur l'immersion Lambert s'intéressait également à l'évaluation de programmes bilingues destinés aux minorités ethnolinguistiques américaines. Ses travaux sur les programmes d'éducation bilingue en Nouvelle Angleterre (Dubé & Hébert, 1975; Lambert, Giles, & Albert, 1976; Lambert, Giles, & Picard, 1975) ont démontré que l'on obtenait des résultats scolaires supérieurs lorsque la scolarisation d'enfants franco-américains incluait le français comme médium d'enseignement. En plus d'obtenir une meilleure connaissance du français ces enfants étaient supérieurs dans toutes les matières académiques et obtenaient des résultats comparables en anglais alors que cette dernière langue n'avait pas été autant utilisée dans le curriculum. Ces résultats ont été confirmés dans d'autres pays: partout où les enfants de minorité sont d'abord scolarisés dans leur langue il semble qu'on obtiennent des résulats supérieurs à ceux obtenus lorsque la scolarisation se fait exclusivement dans la langue de la majorité. Dans ce dernier cas les enfants bilingues obtiennent souvent des résultats scolaires inférieurs à ceux des monolingues.

Les conséquences négatives d'une expérience bilingue précoce ont souvent été décrites en termes de déficits cognitifs. A la même époque ou plusieurs recherches confirmaient l'existence et la nature des avantages cognitifs du bilingue, d'autres études faisaient ressortir l'existence de mauvaises performances académiques chez les enfants minoritaires bilingues. La corrélation entre les résultats scolaires et l'origine ethnolinguistique, donc la bilingualité de l'enfant minoritaire a trop rapidement été interprêtée comme une relation de cause à effet: on attribue les mauvaises performances à un handicap cognitif, lui-même provoqué par un handicap linguistique. Or ces mauvaises performances ne sont pas la conséquence d'un déficit linguistique; comme le fait observé Troike (1984) si la compétence linguistique était responsable des mauvais résultats scolaires chez les minorités alors les hispano-américains qui sont socio-économiquement plus désavantagés que les monolingues anglo-américains blancs mais moins que les monolingues américains noirs devraient obtenir de plus mauvais résultats que ces deux groupes; or si leurs résultats sont inférieurs à ceux des Anglo-Américains ils sont cependant supérieurs à ceux des Noirs Américains. Il devient dès lors difficile d'attribuer l'échec scolaire à un handicap linguistique.

Une des conséquences de la pensée de Lambert a été la démonstration qu'il suffit d'interrompre le cercle vicieux du mythe de l'handicap linguistique pour obtenir des résultats scolaires qui se rapprochent de ceux de la majorité monolingue. De nombreux programmes bilingues pour des groupes minoritaires appliqués dans les dernières années appuient empiriquement cette démonstration. A titre d'exemple, à part les programmes de Nouvelle Angleterre déjà mentionnés, citons le programme bilingue suédois dans lequel on commence la scolarisation des enfants de la minorité finnoise d'abord en finnois pour introduire le suédois à partir de la 3ᵉ année et le maintient des deux langues tout au long du curriculum primaire (Hanson, 1979); le programme Chiapas au Mexique et le programme Rock Point aux Etats Unis ou l'enfant indien est d'abord scolarisé dans sa langue maternelle avant d'utiliser la langue de la majorité (Modiano, 1973; Rosier & Farella, 1976); ou encore, les programmes franco-manitobains où l'on obtient davantage de résultats positifs en utilisant 80% de temps en langue maternelle sans qu'il y ait de perte sur la compétence en L2 (Hébert, 1976); et plus récemment le programme MOTET en Grande Bretagne dans lequel des enfants Mirpuri (un dialecte Punjabi) obtiennent des résultats scolaires supérieurs dans un programme bilingue 50%-50% que ne le font des enfants Mirpuri dans les programmes anglais (Fitzpatrick, 1987).

Pour résumer il semble que, à condition d'introduire la langue maternelle pendant une période suffisamment longue dans le programme scolaire et de permettre à l'enfant de l'utiliser pour effectuer des activités de littéracie on élimine les problèmes scolaires traditionnellement associés à la bilingualité de l'enfant minoritaire. Lorsque l'objectif d'un programme bilingue ne vise plus l'assimilation, mais se rapproche davantage de celui des programmes pour la majorité, à savoir le développement d'une bilingualité fonctionnelle, il semble que l'enfant peut être avantagé sur le plan cognitif par son expérience bilingue.

LA NATURE SOCIO-CULTURELLE DE L'ADDITIVITE-SOUSTRACTIVITE

C'est sur cette toile de fond empirique que la pensée de Lambert et sa théorisation sur le construit d'additivité et de soustractivité prend toute son ampleur. Il a suggéré que les racines de la bilingualité se trouvent dans les différents mécanismes socio-psychologiques impliqués dans le comportement langagier, en particulier ceux pertinents au statut relatif des deux langues et à la perception de ce statut par l'individu.

Les perspectives de Lambert expliquent pourquoi les avantages cognitifs liés à l'expérience bilingue se retrouvent principalement chez des enfants bilingues de famille mixte ou chez des enfants du groupe dominant qui reçoivent leur scolarisation dans une langue moins prestigieuse que la leur; de même qu'elles expliquent pourquoi les enfants de minorité développent une forme soustractive de bilingualité lorsqu'il sont scolarisés dans la langue dominante. Dans le cas de l'additivité les deux langues sont valorisées à même titre, soit parce qu'elles le sont toutes deux dans le milieu familial, soit parce que l'école valorise la langue seconde en l'utilisant comme langue d'enseignement; par contre dans la condition soustractive la langue maternelle déjà dévalorisée par la société l'est encore davantage dans le système scolaire. Ce modèle est concordant avec plusieurs approches sur le développement général de l'enfant, par exemple avec celle de Bruner (1966) pour qui l'environnement culturel joue un rôle de catalyseur dans le développement cognitif dès l'atteinte du stade symbolique. Pour cette raison il est impérieux que l'on ait une meilleure compréhension de ce rôle et notamment des mécanismes qui permettent l'intériorisation des valeurs culturelles.

Suite à ces développements théoriques deux grands axes de recherche se sont développés. Certains chercheurs ont tenté de mieux définir les mécanismes cognitifs qui permettraient d'arriver au développement d'avantages ou de désavantages sur le plan du fonctionnement cognitif, alors que d'autres ont essayé d'analyser les mécanismes socio-psychologiques qui permettraient d'intérioriser les valeurs sociétales et celles de l'entourage.

DEVELOPPEMENTS ULTERIEURS SUR LA NATURE COGNITIVE DE LA BILINGUALITE

Sur le plan cognitif Cummins (1979) a suggéré qu'il existe un double seuil de compétence langagière que l'enfant doit franchir: si un premier seuil de compétence en langue maternelle n'est pas atteint l'introduction d'une langue seconde aura des effets négatifs sur son développement cognitif. Mais ce n'est que lorsqu'un deuxième seuil est atteint et que l'enfant a développé une compétence relativement élevée dans les deux langues qu'il pourra aussi connaitre certains avantages cognitifs. Cummins suggère que le niveau de compétence en L_2 est partiellement fonction de la compétence en langue maternelle au moment où l'enfant est exposé à la L_2. Lorsque certaines fonctions langagières ont été fortement développées en langue maternelle, il est probable qu'une forte exposition à une L_2 mènera à une bonne compétence en celle-ci sans que ce soit au détriment de la langue maternelle. Un haut niveau de compétence en langue maternelle entrainera un haut niveau de compétence en L_2 et un meilleur fonctionnement cognitif. Certaines recherches ont notamment démontrés que des bilingues avec des compétences relativement élevées dans les deux langues obtiennent de meilleurs résultats à des tâches cognitives que ne le font des bilingues non équilibrés ou des monolingues (Duncan & De Avila, 1979; Hakuta & Diaz, 1984). Il semble donc que la compétence langagière soit une variable intermédiaire qui joue un rôle de premier plan pour déterminer l'effet de l'expérience bilingue sur le développement cognitif.

Pour Cummins (1981, 1984) la compétence langagière inclut non seulement les compétences linguistiques mais également une compétence conceptuelle plus profonde, elle même fonction du développement de la littéracie et des compétences académiques. La compétence cognitivo-académique se développerait suivant deux continua indépendants: le premier à trait au support contextuel disponible pour exprimer et comprendre le sens (context-embedded vs. context-free); le second réfère à la complexité cognitive du comportement verbal (cognitively demanding vs. undemanding). Les exigences linguistiques de l'école portent sur des tâches linguistiques qui sont simultanément indépendantes du contexte et exigeantes sur le plan de la complexité cognitive.

Il se peut que dans le cas des minorités nous ayons davantage affaire à des problèmes de développement métalinguistique et de littéracie qu'à un problème linguistique. La conscience métalinguistique est différente de la communication linguistique ordinaire dans la mesure où elle fait appel à des compétences cognitives différentes. Comme nous l'avons déjà mentionné, pour Bialystok et Ryan (1985a, 1985b) tant le développement du langage que le développement cognitif implique un passage progressif d'une connaissance peu analysée et d'un contrôle cognitif réduit vers une connaissance analysée et un contrôle cognitif étendu. Si l'enfant a déjà commencé à développer ces mécanismes, ceux-ci pourraient se développer davantage suite à une expérience bilingue puisque celle-ci fait constamment appel à un niveau d'analyse plus poussée de l'information reçue.

Cette interaction rétroactive a d'ailleurs reçu un appui empirique: Holmstrand (1979) a démontré que des enfants suédois, qui possèdent déjà une bonne compétence linguistique dans leur langue maternelle et qui acquièrent une langue seconde par le biais d'une forme d'immersion, apprennent non seulement à fonctionner en langue seconde, mais améliorent davantage leur compétence en suédois que des monolingues qui n'ont pas eu cette expérience bilingue. De même Kessler et Quinn (1987) ont trouvé que lorsque des enfants bilingues anglais-espagnol sont introduits à des tâches de résolution de problèmes en espagnol, ils deviennent très vite capable de générer des hypothèses plus complexes que ne le font des pairs monolingues anglais; cette compétence cognitive se reflète d'ailleurs dans leur compétence linguistique puisque la complexité syntaxique de leur langage augmente; cette complexité est fortement corrélées avec la capacité à résoudre des problèmes. Les auteurs interprètent ces données comme la preuve que des enfants bilingues développent davantage leur compétence métalinguistique ainsi que les processus créatifs. Ces observations rejoignent celles de Tizard, Schofield, et Hewison (1982) en Grande Bretagne: des enfants d'origine indo-pakistanaise qui ont des difficultés de lecture en anglais, langue d'enseignement, améliorent davantage leur compétence en anglais quand on introduit des activités littéraciées dans le milieu familial, en n'importe quelle langue, que ne le font des enfants comparables qui reçoivent des cours de rattrapage en lecture anglaise. Il semble donc que se soit en développant toutes les fonctions du langage, et en particulier les fonctions liées à la littéracie dans les deux langues que l'additivité cognitive peut se développer.

DEVELOPPEMENTS ULTERIEURS SUR LES ASPECTS SOCIO-PSYCHOLOGIQUES DU DEVELOPPEMENT BILINGUE

Si la bilingualité se manifeste dans le comportement cognitif de l'enfant, celui-ci n'est cependant que le résultat visible d'un processus complexe par lequel l'enfant intériorise et fait siennes les valeurs et représentations de la société (Hamers & Blanc, 1982). A date, les recherches sur les dimensions socio-culturelles du développement bilingue sont moins nombreuses que celles sur la dimension cognitive et les construits théoriques encore moins élaborés.

Les données corrélationnelles entre les comportements cognitifs et l'entourage social dans lequel l'enfant se développent pourraient donner lieu à l'idée d'un déterminisme social. Or ce déterminisme est démenti par plusieurs indications qu'une bilingualité de nature additive peut se développer en milieu soustractif (Lambert, 1987; Landry, 1982; Landry & Allard, 1987); cette modification est obtenue davantage suite à des changements de nature psychologique, notamment en modifiant le rapport de l'enfant avec sa langue maternelle, qu'a des changements sociologiques. Alors que traditionnellement les études sur le bilinguisme se sont limitées à un seul niveau d'analyse on a vu récemment se développer des modèles tentant d'intégrer les approches macrologiques de la sociologie aux approches micrologiques de la psychologie (Blanc & Hamers, 1987; Landry & Allard, 1988; Prujiner, Deshaies, Hamers, Blanc, Clément, & Landry, 1984). Plutôt qu'un modèle de déterminisme social, un modèle d'interactions réciproques entre la société, l'individu et le comportement semble plus approprié pour expliquer les différentes formes de développement bilingue (Hamers, 1987).

Percevant le développement bilingue dans une optique d'auto-régulation de comportement social, Hamers et Blanc (1982) ont suggéré que le type de bilingualité est fonction des mécanismes auto-régulatoires que l'enfant développe suite à l'intériorisation du comportement langagier de son entourage. Dans celui-ci les caractéristiques du réseau social de l'enfant et notamment l'usage et les fonctions des deux langues en interaction avec d'autres caractéristiques du réseau détermineront les représentations du langage que l'enfant développera davantage que ne le font des facteurs macrosociologiques tels l'appartenance à une classe sociale; ces représentations sont à leur tour auto-régulatoires du comportement langagier et ce dernier va constamment modifier ces représentations. Les réseaux sociaux agiraient donc comme un interface entre la structure sociale du monde extérieure et l'élaboration des représentations du langage et de ses langues spécifiques par l'enfant; c'est par eux que l'enfant peut prendre connaissance de la structure et des valeurs sociales et c'est grâce à eux qu'il peut se construire une représentation sociale de sa langue et des autres langues parlées dans sa communauté (Hamers & Blanc, 1989).

Cette approche commence a recevoir un appui empirique. Nous avons notamment pu observer que chez des enfants de Néo-Canadiens, grecs et arabes la compétence en langue ancestrale et le maintien de celle-ci sont fonction non seulement de la fréquence d'usage dans le réseau familial et dans le réseau d'amis mais aussi de la fonction de cette langue dans le milieu familial: si cette langue est utilisée pour des activités littéraciées (livres, cassettes, etc.) l'enfant développera une meilleure compétence dans cette langue et une bilingualité plus équilibrée que si l'usage de cette langue se limite à sa fonction sociale et à un usage folklorique; si le milieu familial limite l'usage de la langue maternelle à l'interaction sociale, il semble que même des cours en cette langue, conçu en dehors du réseau familial et du réseau scolaire ne sont pas suffisant pour développer un usage littéracié chez l'enfant. C'est cet usage là qui se trouve aussi corrélé avec des croyances et des attitudes positives face à la langue ancestrale et aux deux langues officielles (Hamers, in press). Cependant, lorsque une des deux langues n'est pas utilisée pour des interactions sociales, surtout des interactions avec le réseau de pairs, il semble que l'enfant ne développe pas une forme équilibrée de bilingualité (Arnberg, 1984). Ces observations d'Arnberg rejoignent les résultats obtenus par les programmes d'immersion. Il semble donc que pour pouvoir tirer bénéfice de son expérience il faut que les deux langues soient utilisées dans toutes leurs fonctions avec l'enfant.

Pour Landry et Allard (1988) le réseau individuel des contacts linguistiques permet le développement des compétences en langue première et langue seconde ainsi que la formation des croyances, attitudes et valeurs liées aux langues. Ce réseau est lui-même fonction non seulement de la vitalité ethnolinguistique d'un groupe sociologique, puisque ce sont les caractéristiques de groupe (le capital démographique, économique, politique, et culturel pour parler en termes bourdieusiens) qui déterminent l'opportunité de contacts linguistiques mais surtout des croyances par rapport à cette vitalité. Les croyances représentent la dimension socio-cognitive qui contribue au comportement langagier. C'est l'interaction de ces quatre groupes de facteurs, vitalité ethnolinguistique du groupe, réseaux individuels de contacts linguistiques, compétences et croyances ainsi que le comportement langagier lui-même qui détermineront la nature additive ou soustractive de la bilingualité.

Landry et Allard (1987) ont récemment insisté sur le fait que le concept d'additivité-soustractivité a davantage trait au domaine affectif qu'au développement cognitif. D'après eux les gains et les pertes liés à l'expérience bilingue doivent être perçus dans différentes perspectives: cognitive, linguistique, affective et comportementale. Une additivité totale comprendrait un haut niveau de compétence tant dans l'usage communicatif que cognitivo-académique des deux langues; un maintien d'une identité ethnolinguistique forte et de croyances positives envers la langue maternelle, des attitudes positives envers la langue seconde et une capacité d'utiliser les deux langues sans diglossie, c.à.d. qu'aucune des deux langues ne puisse être utilisée exclusivement pour des fonctions ou des domaines moins valorisés dans la société. Chaque fois que ces conditions sont remplies la L2 peut être acquise sans mettre en danger le développement de la langue maternelle et le processus additif peut être enclenché. Inversément chaque fois que l'acquisition de la L2 entrave le développement de la langue maternelle le processus serait soustractif. Donc, pour ces auteurs la bilingualité peut être additive ou soustractive sans que des avantages ou des désavantages cognitifs ne se manifestent. Bien plus, la soustractivité affecte les croyances et l'identité sociale avant d'influencer les compétences linguistiques.

Dans la plus récente version de notre modèle (Hamers & Blanc, 1989), nous avons suggéré que la dimension additivité/soustractivité s'étend sur un continuum résultant de deux dimensions indépendantes, une ayant trait au développement de la fonction cognitive du langage et l'autre relative à la représentation sociale des langues. Au pôle additif du continuum la fonction cognitive est bien développée et les deux langues sont fortement valorisées; l'enfant n'a pas seulement développé une représentation fonctionnelle complète du langage, mais parce qu'il valorise les deux langues au même titre, il les perçoit comme interchangeables; ceci va à son tour faciliter le développement de ses compétences à analyser et contrôler le traitement du langage, donc encourager son fonctionnement cognitif. Seul l'enfant qui aura développer les deux langues sur ces deux axes pourra tirer un maximum de profit de son expérience bilingue. A l'autre bout du continuum, nous trouvons la forme soustractive de bilingualité; dans ce cas, on exige de l'enfant qui n'a pas développé la fonction cognitive et littéraciée du langage dans sa langue maternelle, elle-même dévalorisée pour ce genre de fonction, de le faire dans une autre langue pour laquelle il possède au mieux une compétence à communiquer.

Cette élaboration sur la dimension affective est un apport important au concept d'additivité-soustractivité. Elle insiste sur l'importance de la nature socio-affective du langage et du développement bilingue. Nos connaissances actuelles nous permettent de conclure que tout enfant peut développer une bilingualité additive si les conditions socio-culturelles de son entourage lui permettent de développer les deux langues pour toutes les fonctions langagières et les valorisent pour ces fonctions. Nous commençons à être renseignés sur la nature des avantages cognitifs qu'une bilingualité additive peut amener.

D'autre part, si nous avons relativement bien identifiés les facteurs macrosociologiques qui influencent la forme de bilingualité, nous avons encore relativement peu de connaissances sur les mécanismes qui permettent à l'individu de se créer des représentations à partir de la structure sociale.

REMERCIEMENTS

Je remercie mes collègues Alison d'Anglejan, Fred Genesee et Allan Reynolds pour leurs commentaires et suggestions faits sur une version préliminaire du présent article.

REFERENCES

Arnberg, L. (1984). Mother tongue play groups for pre-school bilingual children. *Journal of Multilingual and Multicultural Development, 5,* 65-84.

Babu, N. (1984). Perception of syntactic ambiguity by bilingual and unilingual tribal children. *Psycho-Lingua, 14,* 47-54.

Baetens Beardsmore, H., & Swain, M. (1985). Designing bilingual education: Aspects of immersion and "European School" models. *Journal of Multilingual and Multicultural Development, 6,* 1-15.

Bain, B. C. (1975). Toward an integration of Piaget and Vygotsky: Bilingual considerations. *Linguistics, 16,* 5-20.

Bain, B., & Yu, A. (1978). Toward an integration of Piaget and Vygotsky: A cross-cultural replication (France, Germany, Canada) concerning cognitive consequences of bilinguality. In M. Paradis (Ed.), *Aspects of bilingualism.* Columbia, SC: Hornbeam Press.

Balkan, L. (1970). *Les effets du bilinguisme français-anglais sur les aptitudes intellectuelles.* Brussels: AIMAV.

Bialystok, E., & Ryan, E. B. (1985a). Toward a definition of metalinguistic skill. *Merrill-Palmer Quarterly, 31,* 229-251.

Bialystok, E., & Ryan, E. B. (1985b). A metacognitive framework for the development of first and second language skills. In D. L. Forrest-Pressley, G. E. MacKinnon, & T. G. Waller (Eds.), *Metacognition, cognition, and human performance.* New York: Academic Press.

Blanc, M., & Hamers, J. F. (1987). Preface. In M. Blanc & J. F. Hamers (Eds.), *Theoretical and methodological issues in the study of languages/dialects in contact at macro and micrological levels of analysis* (Report No. B-160). Québec: International Center for Research on Bilingualism.

Bruner, J. S. (1966). *Towards a theory of instruction.* New York: Norton.

Carringer, D. C. (1974). Creative thinking abilities of Mexican youth: The relationship of bilingualism. *Journal of Cross-Cultural Psychology, 5,* 492-504.

Chun, J. (1979). The importance of the language-learning situation: Is immersion the same as the "sink or swim" method? *Working Papers on Bilingualism, 18,* 131-164.

Cummins, J. (1979). Linguistic interdependence and the educational development of bilingual children. *Review of Educational Research, 49,* 222-251.

Cummins, J. (1981). The role of primary language development in promoting educational success for language minority students. In *Schooling and language minority students: A theoretical framework.* Los Angeles: California State Department of Education, Evaluation, Assessment and Dissemination Center.

Cummins, J. (1984). *Bilingualism and special education: Issues in assessment and pedagogy.* Clevedon: Multilingual Matters.

Cummins, J., & Gulutsan, M. (1974). Some effects of bilingualism on cognitive functioning. In S. T. Carey (Ed.), *Bilingualism, biculturalism and education.* Edmonton: The University of Alberta Press.

Cziko, G. A., Lambert, W. E., Sidoti, N., & Tucker, G. R. (1978). *Graduates of early immersion: Retrospective views of grade 11 students and their parents.* Unpublished manuscript, McGill University, Montreal.

Darcy, N. T. (1953). A review of the literature on the effects of bilingualism upon the measurement of intelligence. *Journal of Genetic Psychology, 82,* 21-57.

Da Silveira, Y. I. (1988). *Développement de la bilingualité chez l'enfant fon de Cotonou.* Unpublished doctoral dissertation, Université Laval, Québec.

Dubé, N. C., & Hébert, G. (1975). *Evaluation of the St. John Valley Title VII Bilingual Education program, 1970-1975*. Unpublished manuscript.

Duncan, S. E., & De Avila, E. A. (1979). Bilingualism and cognition: Some recent findings. *NABE Journal, 4,* 15-50.

Ekstrand, L. H. (1981). Theories and facts about early bilingualism in native and migrant children. *Gräzer Linguistische Studien, 14,* 24-52.

Fitzpatrick, F. (1987). *The open door.* Clevedon: Multilingual Matters.

Gorrell, J. J., Bregman, N. J., McAllistair, H. A., & Lipscombe, T. J. (1982). A comparison of spatial role-taking in monolingual and bilingual children. *Journal of Genetic Psychology, 140,* 3-10.

Hakuta, K., & Diaz, R. M. (1984). The relationship between bilingualism and cognitive ability: A critical discussion and some new longitudinal data. In K. E. Nelson (Ed.), *Children's language* (Vol. 5). Hillsdale, NJ: Lawrences Erlbaum Associates.

Hamers, J. F. (1987). The relevance of social network analysis in the psycholinguistic investigation of multilingual behavior. In M. Blanc & J. F. Hamers (Eds.), *Theoretical and methodological issues in the study of languages/dialects in contact at the macro and micrological levels of analysis* (Report No. B-160). Québec: International Center for Research on Bilingualism.

Hamers, J. F. (in press). *Réseaux sociaux, attitudes et compétences linguistiques chez des enfants néo-québecois.* Québec: International Center for Research on Bilingualism.

Hamers, J. F., & Blanc, M. (1982). Towards a social-psychological model of bilingual development. *Journal of Language and Social Psychology, 1,* 29-49.

Hamers, J. F., & Blanc, M. (1989). *Bilinguality and bilingualism.* Cambridge: Cambridge University Press.

Hanson, G. (1979). *The position of the second generation of Finnish immigrants in Sweden: The importance of education in the home language to the welfare of second generation immigrants.* Paper presented at the Symposium on the Position of Second Generation Yugoslav Immigrants in Sweden, Split, Yugoslavia.

Hébert, R. (1976). *Rendement académique et langue d'enseignement chez les élèves Franco-Manitobains.* Saint-Boniface, Manitoba: Centre de Recherches du Collège universitaire Saint-Boniface.

Holmstrand, L. E. (1979). The effect on general school achievement of early commencement of English instruction. *Uppsala Reports on Education, 4,* 1-15.

Kessler, C., & Quinn, M. E. (1982). Cognitive development in bilingual environments. In B. Hartford, A. Valdman, & C. R. Foster (Eds.), *Issues in international bilingual education: The role of vernacular.* New York: Plenum Press.

Kessler, C., & Quinn, M. E. (1987). Language minority children's linguistic and cognitive creativity. *Journal of Multilingual and Multicultural Development, 8,* 173-186.

Lambert, W. E. (1974). Culture and language as factors in learning and education. In F. E. Aboud & R. D. Meade (Eds.), *Cultural factors in learning.* Bellingham, WA: Western Washington State College.

Lambert, W. E. (1977). Effects of bilingualism on the individual. In P. A. Hornby (Ed.), *Bilingualism: Psychological, social, and educational implications.* New York: Academic Press.

Lambert, W. E. (1987, November). *Persistent issues in bilingualism.* Paper presented at the OISE symposium on the Development of Bilingual Proficiency, Toronto.

Lambert, W. E., & Fillenbaum, S. (1959). A pilot study of aphasia among bilinguals. *Canadian Journal of Psychology, 13,* 28-34.

Lambert, W. E., Giles, H., & Albert, A. (1976). Language attitudes in a rural city in northern Maine. *La Moda Linguo-Problemo, 15,* 129-192.

Lambert, W. E., Giles, H., & Picard, O. (1975). Language attitudes in a French-American community. *International Journal of the Sociology of Language, 4,* 127-152.

Lambert, W. E., Havelka, J., & Crosby, C. (1958). The influence of language acquisition contexts on bilingualism. *Journal of Abnormal and Social Psychology, 56,* 239-244.

Lambert, W. E., & Tucker, G. R. (1972). *Bilingual education of children: The St. Lambert experiment.* Rowley, MA: Newbury House.

Landry, R. (1982). Le bilinguisme additif chez les francophones minoritaires du Canada. *Revue des Sciences de l' Education, 8,* 223-244.

Landry, R., & Allard, R. (1987, September). *Contact des langues et développement bilingue: Un modèle macroscopique.* Paper presented at the conference Contact des langues: Quels modèles, Nice, France.

Landry, R., & Allard, R. (1988, August-September). *Ethnolinguistic vitality beliefs and language maintenance and loss.* Paper presented at the International Conference on Maintenance and Loss of Ethnic Minority Languages, Noordwijkerhout, The Netherlands.

Leopold, W. F. (1939-1949). *Speech development of a bilingual child.* Evanston, IL: Northwestern University Press.

Liedtke, W. W., & Nelson, L. D. (1968). Concept formation and bilingualism. *Alberta Journal of Educational Research, 14,* 225-232.

Modiano, N. (1973). *Indian education in the Chiapas highlands.* New York: Holt, Rinehart and Winston.

Mohanty, A. K., & Babu, N. (1983). Bilingualism and metalinguistic ability among Kond tribals in Orissa, India. *The Journal of Social Psychology, 121,* 15-22.

Okoh, N. (1980). Bilingualism and divergent thinking among Nigerian and Welsh school-children. *The Journal of Social Psychology, 110,* 163-170.

Pattnaik, K., & Mohanty, A. K. (1984). Relationships between metalinguistic and cognitive development of bilingual and unilingual tribal children. *Psycho-Lingua, 14,* 63-70.

Peal, E., & Lambert, W. E. (1962). The relation of bilingualism to intelligence. *Psychological Monographs, 76,* 1-23.

Pintner, R., & Keller, R. (1922). Intelligence tests for foreign children. *Journal of Educational Psychology, 13,* 214-222.

Powers, S., & Lopez, R. L. (1985). Perceptual, motor and verbal skills of monolingual and bilingual Hispanic children: A discriminant analysis. *Perceptual and Motor Skills, 60,* 999-1002.

Prujiner, A., Deshaies, D., Hamers, J. F., Blanc, M., Clément, R., & Landry, R. (1984). *Variations du comportement langagier lorsque deux langues sont en contact* (Rapport No. G-5). Québec: Centre International de Recherche sur le Bilinguisme.

Ronjat, J. (1913). *Le développement du langage observé chez un enfant bilingue.* Paris: Champion.

Rosier, P., & Farella, M. (1976). Bilingual education at Rock Point — Some early results. *TESOL Quarterly, 10*(4), 379-388.

Saer, O. J. (1923). The effects of bilingualism on intelligence. *British Journal of Psychology, 14,* 25-28.

Scott, S. (1973). *The relation of divergent thinking to bilingualism: Cause or effect.* Unpublished manuscript, McGill University, Montreal.

Segalowitz, N. (1977). Psychological perspectives on bilingual education. In B. Spolsky & R. Cooper (Eds.), *Frontiers of bilingual education.* Rowley, MA: Newbury House.

Tizard, J., Schofield, W. N., & Hewison, J. (1982). Collaboration between teachers and parents in assisting children's reading. *British Journal of Educational Psychology, 52,* 1-15.

Torrance, N., Gowan, J. C., Wu, J. M., & Aliotti, N. C. (1970). Oral and literate competences in the early school years. In D. R. Olson, N. Torrance, & A. Hildyard (Eds.), *Literacy, language, and learning: The nature and consequences of reading and writing.* Cambridge: Cambridge University Press.

Troike, R. C. (1984). SCALP: Social and cultural aspects of language proficiency. In C. Rivera (Ed.), *Language proficiency and academic assessment.* Clevedon: Multilingual Matters.

Vygotsky, L. S. (1962). *Thought and language* (E. Hanfmann & G. Vakar, Eds. and Trans.). Cambridge, MA: MIT Press. (Original work published 1934)

8 The Cognitive Consequences of Bilingualism

Allan G. Reynolds
Nipissing University College

> *The rich are different from us.*
> F. Scott Fitzgerald to Ernest Hemingway
> (*ca.* 1923)

> *Bilinguals are different from us.*
> Wallace E. Lambert to Allan G. Reynolds
> (1967, 1968, 1969, 1972, 1977, 1980,
> 1983, 1984, 1985, 1987, 1988, 1989)

Long before he became a research psychologist and long before he repeatedly made that statement to me, Wally Lambert was intrigued by the psychological differences between bilinguals and monolinguals; his fascination has been shared by a host of people in psycholinguistics, anthropology, education, etc. The story of interest in the possible *cognitive* differences between bilinguals and monolinguals began with the first published research studies in the 1920s. In this chapter I'm not going to address in any detail the research prior to the landmark year of 1962; it has been well reviewed by a number of authors (e.g., Baker, 1988; Darcy, 1953, 1963; Diaz, 1983; Hakuta, 1986; Hakuta & Diaz, 1985; Hakuta, Ferdman, & Diaz, 1987; Hamers & Blanc, 1989; Jensen, 1962a, 1962b; Kessler & Quinn, 1982; Lindholm, 1980; MacNab, 1979; McLaughlin, 1984; Peal & Lambert, 1962). Let me simply synopsize the basic plot line of those early studies. The main characters in the story, bilinguals (especially bilingual children, the preferred subjects of research), had lower IQ scores than monolinguals, were socially maladjusted, and trailed monolinguals in academic performance.

This is not exactly the constellation of outcomes that would make you rush out and enroll your child in French immersion!

The methodological problems with those early studies have been recounted numerous times: lack of comparability of the bilingual and monolingual samples in terms of proficiency in the language used for testing (for example, tests were often administered in the bilingual's weaker language); vague or nonexistent criteria for what constituted bilinguality; use of unstandardized tests; and absence of control or matching for age, socioeconomic background, or amount of education. Then came an article, in 1962, by Elizabeth Peal and Wallace E. Lambert entitled "The relation of bilingualism to intelligence." Hakuta and Diaz (1985) called the Peal and Lambert study the "punctuation point" in this line of research. Here is Hakuta and Diaz's description of the study:

> Both bilingual and monolingual samples for the Peal and Lambert study were selected from the same school system in Montreal. All 10-year-old children in the system were included in the initial screening by four measures, the composite of which was used to determine whether the child should be considered monolingual or balanced bilingual. The measures were: (1) the relative frequency of words provided in a word association task in L1 and L2; (2) the relative frequency of words in L1 and L2 detected in a series of letters; (3) the frequency of words recognized in L2 (English) from a subset chosen from the Peabody Picture Vocabulary Test; and (4) subjective self-ratings on ability in speaking, understanding, reading, and writing in L2. Children who fell in the extremes of these scales were determined to be monolingual or balanced bilingual. The final sample consisted of 75 monolinguals and 89 bilinguals; all children were administered a modified version of the Lavoie-Laurendeau Group Test of General Intelligence (Lavoie & Laurendeau, 1960), the Raven's Coloured Progressive Matrices (Raven, 1956; Raven, Court, & Raven, 1976), and a French version of selected subtests of the Thurstone Primary Mental Abilities Test (Thurstone & Thurstone, 1954).
>
> Contrary to the findings of earlier studies, the results of the Peal and Lambert study showed that bilinguals performed significantly better than monolinguals on most of the cognitive tests and subtests, even when group differences in sex, age, and socioeconomic status were appropriately controlled. Bilingual children performed significantly higher than monolinguals on tests of both verbal and nonverbal abilities; the bilinguals' superiority in nonverbal tests was more clearly evident in those subtests that required mental manipulation and reorganization of visual stimuli, rather than mere perceptual abilities. A factor analysis of test scores indicated that bilinguals were superior to monolinguals in concept formation and in tasks that required a certain mental or symbolic flexibility. Overall, bilinguals were found to have a more diversified pattern of abilities than their monolingual peers. (p. 322)

The Peal and Lambert study has had a profound influence on the fields of psycholinguistics and bilingual education. I think there were three reasons for the impact of this study. First, compared to most earlier studies, it was far superior from a methodological point of view. Besides using matching techniques, measures of verbal and nonverbal intelligence, and introducing the practice of using balanced bilinguals as subjects, it was the first study to utilize sophisticated statistical techniques like factor analysis.

Second, from a sociopolitical perspective, the results were extremely significant. The study was performed at a time when Canada was not yet, de jure, a bilingual country. Nonetheless, many citizens spoke both English and French and many geographical regions of the country (like Montreal) were, de facto, bilingual. Unlike earlier studies, the results of this study told psycholinguists and politicians around the world that gaining command of a second language did not doom one to retardation. Bilingual education would not create a "cognitively . . . second-class citizen" (Reynolds & Flagg, 1983, p. 429) or a "social or cognitive Frankenstein" (Hakuta & Diaz, 1985, p. 320); in fact, Peal and Lambert argued that fluent bilingualism has many cognitive benefits for an individual. A critical political implication was that a policy of national bilingualism was not a policy of national intellectual inferiority.

Finally, it is a happy coincidence that the Peal and Lambert study was published in the same year that Lev Vygotsky's theory was thrust into the mainstream of psychological thinking with the English publication of *Thought and Language* (Vygotsky, 1934/1962). Vygotsky's position that language plays a crucial role in cognitive development provided a theoretical rationale for Peal and Lambert's conclusions. He argued that language is initially used by a child as a form of social communication but later also becomes a medium for organizing thought and ordering the components of its abstract symbol system (see Bruner, 1973, 1975, for a more modern counterpart of Vygotsky's theory; see also Vygotsky, 1978, for some ideas on how children might use language to direct actions and plans for solutions to problems). In this volume, Josiane Hamers describes some of the ways that Vygotsky's theory can be applied to bilinguals; for example, Vygotsky (1934/1962) argued that bilinguality allows the child "to see his language as one particular system among many, to view its phenomena under more general categories, and this leads to awareness of his linguistic operations" (p. 110). Segalowitz (1977) has suggested that there would be more than metalinguistic consequences; he felt that bilinguals should also have a superior "mental calculus" arising out of the necessity of switching between two rule systems (from the two languages).

Since the Peal and Lambert monograph, there have been over seven dozen studies, reviews, and book chapters on the effects of bilingualism on cognitive functioning. In the preceding chapter of this volume, Hamers reviews the conclusions of many of the empirical studies and suggests some theoretical rationales for the results (see also Swain, this volume). Although I also offer some theoretical suggestions, what I plan to do, in counterpoint, is to analyze this body of research primarily from a methodological point of view. First, I discuss some common design problems associated with these studies and suggest one or two better designs. Next I look briefly at some issues related to the dependent variables commonly used; I argue that most of them are trivial, theoretically questionable, or psychometrically faulty. Third, I look at the general lack of cognitive theory underlying these studies and suggest some potential theoretical frameworks for this line of research. After this, I propose how this area of research might be extended by investigating the cognitive consequences of bilingualism at the national level. Finally, I conclude by demonstrating how the Peal and Lambert study revitalized this important, but moribund, area of research.

DESIGN CONSIDERATIONS: HAVING A GOOD RESEARCH DESIGN MEANS NEVER HAVING TO SAY YOU'RE SORRY

Let's begin by looking at Table 8-1; this table shows a variety of research designs that have been used, plus some that haven't but should have been. In the course of discussing Table 8-1, I use the terminology for designs and types of validity threats popularized by Campbell and Stanley (1963).

Design 1 is the standard preexperimental design (also often called an ex post facto criterion group design) used by most of the studies prior to 1962 and a discouraging number after (e.g., Cummins, 1977; Dockrell & Brosseau, 1967; Feldman & Shen, 1971; Jacobs & Pierce, 1966; Kakkar, 1976; Okoh, 1980; Whitaker, Rueda, & Prieto, 1985, to name but a few); if there were a Criminal Code for research and penalties for violating the laws of design, the jails would be full. In Design 1, preexisting intact groups (bilinguals and monolinguals) are compared on measures of cognitive performance; because Design 1 is so replete with threats to internal and external validity (e.g., history, selection, etc.), it can be dismissed out of hand (with no regrets). Design 2 is a longitudinal version of Design 1. Designs 3 and 4 are pure experimental designs; each has a control group and random assignment of subjects. Until someone finds a way to randomly assign subjects to language-learning conditions (Hakuta & Diaz's "ideal research design," 1985), these are only dream designs. Because of the impossibility of random assignment, many researchers have opted for some type of quasi-experimental design; some examples of these follow.

The better studies using Design 5 (sometimes called a nonequivalent control group design) tried to solve the internal validity problems (e.g., selection) of the preexperimental designs by matching preexisting intact groups (bilinguals and monolinguals) on key variables like years of schooling, age, or socioeconomic status; however, there is no guarantee that some key confounding variables (such as various social variables) were not omitted in

TABLE 8-1
Research Designs

Design 1

Intact groups (bilinguals vs. monolinguals) one-shot comparison
Matching: None
Example: Most studies prior to 1962 (and many after)

Design 2

Intact groups (bilinguals vs. monolinguals) longitudinal comparison
Matching: None
Example: White & Panunto (1978)

Design 3

Between groups (bilinguals vs. monolinguals) one-shot comparison with random assignment
Example: None

Design 4

Between groups (bilinguals vs. monolinguals) longitudinal comparison with random assignment
Example: None

Design 5

Intact groups (bilinguals vs. monolinguals) one-shot comparison
Matching: Matched on some variables
Example: Peal & Lambert (1962)

Design 6

Intact groups (bilinguals vs. monolinguals) longitudinal comparison
Matching: Matched on some variables (or covariance adjustment)
Example: Barik & Swain (1976)

Design 7

Between subjects (bilinguals) longitudinal comparison (examine changes in cognitive performance over time for groups of bilinguals who originally differed in L_2 proficiency)
Matching: None
Example: Hakuta (1987)

Design 8

Between groups (bilinguals vs. monolinguals) one-shot comparison (monolinguals chosen from French immersion waiting list to attempt to minimize selection or self-selection confounding)
Example: None

Design 9

Between groups (bilinguals vs. monolinguals) longitudinal comparison (monolinguals chosen from French immersion waiting list to attempt to minimize selection or self-selection confounding; examine changes in cognitive performance over time)
Example: None

---

the matching process. Furthermore, there may be subtle interactive effects (such as synergism) when more than one matching variable is used.

Design 6 (the longitudinal version of Design 5) has problems similar to those of Design 5, as well as potential mortality problems. In fact, many problems inherent with matching become especially troublesome with Design 6, which is the typical design used when comparing the performance of French immersion children and control children. Matching is a seductive

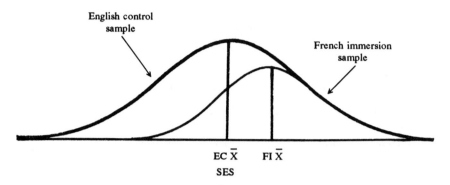

Fig. 8-1.   Typical distribution of SES for immersion (FI) and control (EC) samples.

tool here because we know that the groups differ on some powerful and theoretically relevant variables, for example, socioeconomic status (SES).

Figure 8-1 shows a typical situation a researcher might encounter when trying to compare the performance of a small group of French immersion students (with relatively high family SES) with a larger group of control children (with more varied family SES). We feel forced to match a subsample of the English control sample with our French immersion group on SES because we know that the two groups are not comparable on SES (which we feel might be a relevant variable, itself predictive of school achievement, linguistic performance, or the measures typically used in tests of the cognitive consequences of bilingualism). However, we fail to ask ourselves a key question: "Why would the parents of a child in an English school with the same family SES as the parents of a child in French immersion *not* send the child to French immersion?" There must be something else, something critical we've not matched on. By matching on SES, we create a situation where there must be an overlooked, unmatched variable (e.g., parental attitudes towards bilingualism or education); as well, of course, the English sample is not representative of the larger population from which it was drawn. By the way, statistically matching (by covariance analyses) does not solve these problems; we still have the problem of potentially overlooked variables. Also, if the analysis of covariance is performed on nonrandomly formed groups, it is of limited generality anyway, because these groups are not representative samples.

In Design 6, the most insidious of all the possible threats to internal validity is the dreaded regression to the mean effect. Again, let's imagine a case in which a small sample of French immersion children is matched with a subset of a larger sample of English control children. As in our previous example, we know that the two samples differ on some important dimension (in this case *Otis-Lennon* IQ); we feel compelled to use matching because IQ

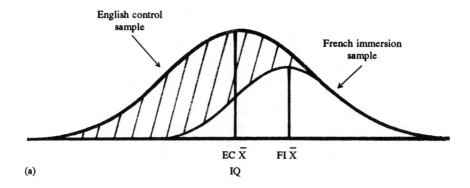

(a)

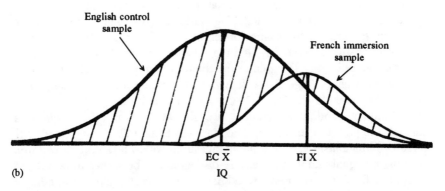

(b)

Fig. 8-2. Two hypothetical situations involving immersion (FI) and control (EC) groups matched on IQ.

is correlated with our dependent variable (which it should be if we want to use IQ as a matching variable).

Figure 8-2 shows two hypothetical situations which might arise. In Figure 8-2a, there is some discrepancy between the mean IQ scores of the two groups and the scores of the control children are contained within the distribution of the immersion children's scores. Figure 8-2b shows the case where there is a greater difference between IQ means; here there is less overlap. Children whose scores fall in the cross-hatched areas of the distributions cannot be matched and, hence, their scores are not included in the analyses of the dependent measure. In a longitudinal study, at posttest, there will be substantial regression to the mean effects for the situation shown in Figure 8-2a, and profound effects for the situation shown in Figure 8-2b. Why? In Figure 8-2a, the control children used in matching are all at the upper tail of their IQ distribution. There will be regression to the mean effects for IQ and, because IQ is positively correlated with the dependent variable, there will also be regression of the dependent variable toward its mean (thus a lower mean score); in contrast, there will be no net regression effects for the French immersion sample because the entire distribution was used. The end result is a high probability of a Type I error; the researcher may find a "significant" difference on the dependent variable when none exists. In Figure 8-2b, there is an even higher likelihood of a Type I error because there will *also* be regression effects for the immersion group (in this case, *upwards*, toward its mean) because of the matched children at the low end of the distibution. There is even the possibility of regression to the mean leading to Type II errors under certain situations. The outcome is affected by a complex mix of factors: the nature of the distribution shapes (variables such as SES and income will probably have grossly skewed distributions; as well, the direction of the skew may well be different for the two samples), the amount of overlap, sample sizes, the nature of the correlation between the dependent variable and the matching variable (the higher the positive correlation, the greater the chance of regression effects; note that there also could be a negative correlation), and the reliability of the dependent variable (the lower the reliability, the greater the chance of a regression effect).

Many researchers (e.g., Barik & Swain, 1976; Cummins & Swain, 1986; Diaz, 1985a; Hakuta & Diaz, 1985) have argued that, because of the impossibility of random assignment, we should look at effects *within* a bilingual sample. For example, Hakuta and Diaz (1985) suggested: "If *degree* of bilingualism can be reliably measured within a sample of children becoming bilingual and if this measure of degree can be shown to be related to cognitive flexibility, then one would have come one step closer to finding a pure relationship between bilingualism and cognitive flexibility" (p. 330). Design 7 exemplifies this approach; it looks at the effects of differences in bilinguals' language proficiency at one point in time upon later cognitive performance.

Because Design 7 is a longitudinal design (like Design 6), again there are potential mortality effects; moreover, differential mortality in the two groups at different parts of their respective distributions could lead to unforeseeable regression to the mean effects. More significantly, researchers using this design overlook the fact that they are still dealing with nonrandomly assigned intact groups (high and low language proficient bilinguals) who may (in fact, will) be different on a host of other dimensions, any one of which may be the true causative agent for subsequent cognitive performance differences.

Finally, Designs 8 and 9: As far as I know, neither of these designs has ever been utilized. I would argue that if a school system were found with such a demand for bilingual or French immersion schooling that a significant number of children had to be refused entry, then the children on the "waiting list" might be the closest thing to a randomly selected control group to be found. With the mushrooming popularity of French immersion education in

Canada and the limited physical and human resources available in some centers to cope with it, there may be a school district somewhere with a waiting list population ready to be tapped for a study that more closely approximates the "ideal research design" than any others I've discussed.

Naomi Holobow and Richard Tucker have suggested to me that many members of one of the English control groups in the original St. Lambert immersion project (Lambert & Tucker, 1972) could be considered, post hoc, as a "waiting list group." When the St. Lambert project began in 1966, only a fraction of the children whose parents wanted them enrolled in immersion could be accommodated; those children who were not admitted into the French immersion pilot class constituted a large percentage of one English control group. Although the samples are small, it would be worthwhile to compare the scores of these children, on the cognitive tests administered, to the scores of the experimental (immersion) group; much of these data are available from published reports describing the outcomes of the St. Lambert project.

Note that waiting list designs are not totally without problems. First, people on waiting lists may engage in some form of "compensatory behaviour"; for example, individuals seeking psychiatric help who are placed on a waiting list for therapy may find another source of counselling— they then do not constitute a real "control group." More to the point for the present suggestions, if a child is placed on a waiting list for immersion education, the parents may find an alternative form of second language teaching, for example, a private tutor. Second, being put on a waiting list can possibly lead to changes in attitudes; to use the psychotherapy example again: People who get the implicit message that they are "not sick enough" to get immediate counselling may change their self-perception about the severity of their distress (with consequent behaviour change); as well, there could be a "sour grapes" reaction: "If I can't get into therapy, it's probably not that helpful after all." In the case of the child placed on a waiting list for French immersion, parents' previously positive attitudes towards second language learning may change to negative ones; this will undoubtedly affect a child's later performance in learning a second language and render such children impure "controls." Third, and most importantly, there are many nonobvious ways in which nonrandomness can creep into designs utilizing waiting lists; for example, there must be no special differentiation between those who are admitted to a high-demand immersion program and those who are placed on a waiting list, for the design to be valid. However, there are some very subtle ways that the criterion of absence of special differentiation can be violated. For example, in the original 1966 St. Lambert immersion study, only those children who had been in French immersion kindergarten were included in the experimental class. In addition, registration for the program was on a "first come, first in" basis and many parents were unable to enroll their children (Olga Melikoff's poignant description of that historic first registration day in St. Lambert tells how registration "opened one spring day at 1 PM, and by 1:05 PM the quota of twenty-six children was reached"; Lambert & Tucker, 1972, p. 226); the waiting list group was definitely not formed in a truly random fashion.

Robert Frender has also pointed out to me that the older siblings of the original St. Lambert experimental group could be considered as a control group. These older brothers and sisters did not have the opportunity to be educated in two languages because there was no program in place when they entered kindergarten. If we assume that their parents would have placed them in French immersion, as they did with the younger siblings, then the older group constitutes a quite acceptable control group (if we are willing to ignore the fact that the older siblings constitute a different cohort, and overlook the possibility that their cognitive behaviour might be affected by the high probability that they are firstborns). Again, although the sample sizes would be very small, it might be worthwhile now, almost 25 years later, to compare the intellectual functioning of adults who did not experience the bilingual educational experience with that of siblings who did.

Other Considerations

There are a number of other, less specific, problems related to design and interpretation in this body of research on the cognitive consequences of bilingualism.

Misreporting in secondary sources. One problem arises from the sheer volume of empirical studies performed, especially since 1962. There has been a proliferation of secondary sources that have, all too often, confused readers by presenting misrepresentations or twisted interpretations of authors' original conclusions, sometimes even presenting conclusions which are the exact opposite of those reached by the original researchers (and at total variance with the original research results).

Procedural shortcomings. Second, there are a variety of procedural shortcomings in this body of research. I have criticized the utility of matching in a previous section; nonetheless, even when matching is employed, it frequently is done in an inadequate manner. SES measures may be derived from occupation alone (rather than from a mix of variables that also includes income, amount of education, and quality of residence) and then often the occupation of only one parent is utilized for matching. As well, when matching is done on Piagetian stage of development, it is often very crude; a child is classified merely as being in one of the four major stages.

Many studies are difficult to evaluate because of inadequate descriptions of the bilingual learning situation, the levels of L_1 and L_2 competence of the subjects, the frequency of use of the two languages at home, or other potentially important variables; in the oft-cited Torrance, Gowan, Wu, and Aliotti (1970) study, for example, little information on IQ, SES, or degree of subjects' bilingualism was provided (see De Avila & Duncan, 1979, for detailed criticisms of some other studies where key linguistic information was lacking or there was no control for linguistic proficiency).

Definition of bilinguality. A third problem relates to the definition of who is a bilingual. Most studies have sidestepped the problem by giving operational definitions of bilinguality (and then often in a less-than-ideal fashion: e.g., by classifying children by surname). Operationalization, alone, merely renders these studies open to the danger of being relatively ungeneralizable. For example, the results of studies that relied exclusively on balanced bilinguals probably should not be generalized to the majority of the North American second language learning population (e.g., in Canada, anglophone children who begin French immersion schooling with no knowledge of French or, in the United States, Hispanic or Asian children who come to bilingual education programs with little or no knowledge of English). These children will stay linguistically unbalanced for many years, perhaps for their entire lives. There is a substantial body of research (see Genesee, 1987, pp. 44-49, for one review) which indicates that many children leaving immersion programs definitely are not balanced bilinguals, whether proficiency is assessed by objective means or by self-report. At a conceptual level, it seems unwise to lump together studies that compare monolinguals and balanced bilinguals (who acquired two languages simultaneously, at an early age, and in a naturalistic context) with studies that compare monolinguals and unbalanced bilinguals (who acquired a second language after the first, when they were older, and in a more formal school setting).

Utilizing balanced bilinguals as subjects not only limits ecological significance but also raises a potentially critical theoretical danger. Cummins (1976) suggested that "there may be a threshold level of linguistic competence which a bilingual child must attain both in order to avoid cognitive deficits and allow the potentially beneficial aspects of becoming bilingual to influence his cognitive functioning" (p. 1). Under Cummins' threshold hypothesis, there could be severe cognitive penalties for many unbalanced bilinguals (e.g., children in immersion programs) that are quite *opposite* to the benefits predicted from studies utilizing balanced bilinguals (for fuller descriptions of Cummins' threshold hypothesis and the related developmental interdependence hypothesis, see Cummins, 1979; Cummins & Swain, 1986; Hamers & Blanc, 1989). A related, key, methodological problem is that looking at bilingual samples as homogeneous entities could well obscure differential effects. As Cummins (1977) put it: "The very different levels of cognitive performance of these two groups [high and low second language proficiency] might mask each other when the performance of only the total group is considered" (p. 10). Thus, he argued, the effects of bilingualism on cognitive development should be examined separately for children with varying second language abilities (i.e., in this context, degree of balance).

The main problem with generalizing from results derived from studies using only balanced bilinguals as subjects is that it can produce a potential confusion of cause and effect. This issue has been reviewed by a number of authors (e.g., MacNab, 1979; Macnamara, 1966, 1970; McLaughlin, 1984); the basic argument is that "balanced bilinguals are a unique class of bilinguals, who, because they are cognitively more able in the first place are more likely to become highly proficient bilinguals. In other words, the question of the direction of the relationship between bilingualism and cognitive . . . development is left begging. Is it that bilingualism affects cognitive development or conversely, that cognitive development affects bilingualism?" (Cummins & Swain, 1986, p. 4). A perfect example of this inability to separate cause and effect is found in Duncan and De Avila's (1979) finding that more proficient bilinguals outperformed less proficient ones on the measures of cognitive development used in that study. Perhaps more intellectually gifted children become more linguistically proficient (bilingually more balanced) or perhaps the reverse is true? In the seminal Peal and Lambert (1962) study, this possibility was acknowledged: "It is not possible to state from the present study whether the more intelligent child became bilingual or whether bilingualism aided his intellectual development" (p. 20); Anisfeld (1964) attempted to control for differences in intelligence in the Peal and Lambert study by a reanalysis that eliminated subjects so that the groups were matched on IQ. She found that the original results were attenuated but still present.

As an aside, the issue of the role of "intelligence" in second language learning is a murky one, indeed. As McLaughlin (1985) pointed out, it is self-evident to many teachers that intelligence is an important factor in determining success in learning another language; for example, Dockrell and Brosseau (1967) found that mental age and second language vocabulary acquisition were positively correlated. Yet vocabulary acquisition is only one aspect of learning a second language and one that is easily predictable, given that a large component of most intelligence tests is verbal (the *Vocabulary* test of the *WAIS* has the highest correlation of any of the tests with the Full Scale score). There has been surprisingly little research done on intelligence as a predictor of second language learning proficiency (e.g., Gardner & Lambert, 1965; Genesee & Hamayan, 1980; Wittenborn & Larsen, 1944).

Genesee and Hamayan (1980) found that intelligence test scores were poorer predictors of second language learning in younger children than in older learners; they suggested that younger children, in an immersion setting or a bilingual classroom, approach the learning situation less analytically than older children in a more traditional high school class setting. Alternatively, the results may be due to lower reliability of intelligence tests or tests of language achievement when these are used with a younger sample.

Genesee and Hamayan's conclusions were supported by Carroll's (1981) survey of a quarter century of research on prediction of language achievement; he felt that "verbal intelligence is more extensively required in the more formal . . . courses taught in high school, college, and university . . . than it is in more audio-lingually and practically oriented courses" (p. 106). Although little relationship between intelligence test scores and *oral* second language skill in young children has been found, Genesee (1976) has suggested that there may be some relationship between intelligence test scores and *literacy skills* in a second language (again this is not surprising, given the way most intelligence tests are standardized). Carroll's survey agreed with this suggestion as well; he speculated that "the extent to which general verbal intelligence is required in foreign language courses depends upon the degree to which the mode of instruction puts a premium on a student's verbal intelligence in order to understand the content of the instruction" (p. 106). Thus there clearly should be a stronger predictive relationship between tests of verbal intelligence and second language achievement when the medium of instruction is the printed word.

Balance and selection artifacts. Many studies utilizing balanced bilinguals as subjects may be victims of unintentional selection artifacts. For example, Diaz (1983) suggested that the Peal and Lambert (1962) study is a possible victim of this kind of artifact because the bilingual sample contained only children who scored above a certain score on the *Peabody Picture Vocabulary Test;* moreover, Diaz pointed out, the bilingual sample belonged to a higher grade level than the monolinguals (thus they had had longer exposure to formal education). He felt that the superiority shown by the bilingual group on the dependent measures might have been due to a selection effect; he cited the fact that the distribution of Raven's test scores was negatively skewed for the bilingual children and positively skewed for the monolinguals, as evidence for his concern. Peal and Lambert were not ignorant of this possibility of selection bias:

> A partial explanation of this [the results] may lie in our method of choosing the bilingual sample. Those suffering from a handicap may unintentionally have been eliminated. We attempted to select bilinguals who were balanced, that is

equally fluent in both languages. However, when the balance measures used did not give a clear indication of whether or not a given child was bilingual, more weight was attached to his score on the English vocabulary test. Thus some bilinguals who might be balanced, but whose vocabulary in English and French might be small, would be omitted from our sample. The less intelligent bilinguals, those who have not acquired as large an English vocabulary, would not be considered "bilingual" enough for our study. (p. 15)

Effects occurring with the manipulations. A final methodological problem concerns potential effects occurring with the experimental manipulation; there are a variety of these. Bilingual children may be more likely to have bilingual parents and there are probably great differences in the ways bilingual and monolingual parents raise their children. Note that in Bain and Yu's (1980) study, a child had to have at least one bilingual parent, and preferably two, in order to be included in the bilingual sample. A similar situation obtains in the Liedtke and Nelson (1968) and Tsushima and Hogan (1975) studies; in both cases the bilingual samples came from bilingual homes. Even monolingual parents may become more involved in trying to further the intellectual development of children in immersion programs than parents of children in nonimmersion programs. This may be due partly to the continued perception that immersion programs are "experimental" and therefore children need extra help at home; it may be due partly to different attitudes towards the educational process on the part of parents of children in immersion programs. I have collected pilot data which suggest strongly that parents of children in French immersion are much more likely to value academic outcomes and other intellectual skills than are parents of nonimmersion children (as well, see Baker, 1988, p. 19). Last, immersion education (or other bilingual education programs) may be better catalysts for intellectual development for reasons covarying with the use of a second language for instruction; these educational settings may be allocated more (and higher quality) resource materials or be staffed by better teachers than nonimmersion classrooms.

Conclusions

In conclusion, with the exception of a handful of studies that have shown no differences, or mixed differences, between bilinguals and monolinguals on measures of cognitive functioning (Bain, 1975; Balkan, 1970; Barik & Swain, 1976; Ben-Zeev, 1977a; Kittell, 1963; Landry, 1974; Torrance et al., 1970; Tsushima & Hogan, 1975; White & Panunto, 1978), most studies since 1962 have shown clear superiority for bilinguals in cognitive tasks. Unfortunately, this generally uniform pattern of results has lulled us into a state of false complacency, because the designs used have all been preexperimental or quasi-experimental designs (this includes the studies listed in the preceding sentence), with all their attendant dangers. The research prior to 1962 has been repeatedly criticized as methodologically inadequate and I fear we are not much better off today; even sophisticated techniques like regression analysis, factor analysis, path analysis, etc., do not compensate for inherently trouble-prone designs. In addition, this body of research is plagued by procedural shortcomings, problems with the definition of bilinguality, and the dangers of selection artifacts and effects occurring with the manipulations.[1] Due to the prevalence of design problems and other logical difficulties I have described, the central question we should be asking ourselves is not whether the thesis that bilinguality affects cognitive performance is true or whether the reverse is true, but whether there is a relationship at all.[2] Turning our attention from issues related to design and independent variables, we find that the situation is not much better when dependent variables are examined.

DEPENDENT VARIABLES: THE HUNT FOR THE HEFFALUMP

The various attempts to measure the cognitive consequences of bilingualism are much like the "hunt for the Heffalump." Kilby (1971) explains that the Heffalump, a character from A. A. Milne's *Winnie-the-Pooh*, "is a rather large and very important animal. He has been hunted by many individuals using various ingenious trapping devices, but no one so far has succeeded in capturing him. All who claim to have caught sight of him report that he is enormous, but they disagree on his particularities" (p. 1). Kilby's allegory perfectly describes the current situation as regards measurement of the cognitive outcomes of bilingualism because researchers have used widely diverse and often inventive instruments to try to capture the essence of this elusive Heffalump.

Let's examine the dependent measures typically used in these studies; in Table 8-2, we see a sampling of these measures. Despite the large number of different indices of cognitive performance in the literature, some measures are used much more frequently than others, for example the *Peabody Picture*

---

[1] In case the reader thinks that I am being too harsh in my judgments about this area of research, it might help to contrast my conclusions with those reached by writers who have surveyed a similar field of research, that of the effectiveness of bilingual education. Willig (1985) discussed three surveys of research on bilingual education; in one of them, 91% of the sample of studies was excluded from the survey because of design faults or other methodological considerations; the rejection rates for the other two surveys were 93% and 95%.

[2] "Research, like life, is tough largely because meaningful relationships are a bitch to find — and then you can't be sure they *are* really meaningful." — Ken Stange

Vocabulary Test and the *Coloured Progressive Matrices* and, hence, I will single them out for special attention. I would argue that, despite their popularity, they are substandard measures from a psychometric point of view. In one of Wally Lambert's immortal phrases, these measures are not "the first team."

TABLE 8-2
A Sampling of Dependent Variables

Intelligence Tests (Verbal and nonverbal)
  Iowa Test of Basic Skills
  Kuhlmann-Finch Intelligence Test
  Lavoie-Laurendeau Group Test of General Intelligence
  Lorge-Thorndike Intelligence Test (frequent)
  Otis-Lennon
  Peabody Picture Vocabulary Test (very frequent)
  Peabody Picture Vocabulary Test-Revised
  Coloured Progressive Matrices Test (very frequent)
  Stanford-Binet
  Thorndike-Hagen Cognitive Abilities Test
  Thurstone Primary Mental Abilities Test
  University of Ibadan Verbal Intelligence Test
  WAIS-R
  WISC
  WISC-R

Divergent Thinking Tests
  Object naming tests
  Patterns test (nonverbal)
  Utility tests (frequent)

Visual-spatial Tests
  Bender Visual-Motor Gestalt Test
  Embedded Figures Test
  Matrix transposition tasks
  McCarthy Perceptual Performance Test
  Spatial relations tasks
  Symbol substitution tasks

Other
  Ability to formulate scientific hypotheses
  Concept formation tasks
  Cooperative Preschool Inventory
  Field dependence/independence tests
  Mathematical reasoning tasks
  Nonverbal memory tasks
  Piagetian conservation tasks (frequent)
  Problem solving tasks
  Rule transfer tasks
  School achievement (grades)
  Torrance Tests of Creative Thinking
  Verbal memory tasks

The original *Peabody Picture Vocabulary Test* was developed solely as a measure of receptive vocabulary. Lyman (1965), writing in *The Sixth Mental Measurements Yearbook*, categorizes it as having moderate reliability and unestablished validity. It was standardized on a sample of white children and adolescents in and around Nashville, Tennessee, and Lyman warns that we should be cautious in interpreting the norms, unless we are testing white children in Nashville. The 1981 revision of the *Peabody Picture Vocabulary Test* does not fare much better in its review (McCallum, 1985) in *The Ninth Mental Measurements Yearbook;* for example, there are no predictive validity data for the revised version (*PPVT-R*). Also, there are very modest correlations (~.40) with standard intelligence tests; thus the reviewer warns that "PPVT-R scores should not be interpreted as intelligence test scores" (p. 1127). Sattler, Avila, Houston, and Toney (1980) and Sattler and Altes (1984) have, in addition, questioned whether the *PPVT* or the *PPVT-R* are appropriate measures of cognitive abilities for bilingual Hispanic children, regardless of whether the test is administered in English or Spanish.

Another very popular test used is the 1956 *Coloured Progressive Matrices* (*CPM*). It was normed on slightly more than 600 Scottish children whose names began with the letters E through L. Comptom (1984) points out that there are inadequate North American norms (new norms have been gathered, however, as recently as 1986), the norms that are provided demonstrate no prognostic value, the test is very prone to impulsive answering, reliability of the test for children below the age of 9 is extremely poor, and there are no predictive validity studies or correlations with other measures of mental development available from the manual. The studies which have been performed relating the *CPM* to other measures often show disappointingly low correlations with standardized tests of intelligence; for example, McNamara, Porterfield, and Miller (1969) reported correlations between the *CPM* and the parts of the *Wechsler Preschool and Primary Scale of Intelligence* ranging from a high of .43 for *Picture Completion* down to .30 for *Full Scale IQ*. Vernon (1969) repeatedly warns against the use of the *CPM* cross-culturally, because of the factors of speededness, understanding instructions, and differences in perceptual style. Finally, there is the basic question of what the test measures. Because a respondent can adopt either a verbal/analytic approach to the test or solve the matrices through visual perceptual discovery, this is not a "pure" test; in fact, different studies on the factor structure of the *CPM* have variously shown one, two, three, or more factors.

Psychometrically superior to these two measures are standardized tests of intelligence, which some researchers have opted to use. Unfortunately, use of standardized intelligence tests can lead to a critical logical problem. By using intelligence test scores as a dependent measure, the researcher is implicitly asking if bilingualism affects IQ. This is a trivial question at best, Macnamara (1972) has argued, because a very large number of factors can affect IQ "without having any *direct* bearing on what we intuitively recognize as intelligence" (p. 70). Much of the problem stems from the fact mentioned earlier that most intelligence tests (including the so-called nonverbal ones) have an enormous verbal component. Regardless of what definition one uses for bilingualism, it ultimately must be linguistically based; hence, there is a built-in correlation between measures of bilingualism and scores on a standardized (especially verbal) intelligence test. The correlation may be positive, zero, or negative, depending on how one assesses bilinguals' language skills. If one demands (in the sample) high proficiency in both languages, the correlation must be positive; if the acceptable level of proficiency in the two languages is lower but still equal, the correlation will tend towards zero; finally, if one accepts very low (but balanced) proficiency, or unbalanced proficiency (with the weaker language being used for intelligence testing), the correlation will be negative.

Let's return to Table 8-2; look again at the variety of dependent measures used. Researchers have been hunting the Heffalump with a veritable arsenal of indices — Piagetian conservation tasks, standardized tasks of intelligence, nonverbal spatial tasks, etc. It's not clear what these dependent variables have in common, psychologically;[3] it is possible that many of them were chosen because of a researcher's familiarity with them or for ease of use, rather than for sound theoretical reasons. The construct validity of many of them is highly questionable; for example, the practice of *arbitrarily* linking a certain measure to "intelligence" or "analytic orientation to language" is discomforting. In fact, we are working very atheoretically here. Since we have no firm predictions about *how* and *why* bilingualism should positively influence cognitive functioning, we end up with this hodgepodge of quite dissimilar measures.

Let us close this section by presenting the remainder of Kilby's (1971) Heffalump allegory: "Not having explored his current habitat with sufficient care, some hunters have used as bait their favorite dishes and have then tried to persuade people that what they caught was a Heffalump. However, very few are convinced, and the search goes on" (p. 1). And the search goes on.

---

[3]As far as I am aware, there has not been a systematic attempt to discover the pattern of shared variance among the various measures described in Table 8-2. Maryann Fraboni has suggested to me that, even if such an enterprise were to be undertaken, it's not clear what the outcome would mean; for example, many of the correlations among the indices might be inflated by virtue of shared method variance and this would tend to obscure the true relationships. On the other hand, this "inflation" could be theoretically meaningful if the method variance were actually task-bound (the method of testing requires the same cognitive processes); however, method variance could be associated with something extraneous, such as common measurement problems in two tests (see Jackson, 1975).

"TOTO, I HAVE A FEELING WE'RE NOT IN KANSAS ANYMORE!": ON THE YELLOW BRICK ROAD TOWARDS A THEORY OF COGNITIVE FUNCTIONING IN BILINGUALS

I don't doubt for a moment that there are tremendous social benefits for bilinguals. They have the personal satisfaction of broadening themselves:

> *To speak another language is to possess another soul.*
>
> King Charles V (1500-1558)

They can act as intergroup mediators and also speak to a diverse cross-section of audiences:

> *I speak Spanish to God, Italian to women,*
> *French to men, and German to my horse.*
>
> King Charles V (1500-1558)

These types of noncognitive benefits have been recognized by people ranging from former Canadian Prime Minister Pierre Trudeau to cartoonist Gary Trudeau (see cartoon).[4]

DOONESBURY   by Garry Trudeau

---

[4] Besides the benefits of self-actualization, communication, and puck control by ethnolinguistic intimidation, there are also other possibilities — self-defense and seduction. In the children's story *Even for a Mouse*, by Lisl Weil, a mouse named Little Ollie saves herself from a cat (Mr. A. H. Cat — A. H. stands for "always hungry") by barking "BOW WOW WOW"; after the terrified cat runs away and climbs a tree, the mother mouse needlessly reminds Little Ollie: "A foreign language is most helpful in life." In the hilarious 1988 movie *A Fish Called Wanda*, the desirable Wanda Gershwitz turns into a quivering, helpless nymphomaniac whenever she hears a man speak in a foreign language — it could be something as mundane as words or phrases like "*mozzarella,*" "Benito Mussolini," or "*glasnost.*"

I have argued that it is an open question whether there really is any relationship between bilinguality and cognitive performance; if, despite all the methodological shortcomings in the research reviewed in this chapter, we nonetheless make a gigantic leap of faith ("We must be over the rainbow!") and accept the hypothesis that bilingualism has cognitive benefits for an individual, how does it do it? Diaz (1985b) argued that "the gap in our own knowledge is due in part to the fact that research has focused mostly on outcome rather than process variables" (p. 19). Hakuta et al. (1987) pointed out (and I agree) that this focus on outcome variables leaves unanswered some major theoretical questions, such as whether bilinguals solve cognitive tasks *differently* than monolinguals or whether the putative positive cognitive effects of bilingualism can be explained by a faster *rate* of cognitive development, caused by the "bilingual experience" (p. 296). Other questions that come to mind include: "Is cognitive development in bilinguals affected by the age at which bilingualism is achieved (i.e., is acquisition at a younger age better)?" and the related question, "If there is a cognitive advantage to being bilingual, does it increase with age (i.e., does more experience with bilinguality lead to greater benefits)?"

In terms of working towards a model of cognitive benefits, we've been acting like Stephen Leacock's character who "flung himself upon his horse and rode madly off in all directions"; we have no theoretical focus. What we need is a theoretical, preferably process-oriented, framework of intellectual functioning within which to conduct our studies and to answer questions like those just posed. I would like to present five possible candidates.

Bloom's Taxonomy

Bloom's (1964) taxonomy of educational objectives (cognitive, psychomotor, and affective) was devised as a means of guiding teachers in devising methods of instruction and evaluation; however, the cognitive elements of the objectives also comprise an implicit model of intellect. These objectives specify the processes related to intellectual activities such as defining, evaluating, recognizing, and reasoning. These cognitive objectives are subdivided into six levels of learning: knowledge (the ability to recall or identify information), comprehension (putting information into one's own words), application (the ability to use an abstraction in a concrete context), analysis (the ability to break down information into its component parts so that the relationship among all the components is clear), synthesis (putting together old knowledge in new ways), and evaluation (making judgments based on knowledge about the value of methods and materials for some purpose).

As far as I know, Bloom's conception of cognition has not been used in any of the research on the cognitive consequences of bilingualism. However, it might be a useful framework within which to devise a set of dependent measures, especially for a study involving children in a school setting (e.g., French immersion).

Piagetian Theory

Piagetian conservation tasks frequently have been used as dependent measures. However, the use of these tasks has not usually been coupled with reference to Piagetian developmental theory. As I mentioned earlier, this seems to be one of those situations where the choice of measures was convenience-driven rather than theory-driven.

Guilford's (1959) Model of Intellect

Again, this view of intelligence frequently has implicitly guided the choice of dependent measures. The utility test of divergent thinking ("How many uses can you think of for a paper clip?") was derived originally from Guilford's battery of tests and is a very popular measure in the studies I reviewed. Unfortunately, Guilford's approach is not in today's mainstream of thinking about cognitive functioning. Perhaps its usefulness should be re-evaluated; it is one of the few multidimensional models of intellectual functioning available.

Information Processing Models

These are promising, I think. They focus on cognitive processes like attention, memory, decision-making, etc. They have two liabilities, however. One is that many of the subtests of politically out-of-fashion standardized intelligence tests are in fact nothing more than information-processing measures; for example, the *Digit Span* test of the *WAIS* is simply a measure of short-term memory. More importantly, I don't think the information processing approach goes far enough; the next, and last, theoretical framework incorporates an information processing approach within a more comprehensive model.

Sternberg's Triarchic Model of Intelligence

As a final framework, I present now the most complete, and modern, approach to intellectual functioning that I've found— Sternberg's (1985, 1988) triarchic model of intelligence. Sternberg's model is composed of three subtheories: a contextual subtheory, an experiential subtheory, and a componential subtheory.

The contextual subtheory describes how the "intelligence" of a behaviour is defined largely by sociocultural context; intelligent behaviour, according to this subtheory, involves adaptation to the current environment (the usual response), selection of another environment, or changing of the present environment to match an individual's values, interests, or skills. This subtheory relates to the question of *what* behaviour is intelligent in a given sociocultural context; for example, intelligent "transportation behaviour" in Manhattan might involve trying to hail a taxi, while this response is clearly inappropriate in the middle of a Saskatchewan wheat field. The experiential subtheory argues that, for any given task, behaviour is not equally intelligent at all points along the continuum of an individual's experience with that behaviour (or similar behaviours). This subtheory suggests that intelligence is demonstrated most clearly either when one is confronted by a relatively novel task or when one is in the process of automatizing performance on a task. There can be interaction between these two possibilities; automatization of processing permits the allocation of cognitive resources for the processing of novelty, whereas adaptation to novelty allows automatization to occur earlier in one's experience with a task. Thus, the experiential subtheory answers the question of *when* behaviour should be viewed as intelligent, because it considers an individual's amount of experience with a task. The final subtheory, the componential subtheory, describes the processes and structures that underlie intelligent behaviour; there are three aspects of this subtheory: metacomponents (which control information processing and allow an individual to monitor and evaluate it), performance components (which execute plans constructed by the metacomponents), and knowledge-acquisition components (which encode new information and compare new information to old information in memory). This subtheory answers the question of *how* intelligent behaviour is generated.

How might Sternberg's model be of explanatory value for the possible cognitive benefits of bilingualism? Table 8-3 presents, in a summary form, some aspects of the development of bilinguality which may enhance intelligence, as Sternberg defines it. In the course of explaining the relevance of Sternberg's model to the cognitive consequences of bilingualism, I interject hypotheses proposed by various researchers; these fragmentary ideas are compatible with Sternberg's more-encompassing approach, as I see it applying to the outcomes of bilingualism.

Contextual subtheory. Because bilinguals have had extensive experience in dealing with separate linguistic (and often social) contexts, they should be more experienced in adapting their behaviours to fit the needs of varying linguistic and cultural milieux. In fact, several studies have indicated that bilinguals exhibit greater social sensitivity and possess a greater ability to react flexibly to feedback (Bain, 1975; Ben-Zeev, 1977a, 1977b; Genesee,

TABLE 8-3
Why Bilinguals Might Be More "Intelligent"
(using Sternberg's Model)

Contextual Subtheory	*Bilingual Possibility*
Adaptation, selection, and shaping of environments	Bilinguals, having experience in separate linguistic (and social) environments, may be more adept at adaptation (e.g., code-switching), selection (e.g., interacting with alternate cultures), and shaping (e.g., language legislation)
Experiential Subtheory	*Bilingual Possibility*
Efficacious adaptation to novelty allows automatization to occur earlier in one's experience with new tasks or situations	Adaptation to novelty of language switching and dual linguistic codes early in life allows easier automatization in dealing with linguistic tasks
Automatization allows resources to be allocated to processing novelty in the environment	Automatization of language processing (necessary in translation, code-switching, etc.) frees resources for novel linguistic tasks
Componential Subtheory	*Bilingual Possibility*
Metacomponents	Necessity of controlling and monitoring two language systems (lexicons, social referents, etc.) improves efficiency of metacomponential system
Performance components	Having command of two languages leads to greater use of verbal mediation and increased use of language as a cognitive regulatory tool. Having two interlocking performance systems for linguistic codes gives double the resources for executing verbal tasks (or tasks with verbal substrates) as well as nonverbal tasks (e.g., spatial tasks) that can be recoded into verbal tasks. Also, there is greater use of learning strategies when learning two languages
Knowledge-acquisition components	Having two interlocking verbal systems allows for ease in encoding new information and combining with one or the other lexicon or verbal semantic memory

Tucker, & Lambert, 1975; by way of warning, note that these studies may be prey to the threats to internal validity described earlier in this chapter). Skutnabb-Kangas (1984) noted:

> The bilingual speaker needs to notice and take account of very small often not verbalized cues and to modify her behavior accordingly . . . . Various very small changes in a social situation may be observed more closely if their effect is to require a code switch; and so the bilingual gets more practise than the

monolingual at paying attention to the fine detail of a social situation and at reacting in various ways. (pp. 232-233)

Balanced bilinguals have the freedom to choose (to some degree) the environment in which they will be players; to the extent that the cultures of the two language communities differ in the values they cherish and the aptitudes and interests they reward, bilinguals automatically have two cultural reference groups open to them for membership. Finally, because of their special linguistic and social status, bilinguals may be influential shapers of society.[5]

Experiential subtheory. While the contextual subtheory focuses on behaviours determined by the sociocultural context, the experiential subtheory describes hypothetical internal processes or metastrategies. Here, bilinguals may be at a general linguistic advantage because they have adapted to the "novelty" of dealing with two code systems (with two grammars, phonological systems, and vocabularies). This may allow easier automatization in dealing with linguistic tasks; as well, the acquired automatization allows the bilingual extra resources to deal with new linguistic tasks.

Componential subtheory. The componential subtheory is the final part of the model. It is closest to the classic information processing approach in that it specifies the structures and mechanisms that underlie intelligent behaviour; from its three parts, one can infer why bilinguals should be more adept at the variety of linguistic, metalinguistic, and nonlinguistic tasks used as dependent measures in this area of research.

The necessity for a bilingual to control two language systems should improve the efficiency of the metacomponential system and performance on various metacognitive and metalinguistic tasks; this should be most evident for young children who learn two languages simultaneously, because they will apprehend the arbitrariness of language earlier than monolinguals. This chapter has not discussed the metalinguistic consequences of bilingualism (for reviews, see Bialystok & Ryan, 1985; Cummins & Swain, 1986; Hamers & Blanc, 1989; McLaughlin, 1984) except to mention, earlier, Vygotsky's suggestions as to how bilingualism frees the child "from the prison of

---

[5] For example, it is extremely unlikely that Canada will ever again have a Prime Minister who is not bilingual in the two official languages; one thing that sticks in my mind from the last Canadian federal election was the television broadcast in which three anglophones (Ed Broadbent, Brian Mulroney, and John Turner) debated each other in French. On a more ironic note, I find it amusing that the Québec politicians who are the most vocal in advocating French-only signs and other measures to protect the French language in Québec (by discouraging the use of English) are, by and large, themselves fluently bilingual.

concrete language forms and phenomena" (1935/1975, as cited in Cummins, 1976, p. 34); Imedadze (1960) described this as the "objectification" hypothesis.

The metacomponential system controls intellectual function by constructing plans and monitoring and evaluating information processing. These "executive processes" are responsible for such aspects of intelligence as *understanding* the nature of a problem, *deciding* which performance components to utilize, *selecting* strategies for the use of various performance components, *deciding* how much time to allocate to different parts of a problem, and *keeping track* of what has been done and what remains to be done in the solution of a problem.

Peal and Lambert (1962) were the first to suggest that bilinguals enjoyed a metacomponential advantage (of course, they did not use this term); they felt that bilinguals should be superior in "performance on tests requiring symbolic reorganization since they demand a readiness to drop one hypothesis or concept and try another" (p. 14). Lambert (1978) has also cited the results of Scott's (1973) research on divergent thinking in bilinguals and monolinguals as evidence for a causal link between bilingualism and flexibility. (Scott's study is unpublished, but there is an excellent summary in MacNab, 1979, pp. 233-234.)

The notion that bilinguals possess greater "cognitive flexibility" has had wide acceptance since Peal and Lambert first proposed the idea; it has been embraced by many investigators (cf. Ben-Zeev's, 1977a, concept of "readiness to reorganize" and De Avila and Duncan's, 1979, notion of a metaset for learning), even though, as Cummins (1976) has pointed out, the vagueness of the term is fraught with conceptual confusion. While many have traced the roots of cognitive flexibility in bilinguals to the early separation of linguistic form from meaning, Ben-Zeev (1977c) saw the increased analytical ability of bilingual children as a consequence of the need to overcome interlingual interference. In a similar vein, Lambert and Tucker (1972) suggested that children developing bilingually practice a form of "contrastive linguistics" (comparing the syntax and vocabulary of their two languages). I agree with this view; I think it is likely that the necessity of monitoring and controlling two (potentially interfering) symbol systems leads to increased metacomponential abilities.

Although it is not described in the foregoing brief outline of Sternberg's model, there are actually three different aspects of the performance components of the componential subtheory. One involves the encoding of task information (perceiving the problem and storing relevant information in working memory). A variety of investigators (e.g., Bain & Yu, 1980; Diaz, 1983; Diaz & Padilla, 1985) have suggested that bilingualism might lead to increasing reliance on verbal mediation in cognitive tasks; this may be partly due to the greater use of language and the increased awareness of "languageness" in bilinguals, leading to a greater use of language as a regulatory tool in cognition. There is suggestive experimental support for this hypothesis; Diaz and Padilla found a positive relationship between degree of bilingualism and use of self-regulatory utterances.

As well, having two interlocking linguistic performance systems doubles the resources available for dealing with verbal tasks (a kind of two-way positive transfer) and should aid also in the performance of many kinds of nonverbal tasks; childhood bilingualism may foster a precocious use of verbal mediation in the processing of information and this would explain bilinguals' improved performance on nonverbal tasks. Again, Peal and Lambert (1962) were the first to suggest this possibility. After factor analyzing their data, they noted that the nonverbal advantages of bilinguals were more evident on tests that required the recognition and manipulation of symbols (rather than on tests requiring spatial or perceptual abilities). Similar results for tasks that require reorganization of a perceptual situation have been reported by Balkan (1970) using the *Figures Cachées* test, which is similar to the *Embedded Figures Test*. It is interesting that the superiority of bilinguals on the *Figures Cachées* was most pronounced for children who acquired both languages before the age of 4 (see also Vaid & Lambert's, 1979, finding of superiority of early bilinguals on an embedded figures test; perhaps simultaneous early bilingualism is crucial for benefits to the performance components of Sternberg's model?). The most well-known example of bilinguals' superiority on nonverbal tasks was provided by Ben-Zeev (1977a), who found that bilinguals outperformed monolinguals on some aspects of a matrix transposition task (those components that were related to linguistic ability).

A second performance component is mapping of higher-order relations, which involves the kind of procedures Piaget describes as formal operational reasoning. It's interesting that, in research with analogy problems, Sternberg (Sternberg & Rifkin, 1979) has found that the mapping of higher-order relations is one of the last skills to enter a child's repertoire; it has been suggested that it causes a major change in how children approach problems.

The third performance ability in Sternberg's model is that of inferring relations (in a problem); an explanation for increased general inferential abilities in bilinguals may be found by utilizing the concept of language-learning "strategies" (for some taxonomies of language-learning strategies and reviews of research, see Bialystok, 1981; Carroll, 1977; O'Neill, 1978; Oxford, 1989; Rubin, 1975; Seliger, 1984; Stern, 1975; Wenden & Rubin, 1987). For example, Seliger (1984) viewed strategies as superordinate, abstract, general processes such as hypothesis-testing and overgeneralization that are used in all language-learning situations; in contrast, "tactics" which language learners use are episodic, short-term processes like rote memorization, or the use of mnemonics, employed to overcome temporary obstacles in language acquisition. Oxford (1989) has listed other strategies (many of them affective or social) used by good language learners; cognitive (performance) strategies include ones like analyzing the problem situation. The existence and the usefulness of over-arching strategies may become especially salient to bilinguals; since all languages are rule-governed, bilinguals, because they use strategies to learn *two* languages, may be more likely to see the power of general, cognitive heuristics (like hypothesis-testing) and more likely to use these in a variety of problem-solving and learning situations, not just for language learning. It would be an interesting experimental project to examine the incidence of these kinds of "strategic" behaviours in children raised bilingually or monolingually.

Knowledge-acquisition components are the third facet of the componential subtheory. These components decide what information is worth learning, help put that information into a meaningful form, and relate new information to previous knowledge; the Diaz and Padilla (1985) study, mentioned in the previous section, also found that degree of bilingualism was correlated with the increased use of language related to the labelling and description of materials and guiding and planning statements. In my opinion, relating new information to existing knowledge is the key to all meaningful learning; Sternberg's model predicts that the doubled linguistic resources available to bilinguals should permit easier encoding of verbal information and its integration with existing vocabulary or semantic memory. Discussion of the issues of the nature of bilingual memory and how information is encoded by the bilingual is beyond the scope of this chapter; for reviews, see Hamers and Blanc (1989) and Paivio (1986, this volume). Note that Lemmon and Goggin (1989) have recently suggested that the nature of the memory storage system of bilinguals may be the basis of any cognitive advantages that bilinguals possess (see also Landry, 1978).

SOME FINAL WILD SPECULATION

In *The Idler,* Samuel Johnson noted: "When speculation has done its worst, two and two still make four." I want to add one more speculative plot line to the complex saga I've been reviewing; as Johnson intimated, this may be a conjecture which is statistically verifiable (conversely, Disraeli pointed out that "there are three kinds of lies: lies, damned lies, and statistics"). I remain unconvinced that there is a proven causal relationship between bilinguality and intellectual performance; nonetheless, in this section I exercise my right to consider one of its possible effects, should it actually exist.

If, as the majority of researchers and theorists in this area have argued, there are significant, positive, cognitive consequences of bilingualism at the level of the individual, should there also not be significant positive intellectual outcomes at the societal level? Might not Lambert's (1974, 1977) concept of additive bilingualism be extended to include not only cognitive benefits for the individual but also cognitive/cultural benefits at the group level?

The impetus for this query was a rereading of McClelland's (1961; McClelland, Atkinson, Clark, & Lowell, 1953) program of research on the achievement motive. Part of McClelland's investigation focussed on a reworking of Weber's (1904/1930) thesis that the Reformation had caused a new work ethic to be born (the "Protestant ethic") and the rise of Protestantism coincided with the rise of capitalistic enterprise and swift economic growth in Germany, England, Switzerland, and the Netherlands. McClelland extended Weber's thesis by proposing a social-psychological mechanism mediating between the two large-scale social forces (the use of Protestantism and the spirit of modern capitalism). He proposed that the ideology of Protestantism should cause parents to practice early independence training; they would stress the importance of achievement and self-reliance to their children (especially sons). This in turn should lead to high achievement motivation (see Figure 8-3).

One prediction of the model in Figure 8-3 is that there should be a link between Protestantism and economic development in the modern world. McClelland (1961) tested this prediction by comparing the levels of development, indexed by average per capita consumption of electric power, in 1950 for all countries in the temperate zones. Even after correcting for differences in availability of natural resources, especially hydroelectric power, there was still a significant difference between Protestant and Catholic nations, with Protestant countries showing more electricity consumption.

Of course, this was only an indirect test of McClelland's extension of Weber's thesis; it did not measure, in any way, the intervening variable of achievement motivation. To do this, McClelland analyzed the stories from children's readers from each of the countries (where they could be obtained), with the assumption that these stories are a primary means by which a

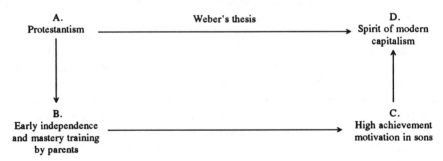

Fig. 8-3.   Weber's thesis and McClelland's modification.

culture transmits its values to a new generation. Two sets of stories were analyzed for achievement motivation themes: one set for the years 1920-29 and one set for 1946 through the 1950s (e.g., a book originally published in 1930 that has a high achievement motivation theme is the still-popular *The Little Engine That Could*). Without going into the intricacies of McClelland's analyses (he used a regression technique and corrections for damage inflicted during World War II), he found that the higher the level of achievement motivation represented in the earlier set of stories (a reflection of cultural values), the greater the increase in economic development (as assessed by electricity production and standardized national income) by the 1950s; note that there was no significant relationship between economic gains and the level of motivation expressed in the stories after 1946. McClelland inferred that the gains had been caused by achievement motivation developed a generation earlier.

What does all this have to do with bilingualism and cognitive performance? The long summary of McClelland's techniques was necessary because most readers will not be familiar with them; it is important, though, to understand McClelland's logic because it can be applied to the study of the relationship between degree of societal bilingualism and national cognitive/intellectual vigour.

Figure 8-4 shows a hypothesized relationship between widespread bilingualism in a country or other definable geographical region and heightened intellectual vitality; of course, it is an analogue to McClelland's extension of Weber's thesis, shown in Figure 8-3. Here the intervening variables are the widespread learning of two languages by many children and the subsequent positive cognitive consequences of bilingualism in these children (the type of outcome predicted by most of the researchers cited in this chapter, and the results of most of the studies, however flawed, that I've reviewed). The relationship described in Figure 8-4 ("Reynolds' thesis"?) suggests that the more widespread the bilingualism in a country or region, the greater the intellectual vitality of that area. This effect is mediated by

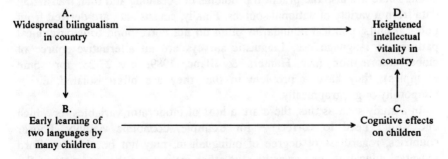

Fig. 8-4. Bilingualism and national intellectual vitality.

widespread bilingualism in children that leads to enhanced cognitive performance. Implicit in this thesis is the prediction that this is a dynamic relationship; that is, a change in degree of societal bilingualism (increase or decrease) will cause, *at a later point in time,* a change in indices of group cognitive/intellectual "performance." How might one assess this societal cognitive "performance"? Some variables that come to mind include (all on a per capita basis): number of books (of various types) published, number of Nobel prizes, number of libraries, library usage, newspaper and magazine circulation (by various types), number of books (of various types) sold, percentage of the population with university degrees (of various kinds), and so on.

The measurement problems involved in compiling various indices of societal intellectual vitality (at two points in time) and in assessing the amount of bilingualism in a variety of geographical regions (again at two points in time) are not trivial. The most straightforward way to measure the amount of bilingualism in a country would seem to be to access national census data banks. However, the questions about mother tongue, language use, and degree of competence in various languages often used in censuses are sometimes poorly worded or otherwise ambiguous, and even may not be the questions most appropriate for the needs of this analysis. Second, the specific questions or the wording of questions about language employed in censuses in a given country change over time, making comparisons between usage patterns at different points in time problematic. Third, censuses in different countries ask different kinds of questions; even the same term may mean quite different things in different national censuses. For example, "mother tongue" in the Canadian census means "the first language used in childhood and still understood," while in the Indian census of 1961 it meant the language spoken by the respondent's mother (Hamers & Blanc, 1989). Fourth, census data may not be reliable due to the self-report nature of the instrument and the possibility of coding inaccuracies. Fifth, many countries have only recently instituted censuses and some countries do not have them at all. There are also the practical problems of obtaining and then translating data from a variety of national sources. Finally, census data are derived from political units; political boundaries often do not correspond to geographical patterns of language use. Linguistic surveys are an alternative source of global information (see Hamers & Blanc, 1989, pp. 27-28, for some examples); they have a problem in that they are often isolated, either temporally or geographically.

In a study such as this, there are a host of moderator variables for which one would need to correct— for example, economic viability. Poorer countries, regardless of degree of bilingualism, may not be able to afford universal education, or universities or other institutions that are part of the infrastructure necessary for a nation to realize full intellectual potential. To compensate for this artifact, one could adopt McClelland's tactic and study only an economically relatively homogeneous sample; note that by surveying only temperate zone countries, he excluded developing Third World nations. Alternatively, the differences in economic power of various countries could be statistically controlled (by covariance analysis). This could lead to a problem in circularity, however; one way in which national intellectual vitality may assert itself is through increased industrial productivity, a positive balance of trade, no international debt, and other facets of a generally healthy economy. Despite the variety of technical problems that I have listed, I think that this hypothesized relationship between societal bilingualism and national intellectual vitality is deserving of exploration.

To this point, the research project I have proposed predicts only a positive relationship between degree of national bilingualism and national intellectual vitality. This is too simplistic; besides the additive form of bilingualism, there is also the possibility of subtractive bilingualism in a country. Subtractive bilingualism, in an individual, occurs when a dominant L_1 is threatened by a more prestigious L_2; Lambert (1977) suggested that the process is "subtractive" because the net competence in the two languages will reflect a subtraction of skill in L_1 and only partial replacement by L_2 competence. In many developing countries, there is a high probability of subtractive bilingualism being prevalent; an indigenous native language may be overshadowed by an imposed, more nationally prestigious L_2. The possibility of a powerful negative relationship between degree of national bilingualism and national intellectual vitality must be explored in those social contexts where the differential prestige of two languages is predictive of a national subtractive bilingualism.[6]

---

[6]After reading an earlier draft of this chapter, Bonifacio Sibayan raised a number of points about the suggestions in the preceding few paragraphs that are especially relevant to bilingualism in Third World countries. First, he pointed out to me that in many formerly colonial territories, bilingualism is of the imposed, or "life or death," variety; failure to attain some degree of bilinguality in the previously imposed second language (e.g., English in the Philippines) dooms one to be a marginal citizen. Second, Sibayan made a distinction between *common*, or ordinary, bilingualism, where one is competent in two indigenous languages (such as Ilocana and Kankaney, in the Philippines) and *intellectual* bilingualism, where one is fluent in an indigenous language and an international language (e.g., English). Only through intellectual bilinguality can an individual tap into the world's stored knowledge in science, mathematics, medicine, etc. Thus, the comments I made above about quantity of bilingualism in a country must be expanded; the specific languages in which the citizenry are bilingual (the quality of the national bilingualism) are important. In addition, Sibayan pointed out, it is critical for there to be a variety of types or registers of intellectual bilingualism (as well as sufficient numbers of "intellectual bilinguals") for there to be positive societal effects; the economic and technological success of countries like the Philippines, Singapore, Malaysia, and Hong Kong could not have happened without large numbers of people bilingual in English and without a variety of theoretical and applied interests.

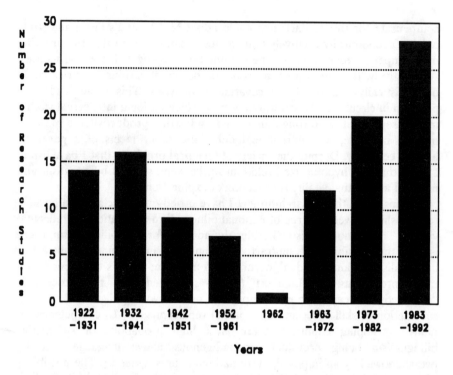

Fig. 8-5.   Number of research studies on the cognitive effects of bilingualism (Note that the total in the last column is derived by extrapolation from the number of studies published from 1983 through 1988).

THE PEAL AND LAMBERT LEGACY: THE SHOW'S NOT OVER TILL THE FAT LADY SINGS

It's time to bring this chapter to a close. History recorded Fitzgerald's admonition ("The rich are different from us.") and Hemingway's reply ("Yes, they have more money."). Research to this point has not yet supplied us with a definitive reply to Wally Lambert's suggestion ("Bilinguals are different from us."), but there's little doubt that the role Wally has played and continues to play in the ongoing search for the cognitive consequences of bilingualism has been a significant one. Almost every paper published since 1962 reflects the Peal and Lambert methodology or theoretical viewpoint and most of them explicitly cite that milestone study as the genesis of a second wave of research in this area.

It is probably both the quantity and the type of bilingualism in these settings that has prevented the negative effects of subtractive bilingualism.

As well, we can also deduce the importance of the Peal and Lambert paper from a quantitative analysis. Figure 8-5 shows the number of empirical studies published on the cognitive consequences of bilingualism since 1922; note that this is a very rough count, gleaned partly from my own collection of articles and partly from bibliographies (the figures for 1963 onwards, especially, are probably underestimates). By the end of the 1950s, activity had just about petered out, and by 1962, there was only one study published, but what a study it was! Since the publication of the Peal and Lambert paper, we have seen a resurgence of activity that shows no signs of abating.

The conclusions of the majority of studies agree with Peal and Lambert's (1962) synopsis:

> The picture that emerges of the . . . bilingual . . . is that of a youngster whose wider experiences in two cultures have given him advantages which a monolingual does not enjoy. Intellectually his experience with two language systems seems to have left him with a mental flexibility, a superiority in concept formation, and a more diversified set of mental abilities . . . . There is no question about the fact that he is superior intellectually. (p. 20)

I hope that the few suggestions I've made will help improve the quality of work in this field and allow us to more rigorously reaffirm the positive conclusions of this theoretically, personally, and politically important area of research.

ACKNOWLEDGEMENTS

I would like to thank Robert Gardner for his helpful comments on this chapter, Jim Mroczkowski for his help with the artwork, and Robert Saltstone for his assistance with some of the psychometric issues discussed here and for innumerable other favours rendered during the writing of this chapter. Special thanks go to my assistants (my dedicated little band of "happy campers"): Lynn Buckley, Chantal Coulombe, Michelann Parr, Suzanne Richard, and, especially, Charlene Tremblay, who kicked some serious butt when it was needed most. Financial support for the preparation of this chapter was provided by Nipissing University College and the Ontario Ministry of Colleges and Universities. Although this book is dedicated to Wally Lambert, this chapter is informally dedicated to George Ferguson, Robert Gardner, and James Ramsay, who taught me the basics of statistics and research design; when you've learned the basics from them, that's about all you need to know.

REFERENCES

Anisfeld, E. (1964). *A comparison of the cognitive functioning of monolinguals and bilinguals*. Unpublished doctoral dissertation, McGill University, Montreal.

Bain, B. C. (1975). Toward an integration of Piaget and Vygotsky: Bilingual considerations. *Linguistics, 160,* 5-20.

Bain, B. C., & Yu, A. (1980). Cognitive consequences of raising children bilingually: 'One parent, one language.' *Canadian Journal of Psychology, 34*(4), 304-313.

Baker, C. (1988). *Key issues in bilingualism and bilingual education.* Clevedon, Avon: Multilingual Matters.

Balkan, L. (1970). *Les effets du bilinguisme français-anglais sur les aptitudes intellectuelles.* Brussels: AIMAV.

Barik, H. C., & Swain, M. (1976). A longitudinal study of bilingual and cognitive development. *International Journal of Psychology, 11*(4), 251-263.

Ben-Zeev, S. (1977a). The influence of bilingualism on cognitive strategy and cognitive development. *Child Development, 48,* 1009-1018.

Ben-Zeev, S. (1977b). The effect of bilingualism in children from Spanish-English low economic neighborhoods on cognitive development and cognitive strategy. *Working Papers on Bilingualism, 14,* 83-122.

Ben-Zeev, S. (1977c). Mechanisms by which childhood bilingualism affects understanding of language and cognitive structures. In P. A. Hornby (Ed.), *Bilingualism: Psychological, social, and educational implications.* New York: Academic Press.

Bialystok, E. (1981). The role of conscious strategies in second language proficiency. *Modern Language Journal, 65,* 24-35.

Bialystok, E., & Ryan, E. B. (1985). A metacognitive framework for the development of first and second language skills. In D. L. Forrest-Pressley, G. E. MacKinnon, & T. G. Waller (Eds.), *Metacognition, cognition, and human performance. Volume 1. Theoretical perspectives.* New York: Academic Press.

Bloom, B. (1964). *Stability and change in human characteristics.* New York: Wiley.

Bruner, J. S. (1973). *Beyond the information given.* New York: W. W. Norton & Company.

Bruner, J. S. (1975). Language as an instrument of thought. In A. Davies (Ed.), *Problems of language and learning.* London: Heinemann.

Campbell, D. T., & Stanley, J. C. (1963). *Experimental and quasi-experimental designs for research.* Chicago: Rand McNally & Company.

Carroll, J. B. (1977). Characteristics of successful second language learners. In M. Burt, H. Dulay, & M. Finocchiaro (Eds.), *Viewpoints on English as a second language.* New York: Regents.

Carroll, J. B. (1981) Twenty-five years of research on foreign language aptitude. In K. C. Diller (Ed.), *Individual differences and universals in language learning aptitude.* Rowley, MA: Newbury House.

Comptom, C. (1984). *A guide to 75 tests for special education.* Belmont, CA: Fearon Education.

Cummins, J. (1976). The influence of bilingualism on cognitive growth: A synthesis of research findings and explanatory hypotheses. *Working Papers on Bilingualism, 9,* 1-43.

Cummins, J. (1977). Cognitive factors associated with the attainment of intermediate levels of bilingual skills. *The Modern Language Journal, 61*(1-2), 3-12.

Cummins, J. (1979). Linguistic interdependence and the educational development of bilingual children. *Review of Educational Research, 49,* 222-251.

Cummins, J., & Swain, M. (1986). *Bilingualism in education. Aspects of theory, research and practice.* London: Longman.

Darcy, N. T. (1953). A review of the literature on the effects of bilingualism upon the measurement of intelligence. *Journal of Genetic Psychology, 82,* 21-57.

Darcy, N. T. (1963). Bilingualism and the measurement of intelligence: A review of a decade of research. *Journal of Genetic Psychology, 103,* 259-282.

De Avila, E. A., & Duncan, S. E. (1979). Bilingualism and the metaset. *NABE Journal, III*(2), 1-20.

Diaz, R. M. (1983). Thought and two languages: The impact of bilingualism on cognitive development. In E. W. Gordon (Ed.), *Review of research in education 10*. Washington: American Educational Research Association.

Diaz, R. M. (1985a). Bilingual cognitive development: Addressing three gaps in current research. *Child Development, 56*, 1376-1388.

Diaz, R. M. (1985b). The intellectual power of bilingualism. *Quarterly Newsletter of the Laboratory of Comparative Human Cognition, 7*, 16-22.

Diaz, R. M., & Padilla, K. (1985, April). *The self-regulatory speech of bilingual pre-schoolers*. Paper presented at the meeting of the Society for Research in Child Development, Toronto.

Dockrell, W. B., & Brosseau, J. (1967). The correlates of second language learning by young children. *Alberta Journal of Educational Research, 13*(4), 295-298.

Duncan, S. E., & De Avila, E. A. (1979). Bilingualism and cognition: Some recent findings. *NABE Journal, 4*(1), 15-50.

Feldman, C., & Shen, M. (1971). Some language-related cognitive advantages of bilingual five-year-olds. *The Journal of Genetic Psychology, 118*, 235-244.

Gardner, R. C., & Lambert, W. E. (1965). Language aptitude, intelligence and second language achievement. *Journal of Educational Psychology, 56*, 191-199.

Genesee, F. (1976). The role of intelligence in second language learning. *Language Learning, 26*, 267-280.

Genesee, F. (1987). *Learning through two languages. Studies of immersion and bilingual education*. Cambridge, MA: Newbury House.

Genesee, F., & Hamayan, E. (1980). Individual differences in second language learning. *Applied Psycholinguistics, 1*, 95-110.

Genesee, F., Tucker, G. R., & Lambert, W. E. (1975). Communication skills of bilingual children. *Child Development, 46*, 1010-1014.

Guilford, J. P. (1959). Three faces of intellect. *American Psychologist, 14*, 469-479.

Hakuta, K. (1986). *Mirror of language. The debate on bilingualism*. New York: Basic Books.

Hakuta, K. (1987). Degree of bilingualism and cognitive ability in mainland Puerto Rican children. *Child Development, 58*, 1372-1388.

Hakuta, K., & Diaz, R. M. (1985). The relationship between degree of bilingualism and cognitive ability: A critical discussion and some new longitudinal data. In K. E. Nelson (Ed.), *Children's language. Volume 5*. Hillsdale, NJ: Lawrence Erlbaum Associates.

Hakuta, K., Ferdman, B. M., & Diaz, R. M. (1987). Bilingualism and cognitive development: three perspectives. In S. Rosenberg (Ed.), *Advances in applied psycholinguistics, Volume 2: Reading, writing, and language learning*. Cambridge: Cambridge University Press.

Hamers, J. F., & Blanc, M. H. A. (1989). *Bilinguality and bilingualism*. Cambridge: Cambridge University Press.

Imedadze, N. V. (1960). Kpsikhologichoskoy prirode rannego dvuyazyehiya (On the psychological nature of early bilingualism). *Voprosy Psikhologii, 6*, 60-68.

Jackson, D. N. (1975). Multimethod factor analysis: A reformulation. *Multivariate Behavioral Research, 10*, 259-275.

Jacobs. J. F., & Pierce, M. L. (1966). Bilingualism and creativity. *Elementary English, 43*, 499-503.

Jensen, J. V. (1962a). Effects of childhood bilingualism I. *Elementary English, 39*, 132-143.

Jensen, J. V. (1962b). Effects of childhood bilingualism II. *Elementary English, 39*, 358-366.

Kakkar, S. B. (1976). Linguistic background and intelligence. *Asian Journal of Psychology and Education, 1*(1), 20-23.

Kessler, C., & Quinn, M. E. (1982). Cognitive development in bilingual environments. In B. Hartford, A. Valdman, & C. R. Foster (Eds.), *Issues in international bilingual education: The role of the vernacular*. New York: Plenum.

Kilby, P. (1971). Hunting the Heffalump. In P. Kilby (Ed.), *Entrepreneurship and economic development*. New York: The Free Press.

Kittell, J. E. (1963). Intelligence test performance of children from bilingual environments. *Elementary School Journal, 64*(2), 76-83.

Lambert, W. E. (1974). Culture and language as factors in learning and education. In F. E. Aboud & R. D. Meade (Eds.), *Cultural factors in learning and education*. Bellingham, WA: Western Washington State College.

Lambert, W. E. (1977). The effects of bilingualism on the individual: Cognitive and sociocultural consequences. In P. A. Hornby (Ed.), *Bilingualism: Psychological, social, and educational implications*. New York: Academic Press.

Lambert, W. E. (1978). Cognitive and socio-cultural consequences of bilingualism. *The Canadian Modern Language Review, 34*, 537-547.

Lambert, W. E., & Tucker, G. R. (1972). *Bilingual education of children. The St. Lambert experiment*. Rowley, MA: Newbury House.

Landry, R. G. (1974). A comparison of second language learners and monolinguals on divergent thinking tasks at the elementary school level. *The Modern Language Journal, 58*, 10-15.

Landry, R. J. (1978). Le bilinguisme: Le facteur répétition. *Canadian Modern Language Review, 34*, 548-576.

Lavoie, G., & Laurendeau, M. (1960). *Tests collectifs d'intélligence générale*. Montréal: Institut de Recherches Psychologiques.

Lemmon, C. R., & Goggin, J. P. (1989). The measurement of bilingualism and its relationship to cognitive ability. *Applied Psycholinguistics, 10*, 133-155.

Liedtke, W. W., & Nelson, L. D. (1968). Concept formation and bilingualism. *Alberta Journal of Educational Research, 14*(4), 225-232.

Lindholm, K. J. (1980). Bilingual children: Some interpretations of cognitive and linguistic development. In K. E. Nelson (Ed.), *Children's language. Volume 2*. New York: Gardner Press.

Lyman, H. B. (1965). Untitled review. In O. K. Buros (Ed.), *The sixth mental measurements yearbook*. Highland Park, NJ: The Gryphon Press.

MacNab, G. L. (1979). Cognition and bilingualism: a reanalysis of studies. *Linguistics, 17*, 231-255.

Macnamara, J. (1966). *Bilingualism and primary education. A study of Irish experience*. Edinburgh: Edinburgh University Press

Macnamara, J. (1970). Bilingualism and thought. In J. E. Alatis (Ed.), *Bilingualism and language contact: Anthropological, linguistic, psychological, and sociological aspects*. Georgetown University Round Table on Languages and Linguistics 1970. Washington, DC: Georgetown University Press.

Macnamara, J. (1972). Bilingualism and thought. In B. Spolsky (Ed.), *The language education of minority children*. Rowley, MA: Newbury House.

McCallum, R. S. (1985). Untitled review. In J. V. Mitchell, Jr. (Ed.), *The ninth mental measurements yearbook* (Vol. II). Lincoln, NE: University of Nebraska Press.

McClelland, D. C. (1961). *The achieving society*. Princeton: Van Nostrand.

McClelland, D. C., Atkinson, J. W., Clark, R. A., & Lowell, E. L. (1953). *The achievement motive*. New York: Appleton-Century.

McLaughlin, B. (1984). *Second-language acquisition in childhood: Volume 1. Preschool children*. Hillsdale, NJ: Lawrence Erlbaum Associates.

McLaughlin, B. (1985). *Second-language acquisition in childhood: Volume 2. School age children.* Hillsdale, NJ: Lawrence Erlbaum Associates.

McNamara, J. R., Porterfield, C. L., & Miller, L. E. (1969). The relationship of the Wechsler Preschool and Primary Test of Intelligence with the Coloured Progressive Matrices (1956) and the Bender Gestalt Test. *Journal of Clinical Psychology, 25,* 65-68.

Okoh, N. (1980). Bilingualism and divergent thinking among Nigerian and Welsh school children. *The Journal of Social Psychology, 110,* 163-170.

O'Neil, H. F., Jr. (Ed.). (1978). *Learning strategies.* New York: Academic Press.

Oxford, R. (1989). *Language learning strategies: Conversation skills through oral histories.* New York: Newbury House/Harper & Row.

Paivio, A. (1986). *Mental representations. A dual coding approach.* New York: Oxford University Press.

Peal, E., & Lambert, W. E. (1962). The relation of bilingualism to intelligence. *Psychological Monographs: General and Applied, 76,* 1-23.

Raven, J. C. (1956). *Coloured progressive matrices: Sets A, Ab, B.* London: Lewis.

Raven, J. C., Court, J. H., & Raven, J. (1976). *Manual for Raven's Progressive Matrices and Vocabulary Scales.* London: Lewis.

Reynolds, A. G., & Flagg, P. W. (1983). *Cognitive psychology* (2nd ed.). Boston: Little, Brown.

Rubin, J. (1975). What the "good language learner" can teach us. *TESOL Quarterly, 9,* 41-51.

Sattler, J. M., & Altes, L. M. (1984). Performance of bilingual and monolingual Hispanic children on the Peabody Picture Vocabulary Test-Revised and the McCarthy Perceptual Performance Scale. *Psychology in the Schools, 21,* 313-316.

Sattler, J. M., Avila, V., Houston, W. B., & Toney, D. H. (1980). Performance of bilingual Mexican-American children on Spanish and English versions of the Peabody Picture Vocabulary Test. *Journal of Clinical and Consulting Psychology, 48,* 782-784.

Scott, S. (1973). *The relation of divergent thinking to bilingualism: Cause or effect.* Unpublished manuscript, McGill University, Department of Psychology, Montreal.

Segalowitz, N. (1977). Psychological perspectives on bilingual education. In B. Spolsky & R. Cooper (Eds.), *Frontiers of bilingual education.* Rowley, MA: Newbury House.

Seliger, H. W. (1984). Processing universals in second-language acquisition. In F. R. Eckman, L. H. Bell, & D. Nelson (Eds.), *Universals of second language acquisition.* Rowley, MA: Newbury House.

Skutnabb-Kangas, T. (1984). *Bilingualism or not: The education of minorities.* Clevedon: Multilingual Matters.

Stern, H. H. (1975). What can we learn from the good language learner? *Canadian Modern Language Review, 31,* 304-317.

Sternberg, R. J. (1985). *Beyond IQ: A triarchic theory of human intelligence.* Cambridge: Cambridge University Press.

Sternberg, R. J. (1988). *The triarchic mind: A new theory of human intelligence.* New York: Viking.

Sternberg, R. J., & Rifkin, B. (1979). The development of analogical reasoning processes. *Journal of Experimental Child Psychology, 27,* 195-232.

Thurstone, L. L., & Thurstone, T. G. (1954). *Primary mental abilities: Ages 7 to 11.* Chicago: Science Research Associates.

Torrance, A. P., Gowan, J. C., Wu, J. M., & Aliotti, N. C. (1970). Creative functioning of monolingual and bilingual children in Singapore. *Journal of Educational Psychology, 61*(1), 72-75.

Tsushima, W. T., & Hogan, T. P. (1975). Verbal ability and school achievement of bilingual and monolingual children of different ages. *Journal of Educational Research, 68,* 349-353.

Vaid, J., & Lambert, W. E. (1979). Differential cerebral involvement in the cognitive functioning of bilinguals. *Brain and Language, 8,* 92-110.

Vernon, P. E. (1969). *Intelligence and cultural environment.* London: Methuen.

Vygotsky, L. S. (1962). *Thought and language* (E. Hanfmann & G. Vakar, Eds. and Trans.). Cambridge, MA: MIT Press. (Original work published 1934)

Vygotsky, L. S. (1975). *Multilingualism in children* (M. Gulutsan & I. Arki, Trans.). Unpublished manuscript, University of Alberta, Center for East European and Soviet Studies, Edmonton. (Original work published 1935)

Vygotsky, L. S. (1978). *Mind in society: The development of higher psychological processes* (M. Cole, V. John-Steiner, S. Scribner, & E. Souberman, Eds.). Cambridge, MA: Harvard University Press.

Weber, M. (1930). *The Protestant ethic and the spirit of capitalism* (T. Parsons, Trans.). New York: Scribner. (Original work published 1904)

Wenden, A., & Rubin, J. (Eds.). (1987). *Learner strategies for language learning.* Englewood Cliffs, NJ: Prentice-Hall.

Whitaker, J. H., Rueda, R. S., & Prieto, A. G. (1985). Cognitive performance as a function of bilingualism in students with mental retardation. *Mental Retardation, 23*(6), 302-307.

White, D., & Panunto, B. (1978). Verbal and nonverbal abilities in English first and second language children. *Psychological Reports, 42,* 191-197.

Willig, A. C. (1985). A meta-analysis of selected studies on the effectiveness of bilingual education. *Review of Educational Research, 55*(3), 269-317.

Wittenborn, J. R., & Larsen, R. P. (1944). A factorial study of achievement in college German. *Journal of Educational Psychology, 35,* 39-48.

9 Second Language Learning in School Settings: Lessons from Immersion

Fred Genesee
McGill University

The 1960s was a particularly fruitful period in Wally Lambert's scientific career. It was during this time that some seminal and now classic studies were conducted by Wally and his colleagues at McGill, including the matched-guise studies (see Giles, this volume), the research with Elizabeth Peal on the cognitive consequences of bilingualism (see Hamers and Reynolds, this volume), studies of children's perceptions of foreign people with Otto Klineberg, and research into the effectiveness of the French immersion programs with Dick Tucker, Alison d'Anglejan, Maggie Bruck, and others. It is the immersion programs that are the focus of my discussion.

It is not my intention to review the findings of the considerable research on immersion— there are extensive and accessible reviews elsewhere (Genesee, 1987a; Lambert & Tucker, 1972; Swain & Lapkin, 1982). Rather, I examine the implications of some of the research findings from the immersion programs for second language learning in school settings in general. I hesitate to summarize even in general terms findings on immersion as a preliminary to my main discussion, but a brief summary is a useful starting point. The most striking and consistent finding from evaluation studies of immersion is that, when compared to carefully selected control students in regular English school programs, immersion students experience no deficits in English language development in the long-term as a result of their immersion in French. This has been observed for all forms of immersion— early, delayed, late, total, and partial— and for students with different learner characteristics, including students who are generally disadvantaged in school. Similarly, the academic development of the

183

participating students is at par with comparable students receiving basic academic instruction through the native language. Finally, the participating students develop functional proficiency in French that surpasses that of students in all other forms of second language instruction in school settings where the learners have little or no contact with peers who are native speakers of the target language.

LESSON 1

The documented general effectiveness of immersion programs indicates that an approach in which second language instruction is integrated with academic or content instruction is a more effective way to teach language skills than an approach in which the second language is taught in isolation. While this may seem very familiar and, indeed, it may be taken for granted now, such a perspective was not always prevalent. It is important to recall both the state of psycholinguistic theory with respect to language development in general and the state of second language pedagogy in particular in the early 1960s when the immersion programs were conceptualized and first instituted, in order to appreciate the true significance of this lesson.

Behaviorist theories were dominant at the time, and behaviorist notions such as stimulus-response, habit strength, reinforcement, and practice were the basis for describing and explaining psychological phenomena in general. This was equally true of linguistic phenomena, as witnessed by the publication of Skinner's book *Verbal Behavior* in 1957. Educational thinking during this period also was influenced heavily by behaviorist theories of learning as well as by then-current linguistic theories which conceptualized language in terms of its constituent structures and the formal rules that described their relationships to one another in grammatical sentences. Second language educators had developed well-articulated and workable methods of second language instruction that were a direct application of behaviorist principles and structural linguistic notions to language teaching in the classroom. It followed logically from behaviorist psychology that language teaching involved tight control of the learners' time so that they heard and practiced correctly formed sentences. Foreign language teachers systematically used stimulus-reinforcement theory to teach sentence patterns. Errors were to be avoided so as to avoid reinforcing the production of incorrect linguistic forms. Language practice tended to be presented out of context or in artificial contexts, such as visiting a foreign country in one's imagination or ordering food in a make-believe restaurant. In short, language tended to be void of any real content and any real communicative interest or value. The impact of this approach is described in Blair (1982):

In 1942, Leonard Bloomfield, an eminent American linguist, had written a short treatise on language learning that had enormous influence in guiding language teaching for decades. In it he stated:

"It is helpful to know how language works, but this knowledge is of no avail until one has practiced the forms over and over again until he can rattle them off without effort. Copy the forms, read them out loud, get them by heart, and then practice them over and over again day after day, until they become entirely natural and familiar . . . "

And two decades later (1964), Nelson Brooks, a professor of foreign language education at Yale, had written:

"The single paramount fact about language learning is that it concerns, not problem-solving, but the formation and performance of habits." (p. 4)

In contrast, the hallmark of the immersion "method" is the integration of language and academic instruction. From a psycholinguistic point of view, such an approach means that second language learning is embedded in a rich and highly meaningful communicative context. The incentive for language learning in immersion is not getting the linguistic forms right, but rather understanding and being understood. And the motivation to learn is maintained by a sense of academic accomplishment and growth rather than the development of linguistic competence per se. The behaviorist notion of "practice" as a means of learning is replaced by the more cognitive notion of "creative construction" as a means of learning— the learners are encouraged to experiment with linguistic forms in order to communicate with one another and their teacher about academic or social matters. Errors in language production are not seen as bad but rather as indications of the learners' creative efforts to master a complex linguistic system. In immersion, the learner is seen as progressing through a series of interlanguage stages toward full target language proficiency.

From a pedagogical point of view, the integration of language and academic instruction means that academic skills and information provide a basis for second language teaching and learning. Language serves as a vehicle for discussing academic matters and to this extent it is a secondary rather than primary focus of instructional attention. Indeed, language teaching and, therefore, language learning are often incidental to academic instruction. The primary basis for instructional planning is not a theoretical structuralist model of language but rather the intellectual skills and knowledge deemed important for every child to learn. In other words, language learning is based on and proceeds according to the academic tasks set out in the program of instruction. Proficiency in the target language is not seen as a prerequisite to communication or academic development but rather as a corequisite.

Recently, there has been a general shift in second language education away from teaching language in isolation towards integrating language and content instruction; for example, witness the growth of communicative approaches to second language teaching such as English for special purposes, content-based English as a second language (ESL), and even integrated ESL (see Enright & McCloskey, 1989, for example). Several theoretical rationales underlie this shift (Snow, Met, & Genesee, 1989). First language acquisition naturally goes hand in hand with cognitive and social development since they occur simultaneously. Moreover, language is an important medium through which social and cognitive development normally proceed. Because language is taught as a subject in isolation, conventional methods of second/foreign language instruction often dissociate language learning from the other aspects of development. Integrated language instruction for young second language learners seeks to bring these domains back together so that language learning is an integral part of social and cognitive development in school.

Language development specialists recognize that language is learned most effectively when it is learned for communication in meaningful and significant social situations. In life at large, people use language to communicate about what they know, what they want to know about, and about their feelings, attitudes, desires, etc. For school children, the academic content of the school curriculum provides the basis for much meaningful and significant communication. But, as Mohan (1986) points out, in subject matter learning in school, we often overlook the role of language as a medium of learning. We see language only as an object of learning. And in language learning, we often overlook the fact that content is being communicated. Integrated language instruction seeks to use academic content as a meaningful basis for language instruction and learning. Viewed differently, academic content provides a motivation for second language learning. Such a motivation is generally lacking in programs of instruction where language is taught as an end in itself. Needless to say, the academic content of the curriculum is an effective motivation for language learning only to the extent that it is interesting or seen to be of some value to the learner.

It has also been argued that the integration of content and language instruction provides a substantive basis for language teaching and learning in that content, academic or otherwise, provides cognitive hangers on which new language structures can be hung. Similarly, classroom discourse about academic matters and classroom activities in general provide substantive bases for learning the communicative functions of the new language. In the absence of real content and real discourse, language is learned as an abstraction devoid of conceptual or communicative substance.

Finally, although language theorists continue to emphasize the universal aspects of language and language learning, there is a growing interest in the specificity of language. In particular, those who study language in context (the functional variationist approach) underline how language use is characterized by unique and complex patterns and that these patterns must be learned in context (Hudson, 1980). Knowing how to use language in one context does not necessarily mean knowing how to use it in another. Particular attention has been given to the differences between language varieties used in school settings versus nonschool settings (Cummins, 1981; Heath, 1983; MacLure & French, 1981). Growing recognition of this characteristic of language has led language educators to devise methods of second language instruction that incorporate specific genres of language use. Thus, English for special purposes is a major focus of attention in ESL education.

Consciously or unconsciously, deliberately or by accident, the immersion programs of the 1960s forecast the development of conceptualizations about language and language learning that have become part of the stock-in-trade of current language development specialists. The St. Lambert immersion program and subsequent variants of it were thus early prototypes of more recently developed integrated or content-based second language instructional approaches. Krashen and Terrell's Natural Approach is a case in point. And, in fact, the immersion programs have often been used as justification for more recent alternative forms of integrated language instruction (see Krashen & Terrell, 1983, for example).

We can now appreciate in retrospect that immersion itself is a specific type of integrated second language program — one that focuses on acquisition of the language skills needed for academic purposes. In fact, it can be said that French immersion programs represent one extreme along a continuum of integrated approaches varying from a focus on language to a focus on content. Immersion falls toward the content end of the continuum in that academic content and skills are the raison d'être of the programs and mastery of academic content is deemed as important as and, indeed, perhaps more important than mastery of the language. That this may be the case is evidenced by the fact that immersion programs are regarded as successful by researchers, educators, and parents alike despite evidence of certain linguistic shortcomings, to be discussed shortly, because the academic achievement of the students is at par with comparable students educated through English.

The immersion programs have also been prototypical with respect to the role of research and evaluation — to this day the evaluations of immersion comprise one of the very few systematic, and certainly the most comprehensive, assessments of any type of second language instruction anywhere. The success of the immersion programs as an integrated approach to second language instruction is evidenced by research findings that the participating students acquire the second language skills needed to master the academic skills and knowledge appropriate to their age level. This is no mean achievement considering that this is true for such academically advanced subjects as high school mathematics, chemistry, and history (Genesee, 1976).

LESSON 2

Research has consistently indicated also that there are no negative effects to the native language development and academic achievement of immersion students (see Genesee, 1987a, chap. 3). As a result, researchers have progressively shifted their attention toward a closer examination of the students' second language development. They have increasingly asked whether the integration of academic and language instruction alone is sufficient to optimize second language learning in immersion and, therefore, in other integrated programs. The answer that appears to be emerging is that it is probably not merely the integration of content and language instruction that is important, but rather how they are integrated.

In this regard, Krashen (1985) has argued that "humans acquire language in only one way— by understanding messages, or by receiving 'comprehensible input'" and that "listening comprehension and reading are of primary importance in the second language program" (p. 2). Krashen's basic argument that input must be comprehensible in order for it to contribute to second language acquisition is relevant here because it requires that the content of integrated second language instructional programs be taught using language that makes it comprehensible and, therefore, meaningful. It can probably be said with some certainty that immersion programs provide extensive comprehensible input; otherwise, how could one explain the impressive academic outcomes noted earlier? And indeed, it has been found that immersion students often perform as well as native French-speaking students on tests of reading and listening comprehension. It is important to note here that these findings pertain to comprehension of school-type language. Whether or not immersion students would demonstrate the same high levels of proficiency with less formal, more colloquial forms of French is an open question. The students themselves report in surveys of their language usage that they have difficulty understanding and using French in extracurricular settings.

On the one hand, it is probably generally true and largely noncontroversial that comprehensibility is a necessary condition for second language learning. On the other hand, whether comprehensibility alone is sufficient for optimal second language learning is arguable (see also Swain, 1985; White 1987). Krashen (1981) sees comprehensible input as both a necessary and sufficient condition for second language learning: "The ability to speak (or write) fluently in a second language will come on its own with time. Speaking fluency is thus not 'taught' directly; rather, speaking ability 'emerges' after the acquirer has built up competence through comprehending input" (p. 59). According to Krashen (1985), production is simply a means of increasing comprehensible input.

To equate language production with comprehension, as Krashen does, is to imply that the means for learning to comprehend language are the same as those for learning to produce language. It seems unlikely that this is the case. There are neurophysiological reasons for believing that language comprehension and language production are separate systems. It has been well established that damage to certain areas of the brain differentially impairs language comprehension and language production (Penfield & Roberts, 1959). The extant evidence also suggests that the neurophysiological substrates that subserve comprehension and production are not totally distinct (Caramazza & Zurif, 1976)— there is overlap in the neurophysiological locus of representation of comprehension and production. Notwithstanding such overlap, evidence that language production and comprehension have somewhat distinct loci of neurophysiological control suggests that they develop somewhat independently.

Language production may be an important and critical means for language learning because it provides the learner with means for discovering, testing out, and practicing the elements and rules of language use (see also Swain, 1985). Knowledge of the specific rules of a language is not always necessary for accurate comprehension because many rules are strictly grammatical and serve no real semantic purpose. For example, in most cases the third person singular ending on verbs in English is usually redundant with information contained in the pronoun or subject of the sentence and, therefore, can be ignored. Indeed, it has been argued that pidgins and creoles, especially basolectal forms, generally lack such purely grammatical elements of language because they are not essential for conveying meaning (Hudson, 1980). The meaning of many verbal messages can also be derived from context and does not depend upon a precise grammatical analysis of the utterance. For example, it is not difficult to understand that one is being offered a cigarette by a stranger who speaks a foreign language, simply on the basis of the stranger's physical gestures.

Contrary to facilitating acquisition, in some cases comprehensibility may actually impede it by making certain linguistic forms transparent. That is to say, to the extent that the meaning of certain messages is obvious, on the basis of context or salient linguistic elements, then unknown elements may go unnoticed and, therefore, unacquired. Thus, in some cases, incomprehensible input may actually promote acquisition because the learner must attend to unknown meaning-bearing linguistic elements in order to make sense of the message. And, although precise knowledge of purely grammatical rules is not necessary for accurate comprehension, knowledge of such rules is necessary if the learner is to produce grammatically correct, nativelike utterances in the target language. To fail to acquire such productive competence may mark the learner with all of the attendant negative attitudes and stereotypes associated with nonnative language styles (Ryan & Giles, 1982).

The importance of productive language use is underlined by theorists who have argued that the process of language development is the same as the process of language use. Ellis (1984), for example, argued that "output is the product of taking part in discourse. In order to explain . . . output it is necessary to examine how the learner takes part in discourse" (p. 176). In a similar vein, Widdowson (in Ellis, 1984) contends that "we draw upon our knowledge of rules to make sense. We do not simply measure discourse up against our knowledge of pre-existing rules, we create discourse and commonly bring new rules into existence by so doing" (p. 176). In other words, the process of language learning is embedded in discourse processes. Discourse is a fundamentally social process that is negotiated and interactive and, therefore, necessarily entails production or output as well as comprehension or input.

It has been found that immersion students do not usually achieve the same high levels of proficiency in speaking and writing as they achieve in comprehension. And yet, as was pointed out earlier, immersion students arguably have extensive exposure to comprehensible input. The question that arises is: Can we account for these findings, in part at least, in terms of the discourse characteristics of immersion classrooms?

In fact, there has been little systematic documentation of how language is used in immersion classrooms by either students or teachers (however, see Swain & Carroll, 1987; Weber & Tardif, 1988). Thus, we have an insufficient empirical basis on which to draw firm conclusions about the discourse characteristics of immersion classrooms and, therefore, about the impact of classroom interaction styles on second language learning. It would, in fact, be difficult to collect such evidence given the highly variable nature of classroom interaction patterns. The scant evidence that is available suggests that students in many immersion classes are given limited opportunity to actively engage in discourse. Specifically, they are given few chances to speak at all during class and even less opportunity to initiate the use of language; most student language use appears to be in response to questions or comments initiated by the teacher. The generally limited opportunities for productive language use in immersion can best be illustrated anecdotally by describing a research project that we undertook several years ago (Lengyel & Genesee, 1975).

The purpose of this project was to document the language development of an individual immersion student over the course of an academic year and to examine the linguistic environment in which this development took place. This project was conceptualized to complement the emphasis on "group" research which has pervaded evaluations of immersion programs. To this end, a young boy in a Grade 1 early total immersion program was identified and equipped with a very powerful wireless transmitter for one hour every second week during his Grade 1 year. We were careful to select nonlanguage classes for our recordings in order to obtain representative examples of language use. For comparison purposes, another young boy, this time in kindergarten of an all-French school, was similarly identified and recorded. We chose Grade 1 in the case of the immersion student because we wanted to begin our observations at a time when his second language proficiency would have developed sufficiently to permit him to begin to use the language actively. We felt that kindergarten in an all-French school would be equivalent.

We diligently recorded, week after week; our young subjects, stoically at first and with much pleasure later on, endured our careful scrutiny. Our intention was to transcribe the entire corpus of our young subjects' verbal performance and that of their classmates and teachers and, thereby, to create a written record of their language development. Our recording equipment was sufficiently powerful to track all verbal behaviors within the classroom. What was most striking from our data was the scant verbal output and, in fact, the limited opportunity for output, not to mention interactive discourse, on the part of each of our subjects, and particularly our immersion subject. There were insufficient data from either boy to analyze and describe alone; most of our analysis and description focused on teacher language which dominated our recordings.

In a related vein, Swain (1988) has calculated, based on tape recordings of Grade 3 and Grade 6 immersion classes, that only about 14% of the times that immersion students talk in teacher-fronted classrooms are their utterances longer than a clause. Thus, these and other observational data suggest that the nonnativelike production skills of immersion students may result from learning environments in which there is a lack of opportunity to engage in extended discourse. Such limitations are undoubtedly less influential in the language development of native speakers because they have many other opportunities to use language outside school or in school with their peers.

The importance of discourse for second language development is evidenced by a recent study in which we compared the second language achievement of subgroups of anglophone students attending all-French schools in which they were the majority, with that of comparable students in all-French schools in which they were the minority (see Genesee, Holobow, Lambert, & Chartrand, 1989). We found that the "minority" anglophone students outperformed the "majority" anglophone students. This was true for the students' listening and speaking skills but not their reading and writing skills. It is precisely in the oral/aural domain that one would expect the former to excel because they have increased opportunity to interact informally with francophone students the same age. Since both groups of students were in regular French schools under the jurisdiction of the Ministère de l'éducation du Québec, both were exposed to the same academic curriculum. Thus, one would expect relatively few differences in reading and writing experiences. As well, any advantage that might accrue to increased interaction with francophone students as a result of modelling effects would be expected to be more apparent on examination of oral language as opposed to written language.

It is not possible in this study to dissociate the potential effects of discourse from those of peer modelling because the presence of peers in these classes increased not only opportunities for language use but also native-language modelling. We have additional evidence that, notwithstanding the advantages of native-speaker models for second language learning, extended opportunities for discourse even with nonnative speakers is advantageous (but see White, 1987). This evidence comes from an earlier evaluation by Stevens (1976) of two alternative late immersion programs— one an activity-centred immersion program and the other a conventional teacher-centred program. The activity-centred program was a half-day program and consisted of language arts, mathematics, and science taught in French; the other subjects were taught during the remainder of the day in English. The program was individualized so that the students were free to choose how they would complete their academic requirements in each of these subjects. In effect, this meant that the students could choose which topics to study, how, and when. The program promoted verbal interaction in French in that the students were allowed to work on projects together or they could consult one another on their individual projects. Typically the classroom was filled with lively and vocal students chattering away in French. The projects chosen by the students usually included hands-on-experiences (e.g., building models, preparing blueprints, or gathering collections of objects) in addition to cognitive work (e.g., library search). Thus, much of the students' language use occurred in conjunction with immediate and concrete physical activity.

The teachers in these classrooms acted more like consultants and advisors rather than disseminators of information, as tends to be the case in conventional teacher-fronted classrooms. In conventional classrooms, all students tend to work on the same projects at the same time and in the same way; there tends to be much less active involvement and more passive involvement in school work. The immersion classes that comprised the comparison groups were characterized by this teacher-centred style. An additional difference was that it was a full-day program that comprised 80% of the school day; in comparison the activity-centred program comprised approximately 40% of the school day.

Notwithstanding the time differential in favour of the teacher-centred classroom, Stevens' results revealed that the students in the activity-centred program attained the same levels of proficiency in speaking and listening and almost the same levels of proficiency in reading and writing French as the students in the more extended teacher-centered program. Stevens (1983) attributed the success of the program to the motivation provided by the use of language in situations of personal choice and to the opportunities for extended discourse in French with peers in a stimulating and enjoyable atmosphere. Ellis (1984) adds that activity-oriented interactions may be advantageous for language learning because they "result in a greater variety of address-types and offer the pupil the opportunity to act as the Initiator to a much greater extent" (p. 112) than medium-oriented interactions.

In summary, the second lesson emerging from our investigations of immersion is that integrated language programs that promote discourse, especially activity-oriented discourse which the students have been responsible for selecting, may be particularly beneficial for second language learning in school settings. At the same time, learning style differences among individual children and cultural differences in preferred learning style among subgroups of children must also be considered when discussing optimal instructional approaches to second language teaching (Wong-Fillmore, 1989).

LESSON 3

The final lesson I discuss here concerns time and second language learning. Considerable attention has been given to the role of time in accounting for educational results in general and second language results in particular. Thus, for example, the notion of time-on-task which enjoyed widespread support underlined the importance of the amount of time spent on specific tasks. In the domain of second language education, amount of time in second language study was also held to be an important determinant of second language achievement. In an international study of achievement in French as a second language in eight different countries, Carroll (in Swain, 1981), for example, concluded that "the primary factor in the attainment of proficiency in French . . . is the amount of instructional time provided" (p. 276). Certainly educational planners and parents alike regard time as an important factor in achievement; witness the sometimes obsessive attention given picayune allotments of time to specific school subjects in curriculum planning. The prevailing *Zeitgeist* usually maintains that more time is better.

Recent research findings from immersion indicate, in contrast with Carroll's 1975 conclusion, that there is no simple or consistent relationship between amount of time in immersion and achievement. In some cases, it has been found that there is a positive association between time and relative level of achievement. Thus, for example, comparative evaluations of early total and early partial immersion and of one-year and two-year late immersion programs have found that the alternatives which offer more time in French result in higher levels of achievement. However, other comparisons have not yielded findings in this direction. A particularly striking example is that of early versus two-year late immersion; research in Montreal by Genesee (1981) and Adiv (1980) failed to find consistent differences in favour of early immersion students even though they had accumulated more than twice as much time in French as late immersion students at the time of the evaluation. More recently, in an evaluation of the performance of anglophone students in all-French schools, we found that these students did not attain significantly higher scores on a variety of French language tests than students in an early total immersion program. The anglophone students in the all-French schools had received all of their instruction in French throughout their elementary schooling (K to 6) with the exception of English language arts instruction for 2.5 hours per week in Grades 4, 5, and 6. The early immersion students, in contrast, had had all instruction in kindergarten and Grades 1 and 2 in French; this was reduced to 80% in Grade 3, 60% in Grade 4, and 40% in Grades 5 and 6.

Time itself is not a psychological variable and, therefore, there is no reason to believe that considered alone it will have consistent effects on psychological processes such as language learning. The effects of time are likely to depend upon other factors of a more psychological nature that are coextensive with the time during which second language instruction occurs. For example, the time spent studying a second language might be expected to have different effects at different ages because the learner is at different points in his/her general development. And, indeed, we have seen that older learners in late immersion programs learn as much or more than younger learners from early immersion programs given the same amount of time, or even less time, in studying through French. These findings are not unique. In fact, a review of research studies that have compared older and younger learners generally confirms this finding, provided that the context of second language learning is school (Genesee, 1987b). This is not the case when second language learning takes place in nonschool settings. The apparent language learning efficiency of older school learners has been attributed to: (1) their generally advanced cognitive development which facilitates all learning (Genesee, 1987a); (2) advantages associated with a well-developed first language (Keller-Cohen, 1981), especially literacy; and (3) even their greater commitment to language learning.

Notwithstanding the effects of other concomitant psychological factors, time is important from a psycholinguistic point of view because it is a correlate of language development— language development takes place over time. In educational terms, the language development of immersion students can be said to depend in critical ways on two distinct aspects of the language learning environment of the school: the explicit language curriculum and the implicit language curriculum. The explicit curriculum is comprised of language arts instruction and those classes during which predesignated aspects of language are taught for limited and specified periods of time. Language arts is like other subjects in the program of study— it is taught and learned formally. It usually has explicit objectives and time lines for teaching those objectives.

The implicit language curriculum comprises all other instruction in which language is the medium of instruction but not the object of instruction— mathematics, science, social studies, etc. Unlike the explicit language curriculum, the implicit language curriculum is not defined nor is it relegated to specified instructional times. Moreover, it is not taught formally or consciously. In most cases, the learner is simply exposed to it and learns it incidentally in the process of learning academic subjects. This is clearly not the case all the time; some formal and conscious instruction in language and, therefore, some language learning does take place during academic instruction. The implicit language curriculum is embedded in the academic content and materials of the program of study and in the ways in which teachers use instructional materials to teach academic content. In other words, it will be reflected in any and all of the language that is used to teach the academic curriculum. The unique and, I would hazard to guess, the psycholinguistically most significant aspect of language development in immersion depends on the implicit language curriculum. Indeed, the rationale behind immersion is that the students will learn the language skills required to learn their academic subjects.

What about the actual second language development of immersion students? In fact, we know surprisingly little about this. Most of the research in immersion has focused on achievement— we know the level of second language achievement of immersion students relative to that of control students in core French programs or relative to that of French-speaking students in French schools. And, we can characterize their general proficiency in using French in different domains— speaking, reading, writing, and listening. In this regard, we know, as noted earlier, that immersion students develop high levels of functional proficiency. A somewhat different picture emerges from indepth studies of their language development. Studies by Spilka (1976) and Harley and Swain (1984), for example, suggest two generally sober characterizations of their oral language development. First, their grammar is less complex and less redundant than that of native speakers. Second, their second language usage is decidedly nonidiomatic; that is to say, their use of lexical and syntactic forms deviates from native usage in ways that cannot be labelled as incorrect but which is simply uncommon or highly unlikely in the case of native speakers. Genesee, Holobow, Lambert, Cleghorn, and Walling (1985) have reported similar nonidiomatic usage in written French. Other researchers have characterized their spoken language as pidginized or fossilized (Selinker, Swain, & Dumas, 1975) and have suggested that there may even be some linguistic "backsliding" so that structures that are used correctly early in development are used incorrectly later (e.g., use of *être*, instead of *avoir*, in stative expressions of age and body temperature). In general, then, there is the suggestion that the language development of immersion students is linguistically truncated, albeit functionally effective (see Genesee, 1987a, chap. 4, for a complete review of second language outcomes in immersion).

Assuming, for the sake of the present discussion, that these outcomes do not simply reflect absolute limitations of language learning in school settings, they raise important questions about the language curriculum of immersion and, therefore, probably other second language programs in which language and content instruction are integrated. One would expect continuous and more complete linguistic development in integrated second language programs to the extent that the curriculum demands or allows for continuous and nativelike development. More specifically, this means that the academic tasks that embody the implicit language curriculum must themselves be developmental in some linguistic sense. As well, the way in which the academic curriculum is taught must be developmental in some linguistically significant ways. As Swain (1988) has documented, there may be shortcomings to content teaching that does not consider language development systematically: language use might be functionally restricted; correction of content may take precedence over correction of linguistic form; correction of linguistic form may be inconsistent; and students' opportunities to engage in extended discourse may be limited, as noted earlier. Thus, reliance on the regular academic curriculum and on normal academic instruction is unlikely to maximize second language development. This is probably the case even if academic instruction is extended over many grades and the academic material becomes cognitively more complex and demanding. Students may be able to handle increasingly complex academic material by simply "recycling" basic language skills. Indeed, the scant available evidence suggests, albeit tentatively, that immersion students may reach a plateau in their language development in the middle elementary grades. For example, Adiv (1980) carried out detailed error analyses of oral language samples of students in Grades 1, 2, and 3 of an early total immersion program and found that, by Grade 3, the students had not mastered most of the 17 linguistic structures that she examined (e.g., prepositions, adjectives, object pronouns). Much more truly developmental research is needed in order to validate this hypothesis.

The implication here is that in order to enhance the language learning impact of an integrated curriculum, the academic tasks presented to the students and the instructional strategies used by the teachers need to keep both language development and academic development in mind (Snow et al., 1989). What is called for is a psycholinguistic model of language development that can serve to guide curriculum writers and teachers in this work. It is difficult to imagine at this time what such a model would look like, however. Lacking a psycholinguistic model, a "plan" for language development would be useful in the selection and structuring of academic tasks so as to better promote language development. Observational work by Swain & Carroll (1987) indicates that, in the absence of such a plan, content teachers may provide language learners with inconsistent and possibly even random information about target language forms. It is interesting to speculate here about the general developmental characteristics of teacher language use in the content classroom: Does the language used by teachers to teach content material at progressively higher grades change in ways that are relevant for development, as the material itself becomes progressively more complex? Moreover, do content teachers or the academic tasks they set for their students demand progressively more sophisticated language from their students as the material increases in complexity? It seems unlikely that the students' language will develop over time if the teachers themselves do not model or demand development.

At present, we know surprisingly little about what immersion teachers do and do not do with language. The research by Swain and Carroll is unique in its interest in teacher language behavior and underlines the need for more such descriptive research (see also Weber & Tardif, 1988, for an ethnographic study of kindergarten immersion students strategies for making sense in the immersion classroom). Moreover, we know surprisingly little about what kinds of linguistic interventions work in second language classrooms in general and in integrated classrooms in particular. The extant evidence suggests that teacher intervention in the form of error correction can influence the rate of language acquisition but not the pattern (Long, 1983). Training studies in which intervention strategies are tried out and evaluated would be valuable here (see Harley, Allen, Cummins, & Swain, 1987, for an example). Finally, we do not know what kinds of linguistic interventions are workable in the classroom. To prescribe that teachers actively intervene in the language learning process is to recommend psycholinguistic engineering of sorts. Such a recommendation entails certain assumptions. One such assumption is that we know what the critical intervention points are (Long & Crookes, 1986). Another is that teachers are able to monitor and manipulate their language behavior in significant ways while actively involved in meaningful communication. These are important assumptions that need empirical verification.

Generally speaking, these recommendations move us away from the originally somewhat laissez-faire approach to language learning in immersion toward a more systematic and interventionist approach. Whether or not such an approach is feasible and effective needs to be examined. This shift should not be construed as recommending less focus on meaning and more focus on formal language instruction. Rather it is a call for a more systematic focus on the way in which language is used to express meaning (Lightbown, 1989). These recommendations also call for a shift away from an almost exclusive research focus on the language learner and particularly on second language achievement which has dominated investigations of immersion to date, toward a program of research which also includes a focus on the teacher, the curriculum, and developmental aspects of second language acquisition (see also Tardif & Weber, 1987).

To return to the starting point of this section, the issues of language development that have been discussed herein are relevant to the issue of time because language development entails the effective use of time for language teaching. At issue is how best to make use of time in integrated programs of second language instruction. The immersion classroom provides an ideal research setting in which to explore these issues further.

SUMMARY

A review of research results emanating from evaluations of alternative forms of second language immersion along with a consideration of other relevant literature suggests at least three lessons of general relevance to second language learning and teaching in school settings:

1. Instructional approaches in which content and language instruction are integrated are likely to be more effective than approaches in which language is taught in isolation.

2. The use of instructional strategies and academic tasks that encourage extensive interaction between learners and between learners and the teacher are likely to be especially beneficial for second language learning.

3. Explicit and systematic planning for, and attention to, language development are called for in the development of the academic curriculum in order to maximize language learning.

ACKNOWLEDGMENTS

I would like to thank the following people for helpful comments on an earlier draft of this chapter: Patsy Lightbown, Merrill Swain, Dick Tucker, and Rosemary Weber.

REFERENCES

Adiv, E. (1980). *An analysis of second language performance in two types of immersion programs.* Unpublished doctoral dissertation, McGill University, Montreal.

Blair, R. W. (Ed.). (1982). *Innovative approaches to language teaching.* Rowley, MA: Newbury House.

Bloomfield, L. (1942). *Outline guide for the practical study of foreign languages.* Baltimore, MD: Special Publication of the Linguistic Society of America.

Brooks, N. H. (1964). *Language and language learning theory and practice.* New York: Harcourt Brace.

Caramazza, A., & Zurif, E. (1976). Dissociation of algorithmic and heuristic processes in language comprehension: Evidence from aphasia. *Brain and Language, 3,* 572-582.

Cummins, J. (1981). The role of primary language development in promoting educational success for language minority students. In *Schooling and language minority students: A theoretical framework.* Los Angeles: California State Department of Education, Evaluation, Dissemination and Assessment Center.

Ellis, R. (1984). *Classroom second language development.* Oxford: Pergamon Press.

Enright, D. D., & McCloskey, M. L. (1989). *Integrating English: Developing English language and literacy in the multilingual classroom.* Reading, MA: Addison Wesley.

Genesee, F. (1976). *Addendum to evaluation of the 1975-76 grade 11 French immersion class.* Report submitted to the Instructional Services Department, The Protestant School Board of Greater Montreal.

Genesee, F. (1981). A comparison of early and late second language learning. *Canadian Modern Language Review, 13,* 115-128.

Genesee, F. (1987a). *Learning through two languages: Studies of immersion and bilingual education.* Cambridge, MA: Newbury House.

Genesee, F. (1987b). Neuropsychological perspectives. In L. Beebe (Ed.), *Issues in second language acquisition: Multiple perspectives.* Cambridge, MA: Newbury House.

Genesee, F., Holobow, N. E., Lambert, W. E., & Chartrand, L. (1989). Three elementary school alternatives for learning through a second language. *Modern Language Journal, 73,* 250-263.

Genesee, F., Holobow, N., Lambert, W. E., Cleghorn, A., & Walling, R. (1985). The linguistic and academic development of English-speaking children in French schools: Grade 4 outcomes. *Canadian Modern Language Review, 41,* 669-685.

Harley, B., Allen, P., Cummins, J., & Swain, M. (1987). Functional grammar in French immersion: A classroom experiment. In B. Harley, P. Allen, J. Cummins, & M. Swain (Eds.), *The development of bilingual proficiency.* Toronto: Ontario Institute for Studies in Education.

Harley, B., & Swain, M. (1984). An analysis of verb form and function in the speech of French immersion pupils. *Working Papers in Bilingualism, 14,* 31-46.

Heath, S. B. (1983). *Ways with words.* Cambridge: Cambridge University Press.

Hudson, R. A. (1980). *Sociolinguistics.* Cambridge, MA: Cambridge University Press.

Keller-Cohen, D. (1981). Input from the inside: The role of a child's prior linguistic experience in second language learning. In R. Andersen (Ed.), *New dimensions in second language acquisition research.* Rowley, MA: Newbury House.

Krashen, S. D. (1981). Bilingual education and second language acquisition theory. In *Schooling and language minority students: A theoretical framework.* Los Angeles: California State Department of Education, Evaluation, Dissemination and Assessment Center.

Krashen, S. D. (1985). *The input hypothesis: Issues and implications*. London: Longman.

Krashen, S., & Terrell, T. (1983). *The natural approach: Language acquisition in the classroom*. Oxford: Pergamon Press.

Lambert, W. E., & Tucker, G. R. (1972). *Bilingual education of children: The St. Lambert experiment*. Rowley, MA: Newbury House.

Lengyel, C., & Genesee, F. (1975). *A case study of early second language learning through immersion*. Unpublished manuscript, McGill University, Montreal.

Lightbown, P. M. (1989). Process product research on second language learning in classrooms. In B. Harley, J. P. B. Allen, J. Cummins, & M. Swain, (Eds.), *The development of bilingual proficiency*. Unpublished manuscript, Ontario Institute for Studies in Education, Toronto.

Long, M. H. (1983). Does second language instruction make a difference: A review of research. *TESOL Quarterly, 17*, 355-382.

Long, M. H., & Crookes, G. (1986, April). *Intervention points in second language classroom processes*. Paper presented at the ELC Seminar on Patterns of Classroom Interaction, Singapore.

MacLure, M., & French, P. (1981). A comparison of talk at home and at school. In G. Wells (Ed.), *Learning through interaction: The study of language development*. Cambridge: Cambridge University Press.

Mohan, B. (1986). *Language and content*. Reading, MA: Addison-Wesley.

Penfield, W., & Roberts, L. (1959). *Speech and brain mechanisms*. New York: Atheneum.

Ryan, E., & Giles, H. (1982). *Attitudes toward language variation: Social and applied contexts*. London: Arnold.

Selinker, L., Swain, M., & Dumas, G. (1975). The interlanguage hypothesis extended to children. *Language Learning, 25*, 139-152.

Skinner, B. F. (1957). *Verbal behavior*. New York: Appleton, Century, Crofts.

Snow, M. A., Met, M., & Genesee, F. (1989). A conceptual framework for the integration of language and content in second foreign language instruction. *TESOL Quarterly, 23*, 201-217.

Spilka, J. (1976). Assessment of second language performance in immersion. *Canadian Modern Language Review, 32*, 543-540.

Stevens, F. (1976). *Second language learning in an activity-centred program*. Unpublished master's thesis, Concordia University, Montreal.

Stevens, F. (1983). Activities to promote learning and communication in the second language classroom. *TESOL Quarterly, 17*, 259-272.

Swain, M. (1981). Time and timing in bilingual education. *Language Learning, 31*, 1-16.

Swain, M. (1985). Communicative competence: Some roles of comprehensible input and comprehensible output in its development. In S. M. Gass & G. G. Madden (Eds.), *Input in second language acquisition*. Rowley, MA: Newbury House.

Swain, M. (1988). Manipulating and complementing content teaching to maximize second language learning. *TESL Canada Journal, 6*, 68-83.

Swain, M., & Carroll, S. (1987). The immersion observation study. In B. Harley, P. Allen, J. Cummins, & M. Swain (Eds.), *The development of bilingual proficiency*. Toronto: Ontario Institute for Studies in Education.

Swain, M., & Lapkin, S. (1982). *Evaluating bilingual education: A Canadian case study*. Clevedon, Avon: Multilingual Matters.

Tardif, C., & Weber, S. (1987). French immersion research: A call for new perspectives. *The Canadian Modern Language Review, 44*, 67-77.

Weber, S., & Tardif, C. (1988). *An ethnography of French immersion kindergarten: Sense-making strategies in second language classrooms*. Paper presented at the 8th Second Language Research Forum, University of Hawaii, Manoa.

White, L. (1987). Against comprehensible input: The input hypothesis and the development of second language competence. *Applied Linguistics, 8,* 95-110.

Wong-Fillmore, L. (1989). Language learning in social context: The view from research in second language learning. In R. Dietrich & C. F. Graumann (Eds.), *Language processing in social context.* North-Holland, PA: Elsevier Science Publisher.

10 Additive Bilingualism and French Immersion Education: The Roles of Language Proficiency and Literacy

Merrill Swain
Sharon Lapkin
Ontario Institute for Studies in Education

In 1975, Wallace Lambert introduced the terms "additive" and "subtractive" bilingualism. He used the term additive bilingualism to refer to the situation where an individual's first language is a societally dominant and prestigious one, and in no danger of replacement when a second language is learned; individuals add another socially relevant language to their repertoire at no cost to their first language competence. Lambert contrasted this form of bilingualism to that of subtractive bilingualism where an individual's first language is a minority, nonprestigious language such that the bilingual's competence in his or her two languages is likely to reflect some stage in the subtraction of the first language and its replacement by the second, majority language.

These concepts have been useful in accounting for positive and negative consequences of bilingualism; additive bilingualism has typically been associated with positive social and cognitive characteristics of bilinguals, while subtractive bilingualism has typically been associated with negative social and cognitive characteristics (Cummins & Swain, 1986; Lambert, 1977).

French immersion education, originally utilized almost exclusively by English-speaking students, has been considered a prime example of an educational program which promotes additive bilingualism. The students are speakers of a prestigious, majority language and are learning a second language which carries with it potential political, economic, and social rewards for its learners.

This chapter considers certain linguistic outcomes of French immersion education in an attempt to show how truly "additive" the program has been. Specifically, it examines aspects of immersion students' first language performance that indicate an enhancement of linguistic skills over those of unilingual English students. (Aspects of cognitive and social enhancement are treated elsewhere in this volume.) This is followed by an examination of the French language skills of those students for whom French is a third rather than a second language. Taken together, the results indicate that the conditions which create an additive form of bilingualism involve, as Lambert argued, first language development and maintenance. What this chapter suggests, however, is that literacy may also play a crucial role.

ENGLISH LANGUAGE PERFORMANCE

In an early French immersion program, students are initially instructed in French— a language with which most children will not have had any previous contact. All instruction is in French throughout kindergarten and Grade 1 and, in some programs, Grade 2. Beginning in Grade 2 or 3, English Language Arts is introduced into the program. Gradually more instruction in English is introduced, such that by Grade 6, usually about half the program is in English and half in French. Clearly, then, French immersion students will have had less exposure to English in the school setting than children in a regular English program. As well, they will have had no formal literacy instruction in their native language until Grade 2 or 3.[1]

Interestingly, in spite of the restricted instruction in English, a body of research is accumulating which suggests that aspects of the immersion students' English are enhanced. The early research is largely based on results from standardized tests of achievement such as the *Canadian Test of Basic Skills* (*CTBS*). More recent research has used materials specifically constructed to test particular skill areas. In this section these studies are reviewed.

Studies conducted in the 1970s were typically evaluations of immersion programs in operation in various school boards (Genesee, 1987; Swain & Lapkin, 1982). Students in the immersion program were compared to a similar group of students in the regular English program. Generally speaking, where English speaking or listening comprehension have been assessed (Lambert & Tucker, 1972), results indicate similarities between the groups. A notable exception is the study conducted by Genesee, Tucker, and Lambert

---

[1] Although not precisely documented, it is considered to be common practice for immersion children (and children in the English-educated comparison groups) to be read to in English at home.

(1975) where immersion and unilingual English kindergarten, Grade 1, and Grade 2 children were asked to explain the rules of a game, in one case to a blindfolded listener, and in the other case to a sighted listener. The immersion students were more likely than the unilingual students to take the listener's handicap into account. The sensitivity of the immersion students was attributed to the immersion experience, "wherein the normal assumptions about communicating in one's native language are not operative, and therefore one becomes more aware of and responsive to the parameters of interpersonal communication" (Genesee, 1987, p. 35).

From repeated administrations of standardized achievement tests, a clear pattern of results has emerged. In kindergarten through Grade 3, immersion students lag behind their peers in the regular English program in some aspects of English language skills. In Grade 1, for example, in studies conducted in Ottawa and Toronto, immersion students' scores are lower on tests of word knowledge, word discrimination, and reading. This pattern of results persists through Grades 2 and 3, where immersion students also fail to score as well as their regular program counterparts in more technical skills such as spelling, capitalization, and punctuation (e.g., Barik & Swain, 1975; Barik & Swain, 1976; Polich, 1974; Swain & Barik, 1976).

Such findings are not surprising, since no formal English language instruction is provided before Grade 2 or 3. In spite of this, when a linguistic analysis was undertaken of stories written by Grade 3 immersion and non-immersion students, it was found that their abilities in spelling, punctuation, capitalization, and vocabulary use were comparable. Additionally, the immersion students used proportionately more complex and compound-complex sentences than their unilingual counterparts (Swain, 1975).

By the end of Grade 5, immersion children perform as well as or better than their English-educated peers on all aspects of English language skills measured by standardized tests (see, for example, Barik & Swain, 1978). From Grade 5 on, in almost all instances where there have been significant differences between immersion and comparison students, immersion students have outperformed their comparison groups in such areas as punctuation, spelling, vocabulary, and grammatical usage (see, for example, Swain, Lapkin, & Andrew, 1981).

It has been suggested that the advantages in English demonstrated by early immersion students in the middle and upper elementary grades may in part be due to their knowledge of two language systems, a knowledge which permits them to compare and contrast French and English, thus leading to a heightened overall linguistic awareness. Lambert and Tucker (1972) suggested that the French immersion experience encourages students to engage in "incipient contrastive linguistics," which has positive effects on skills in English and helps students both "to build vocabulary and to comprehend complex linguistic functions" (p. 208). Vygotsky (1934/1962) hypothesized that learning a second language in childhood "facilitates mastering the higher forms of the native language. The child learns to see his language as one particular system among many, to view its phenomena under more general categories, and this leads to an awareness of his linguistic operations" (p. 110). As well as leading to a greater sensitivity to the grammatical system, this leads to a greater ability to separate form and meaning in language use.

Studies conducted in contexts other than immersion that support these hypotheses have been reviewed elsewhere in this volume (Hamers, Reynolds) and, indeed, Reynolds has discussed what some of the cognitive underpinnings of these phenomena might be. In the context of immersion education, one recent study is of particular interest.

The study, undertaken by Harley, Hart, and Lapkin (1986), sought to identify specifically those first language skills of immersion students where performance was enhanced by their bilingualism. The study involved two phases. First, existing data from the annual evaluations of a Toronto and an Ottawa immersion program were analyzed longitudinally— Grades 1 through 6.[2] Second, based on the findings of the longitudinal study, specific tasks where superior performance of immersion students had been indicated relative to English-educated peers were developed and administered to groups of Grade 6 students.

In the longitudinal study, it was possible to examine the issue of degree of bilingualism. Cummins (1979), building on the notions of additive and subtractive bilingualism, has proposed that there are minimal or threshold levels of competence in each language: lower ones which are sufficient to avoid any negative cognitive effects, and higher ones which may be necessary for positive effects to accrue. By observing first language performance at different levels of second language proficiency, it is possible to determine whether the impact of bilingualism on first language skills is dependent on the degree of second language proficiency.

The students whose performance was studied longitudinally were selected from the sample of students tested in the cross-sectional studies mentioned earlier that were carried out in Toronto and Ottawa. The immersion and regular program students were individually matched as closely as possible for the entry-level characteristics of cohort, school board, individual school, sex, age, and IQ.

The longitudinal results indicate that, beginning in Grade 3, there are scattered differences (that reach statistical significance) in reading and punctuation that favour the immersion students. Although not statistically

---

[2] See Swain and Lapkin (1982) for a listing of the published reports of the annual evaluations undertaken by Swain and her colleagues at OISE.

significant, there is also a consistent pattern of all mean scores from Grade 3 on— for vocabulary knowledge, reading, punctuation, and grammar— to be higher for immersion students relative to their unilingual English counterparts. The tests (subtests of the *CTBS*) measure vocabulary knowledge which involves the selection of a synonym to match a stimulus vocabulary item, reading comprehension which involves reading short passages and answering multiple-choice questions based on them, the identification of incorrect punctuation, and the identification of grammatical errors in sentences.

Given the threshold hypothesis, it was expected that those immersion students who scored relatively well in French would be more likely to manifest enhancement in English skills relative to their matched pairs in the regular English program than were those whose French scores were lower. Thus, the sample of immersion students was divided into a high French group and a low French group based on a test of French achievement (*Test de rendement en français: 3 [e]*) given at Grade 3. The high French achievement group and the low French achievement group did not differ in IQ in Grade 1.

The results indicate that the high French proficiency group did not lag behind the matched English-schooled children in measured English skills (*Metropolitan Achievement Test*) in Grade 1. In Grades 2 and 3 both the upper and lower French proficiency groups were at par with their matched counterparts. In Grades 4 to 6 there was a general, but nonsignificant tendency for immersion students in both the upper and lower French proficiency groups to score better in English than their counterparts in the regular English program— in 16 out of 18 test results for the upper French proficiency group and in 15 out of 18 test results for the lower French proficiency group.

In Grades 4 to 6 the results indicate a trend for the high French achievement group to show enhancement in English language skills (as measured by the *CTBS*) relative to their matched pairs *earlier* than the low French achievement group. That is, for the high French group there were significant (vocabulary [Grade 4], reference skills [Grade 6]) and near-significant (punctuation [Grade 4], vocabulary [Grade 5], punctuation [Grade 6]) results in their favour in Grades 4, 5, and 6, whereas for the low French group, such results first appeared in Grade 5 (significant only for reference skills) and were mainly found in Grade 6 (nearly significant for reading, punctuation, and usage).

Based on the results of the longitudinal study— including detailed item analyses— several specific hypotheses were formulated for testing cross-sectionally at the Grade 6 level. The hypotheses with respect to vocabulary knowledge were that immersion students would show greater vocabulary knowledge in English where there exists a French cognate, and would overall show a generally greater lexical range than regular program students. In the area of grammar, it was hypothesized that immersion students would show greater sensitivity to number marking and other grammatical forms such as double negatives, past tense forms, and erroneous pronoun usage than unilingual English students.

On the one hand, the hypotheses with respect to vocabulary were not confirmed. No special advantage in lexical range or in knowledge of words with French cognates was shown by the immersion students. Perhaps, as the authors suggested, explicit instruction that draws attention to cognate relationships between French and English is needed.

On the other hand, the hypotheses with respect to grammatical usage were confirmed. It is interesting that it is in the area of grammatical form rather than lexical meaning where immersion students' performance is significantly better than that of the unilingual students. Other studies (see Hamers, this volume) have also indicated an association between bilingualism and a superior ability to make grammatical judgments in the first language. Perhaps this is because of the salience of grammatical contrasts relative to meaning contrasts in natural language use. Whereas there are major overlaps in meaning systems, this is much less the case for at least the surface manifestations of grammatical systems. It is certainly an issue that deserves further investigation.

To summarize to this point, results of numerous studies show a tendency toward enhanced first language skills among immersion students — beginning at around Grade 3 — relative to English unilingual children. Longitudinal data examined suggest that the enhancement of first language skills is possibly related to the attainment of a threshold level of L_2 proficiency. The results, although suggestive, are not yet powerful enough to argue that the direction of causality is from L_2 to L_1. They do, however, support the notion of an underlying interdependence between a bilingual's two languages (Cummins, 1979), whereby (cognitive academic) language proficiency in one language supports that in other languages. Specific tasks developed to reveal expected differences between English-French bilingual children and English-only children suggest that first language advantages may lie more in grammatical rather than semantic knowledge.

FRENCH LANGUAGE PERFORMANCE

Considering the issue of additive bilingualism then, the data suggest that these majority language children whose first language is strongly reinforced by their environment — that is, where their first language is used in most out-of-school contexts, as well as in-school contexts (as a language of the *school* in the primary grades and as a language of instruction in the *classroom* from Grades 2 or 3 onwards) — and where a threshold level of performance has been achieved in their second language, there is a tendency for first language performance to be enhanced. There appears, thus, to be a reciprocal interaction between firmly established first language skills and threshold levels of second language performance which engender further development of first language knowledge, particularly within the grammatical domain.

However, among minority language children, the development and maintenance of the first language is often at risk due to psychological and societal pressure to develop L_2 skills with little or no institutional support provided for L_1 skills. When L_1 is used, taught, and valued in an educational setting, numerous studies have demonstrated that second language learning and academic achievement have been enhanced (e.g., Cummins, 1981; Genesee, 1987; Hakuta, 1986; Krashen & Biber, 1988; Rosier & Farella, 1976; Troike, 1978; Willig, 1985).

For minority students in immersion programs, French is typically their third language. They may have acquired English, their L_2, at home from their siblings, on the street from their friends, and/or at school. How do these children fare in an immersion program? To what extent does their first language proficiency— including literacy— contribute to their success in immersion? There are, to our knowledge, only two studies which address these questions in the context of French immersion programs.

Both studies (Bild & Swain, 1989; Swain, Lapkin, Rowen & Hart, in press) involve minority (heritage) language children in a mid-immersion program in Toronto. In the mid-immersion program, students study in English through to Grade 4. During that time they take French as a second language for twenty minutes a day as part of their regular program. In Grade 5, they begin a program in which half of their instructional day is in French and half is in English. Throughout their schooling, minority language children have the option of participating in a Heritage Language Program. These are classes which instruct students in and about their native language and culture, and are offered outside of school hours for a half hour each day, or two and a half hours on Saturday mornings.

In the first study (Bild & Swain, 1989), we sought to determine how well minority language children in this mid-immersion program learned French relative to children whose first language was English. There were three groups of immersion students: a Grade 8 English-background group and two Grade 8 minority language background groups. One minority language group consisted of students whose first language was Italian. The second group was a heterogeneous group of non-Romance language speakers: 1 Armenian, 6 Croatians, 1 Czechoslovakian, 1 German, 1 Greek, 1 Polish, 3 Slovenians, and 1 Ukrainian. There were two hypotheses. First, due to the historical linguistic connection among Romance languages, it was anticipated that the Italian speakers would, through positive linguistic transfer, perform better on measures of French proficiency than the non-Romance language speakers. Second, as the interdependence hypothesis would predict, learning a third language should be facilitated from other language learning, particularly with respect to literacy-related skills.

Students were selected on the basis of background information obtained from their teachers, school records, and a questionnaire which asked for information concerning language use patterns, own and parents' birthplaces, and parents' languages, level of education, and occupation. From the questionnaire it was determined that the home language use patterns of the minority language children involved the use of the minority language between the parents, between the student and at least one parent (often both), often between the student and grandparents, and only rarely between the student and siblings. According to self-ratings of written proficiency in the minority language, the non-Romance group rated themselves significantly higher than did the Italian group. Additionally, the Italian group had a significantly lower mean parental occupation score than did the English group.

Four different measures of French proficiency were used: 2 story retelling tasks and 2 cloze tasks. Scores for the story retelling task were calculated for such features as verb, prepositional, and syntactic accuracy, lexical diversity and lexical uniqueness, accent, fluency, and discourse and strategic performance.

The results indicate that the two groups of minority language students were significantly better than the English group on the French cloze tests and on most of the oral measures. This was the case in spite of the lower SES (as indicated by parental occupation) of the Italian group. Interestingly, the minority groups were superior on all grammatical measures but not on measures of lexical uniqueness and lexical diversity. Thus, once again, bilinguals show superior performance in the area of grammatical knowledge but not in lexical knowledge— in this case demonstrated in their learning of a third language.

The results also indicate that the Italian group consistently performed better than the non-Romance group. However, no statistically significant differences were noted. As seen in the next study, literacy knowledge in the minority language appears to be a significant factor in French language performance. Thus, it may be that the higher minority language written proficiency (as indicated by self-ratings) of the non-Romance group relative to the Italian group has compensated for the greater "language distance" between their home and target languages. A significant positive correlation (found in the current study) between the number of years in heritage language classes and French proficiency, supports this conjecture.

The second study (Swain et al., in press) was carried out in the context of a much larger study (Hart, Lapkin, & Swain, 1987), the intent of which was to compare the French performance of Toronto early and mid-immersion students and to study the characteristics of the students who entered each type of program. We would like to have examined the French performance of minority students in the early immersion program relative to non-minority language students, but there were simply not enough minority language students in the early immersion sample to warrant such a study. However, in the Board of Education which housed the mid-immersion program, there were a large number of minority students enrolled in the program and therefore we were able to compare their performance in French relative to majority language students in the same program. In all, data were collected from 16 Grade 8 bilingual classes.

Our questions concerning minority language students' French performance relative to non-minority language students' (i.e., English background) performance were threefold. First, we wanted to determine if the findings of the previous study were replicable— specifically whether minority language students' French proficiency would be superior to that of English background students, and whether Romance and non-Romance students' performance would be similar. Second, we wished to explore the role of literacy in the minority language on third (i.e., French) language proficiency. Is there an additional impact that minority language literacy has above and beyond that provided by its oral use? And third, if there is a particular advantage in third language learning associated with first language literacy, could it be that SES is the critical variable rather than literacy per se? The relationship between SES and literacy in the minority language was therefore examined to be able to exclude SES as a confounding variable.

The set of French assessment instruments included a sentence repetition task, a listening comprehension test utilizing authentic passages from the radio, a cloze test, the writing of an opinion essay, and discussion about a controversial but personal topic (parental strictness). The instruments, therefore, involved reading, writing, speaking, and listening.

Listening comprehension scores were based on both the comprehension test (multiple-choice) and the extent to which sentences were repeated in the sentence repetition task, thus indicating an understanding of what had been said, even if a precise repetition had not been given. For speaking, the discussion was scored for fluency, and the sentence repetition task was scored for various grammatical and discourse features. The opinion essay was scored for number of words written, nonhomophonous grammatical errors (that is, errors which would sound incorrect if spoken), and a global judgement of "good" writing involving two dimensions: complexity of sentence structure and phrasing, and incidence of spelling, grammatical, and syntactic errors. Reading ability was assessed by the cloze score. Unfortunately, no measure of vocabulary knowledge was obtained.

Students were asked a number of questions (via a questionnaire) to determine minority language use patterns. To obtain categories that would indicate literacy knowledge in the minority language, information from several questions was combined. The questions asked students to list what languages, not counting English and French, they understand in written and spoken form and to indicate the main ways in which they use these languages (e.g., speaking to parents, writing to relatives, watching TV, reading letters or newspapers). Using this information, four categories were derived: 1) no minority language; 2) has a minority language but is unable to understand the written form of it; 3) understands the minority language in the written form but does not indicate any use of it; and 4) understands and uses the minority language in the written mode.

The results are striking. First, those students who do not have a minority language and those who do have a minority language but claim not to read or write in it are similar in their French test results; however, those students who read and/or write in their minority language *whether they claim to be currently making use of these skills* are similar in their French test results. Second, with one exception, the literate minority language groups significantly outperform the English background group and the nonliterate minority language group on all measures of French language performance. The one exception is with respect to nonhomophonous grammatical errors where no significant differences were found. In other words, having a minority language in which one can or cannot engage in literacy activities appears to make no difference to the number of nonhomophonous grammatical errors the students make while writing in French. Why this finding should be unique to this measure is not at all clear.

In short, it appears that minority language literacy has a generalized positive effect on third language learning; that is, its positive impact is not limited to literacy-related activities in the third language. The results suggest that the effect is related to literacy knowledge rather than oral proficiency in the minority language.

One issue in interpreting these findings is whether the results could be due simply to a general high level of proficiency in the minority language, or whether they are specifically due to the impact of minority language literacy. In order to tease apart general minority language proficiency and minority language literacy, we examined test scores as a function of frequency of use of the minority language and literate versus nonliterate background. Doing so involved making the assumption that students who report frequent use of the minority language in the home are proficient in that language. Specifically, we looked to see if, among those who reported their minority language to be frequently used in the home, there was a tendency for those who are also literate in their minority language to do better on test measures relative to those who are not literate. The results significantly favour the literate group.

Thus, it appears that minority language literacy has an enhancing effect on third language learning *independent of overall general minority language proficiency*.

Another issue in interpreting the above findings is a possible confounding of SES with literacy. If SES and literacy in the minority language are associated, then the higher French scores observed may be due to factors associated with social and economic class rather than literacy per se. The SES variables examined were father's educational level, mother's educational level, father's occupation, and mother's occupation. The results show that students who are literate in their minority language are at least as likely to come from the lower categories of the SES variables as from the higher. That is, with respect to the educational attainment of fathers, those children who are literate in their minority language are at least as likely to come from families where the father has had only elementary school or some high school (approximately 32% of our sample) as they are to come from families where the father has completed a university, graduate, or professional degree (approximately 27%).

Similarly, with respect to the father's occupation, those children who are literate in their minority language are at least as likely to come from families where the father is a semiskilled or unskilled worker (approximately 33%) as they are to come from families where the father is a manager or a professional (approximately 19%).[3] Thus, among students who have a minority language, differences in third language proficiency associated with minority language literacy do not appear to be due to SES.

The final question that this study addressed was whether students speaking a Romance language would outperform their non-Romance peers in French. For this purpose, students were divided into two groups: a Romance group including students who reported using Italian, Spanish, or Portuguese, and a non-Romance group including students who reported using German, Polish, Hebrew, Filipino/Tagalog, Chinese, Greek, or Korean. As with the previous study, we found a trend for Romance background students to do better on the French measures than the non-Romance background students, but the differences were statistically significant on only two measures: fluency and global comprehension.

Taken together, these two studies show an enhanced proficiency in French among minority language students who read and/or write in their first language. This was suggested in the first study by a significant correlation between years in a Heritage Language Program (in which literacy skills are usually taught) and French performance. In the second study, the link between being literate in one's first language— as opposed to just having

---

[3] The pattern is similar as concerns mothers' educational attainment and occupation.

oral/aural skills in that language — and enhanced third language learning is quite clear. Moreover, the link does not appear to depend on generally high levels of oral/aural first language proficiency, SES, or the linguistic/historical relationship between the two languages.

ADDITIVE BILINGUALISM AND IMMERSION EDUCATION

In the first part of this chapter, it was suggested that early French immersion education resulted in enhanced first language skills, possibly following the attainment of a threshold level in L_2. In the second part of this chapter, it was suggested that first language skills, which include literacy knowledge, enhance the attainment of L_3 skills among minority language students. It might therefore be expected that the consequence for minority language children literate in their first language would be further enhancement of their first language skills. We know of no study which has examined this third link. Clearly, such studies are needed in the context of French immersion education.

Even without such studies, however, it can be concluded that French immersion education is "additive" in two ways. First, for majority language children, not only does it add a second language but it appears to have the potential of enhancing their first language. Second, for minority language children who have maintained their first language and supported it with literacy knowledge, superior third language performance can be expected relative to anglophones, or other minority language children who do not read or write in their minority language.

The pattern of results does not argue strongly for a unidirectional causal link from L_1 to L_2, from L_2 to L_1, or indeed from L_1 to L_3, in the case of minority language students. Rather, it suggests the possibility of a positive reciprocal interaction between bilinguals' developing language competencies. Whether the nature of the reciprocity will be found in the concept of a common underlying, interdependent proficiency is not clear. What is clear is that the nature of the reciprocity, and the psychological and societal conditions which foster it, deserve further attention.

ACKNOWLEDGEMENTS

We would like to thank Fred Genesee, Allan Reynolds, and Dick Tucker for their thoughtful and insightful comments on an earlier draft of this chapter.

REFERENCES

Barik, H. C., & Swain, M. (1975). Three-year evaluation of a large scale early grade French immersion program: The Ottawa study. *Language Learning, 25,* 1-30.

Barik, H. C., & Swain, M. (1976). Primary-grade French immersion in a unilingual English-Canadian setting: The Toronto study through grade 2. *Canadian Journal of Education, 1,* 39-58.

Barik, H. C., & Swain, M. (1978). Evaluation of a French immersion program: The Ottawa study through grade five. *Canadian Journal of Behavioural Science, 10,* 192-201.

Bild, E-R., & Swain, M. (1989). Minority language students in a French immersion programme: Their French proficiency. *Journal of Multilingual and Multicultural Development, 10*(3), 255-274.

Cummins, J. (1979). Linguistic interdependence and the educational development of bilingual children. *Review of Educational Research, 49,* 222-251.

Cummins, J. (1981). The role of primary language development in promoting educational success for language minority students. In *Schooling and language minority students: A theoretical framework.* Los Angeles: California State Department of Education, Evaluation, Dissemination and Assessment Center.

Cummins, J., & Swain, M. (1986). *Bilingualism in education.* London: Longman.

Genesee, F. (1987). *Learning through two languages: Studies of immersion and bilingual education.* Cambridge, MA: Newbury House.

Genesee, F., Tucker, G. R., & Lambert, W. E. (1975). Communication skills of bilingual children. *Child Development, 46,* 1010-1014.

Hakuta, K. (1986). *The mirror of language: The debate on bilingualism.* New York: Basic Books.

Harley, B., Hart, D., & Lapkin, S. (1986). The effects of early bilingual schooling on first language skills. *Applied Psycholinguistics, 7,* 295-322.

Hart, D., Lapkin, S., & Swain, M. (1987). *Early and middle French immersion programs: Linguistic outcomes and social character.* Toronto: Metropolitan Toronto School Board.

Krashen, S., & Biber, D. (1988). *On course: Bilingual education's success in California.* Sacramento: California Association for Bilingual Education.

Lambert, W. E. (1975). Culture and language as factors in learning and education. In A. Wolfgang (Ed.), *Education of immigrant students.* Toronto: Ontario Institute for Studies in Education.

Lambert, W. E. (1977). The effects of bilingualism on the individual: Cognitive and sociocultural consequences. In P. A. Hornby (Ed.), *Bilingualism: Psychological, social, and educational implications.* New York: Academic Press.

Lambert, W. E., & Tucker, G. R. (1972). *The bilingual education of children: The St. Lambert experiment.* Rowley, MA: Newbury House.

Polich, E. (1974). *Report on the evaluation of the lower elementary French immersion program through grade 3.* Montreal: Protestant School Board of Greater Montreal.

Rosier, P., & Farella, M. (1976). Bilingual education at Rock Point — Some early results. *TESOL Quarterly, 10*(4), 379-388.

Swain, M. (1975). Writing skills of grade three French immersion pupils. *Working Papers on Bilingualism, 7,* 1-38.

Swain, M., & Barik, H. C. (1976). A large scale program in French immersion: The Ottawa study through grade three. *ITL: A Review of Applied Linguistics, 33,* 1-25.

Swain, M., & Lapkin, S. (1982). *Evaluating bilingual education: A Canadian case study.* Clevedon, Avon: Multilingual Matters.

Swain, M., Lapkin, S., & Andrew, C. M. (1981). Early French immersion later on. *Journal of Multilingual and Multicultural Development, 2,* 1-23.

Swain, M., Lapkin, S., Rowen, N., & Hart, D. (in press). The role of mother tongue literacy in third language learning. In S. P. Norris & L. M. Phillips (Eds.), *Foundations of literacy policy in Canada.* Calgary, Alberta: Detselig Enterprises.

Troike, R. C. (1978). *Research evidence for the effectiveness of bilingual education.* Arlington, VA: National Clearinghouse for Bilingual Education.

Vygotsky, L. S. (1962). *Thought and language* (E. Hanfmann & G. Vakar, Eds. and Trans.). Cambridge, MA: MIT Press. (Original work published 1934)

Willig, A. C. (1985). A meta-analysis of selected studies on the effectiveness of bilingual education. *Review of Educational Research, 55,* 269-317.

11 "And Then Add Your Two Cents' Worth"

Wallace E. Lambert
McGill University

My assignment was to listen to, read carefully, and digest the preceding contributions and then to add my own "two cents' worth." That sounds easier than it turned out to be because there is a good deal to digest here, and I have a peculiar tendency to watch carefully how I spend my pennies. Furthermore, I have to comment on the brain work of 13 very talented people whose current work tests the limits of any reader's cognitive system, not to mention the digestive. However, these contributors are all friends of mine, most of them former graduate or undergraduate (in the case of Geoff Hall) students. There are also two "grand-students": Don Taylor, who obtained his undergraduate and graduate degrees under the direction of Bob Gardner (who was "my" graduate student), and Fred Genesee, who completed his doctoral work with Dick Tucker (who was also "my" student). In fact, there is a "double grand-student/student" in the case of Al Reynolds who completed an undergraduate thesis with Al Paivio (also "my" student), his master's degree with Bob Gardner, and his doctoral work with me! Thus most of us are interconnected because of interlocking academic backgrounds and shared research interests. So what amazes me is the originality and individuality of each contribution in this book and the fascinating new directions each has taken in the study of one or more aspects of this rapidly developing research domain. I never anticipated such a development of the study of bilingualism and multiculturalism thirty-five years ago.

How can I best add my own two cents' worth? My decision was not to try to tease out recurrent themes in these separate contributions, although that could easily be done, nor to come to tentative summary-type conclusions

217

about where we now stand. That too could be done, but I view it all in motion, in process, no way near its ultimate stop points. In fact, I wonder about the unanticipated changes and alternative approaches there will be in this field three and half decades from now, changes that would amaze us all because we never thought about them in our time. Instead, I will protect the individuality of each chapter by reacting to each one as a separate entity as if it were a presentation in one of our old seminars at McGill. I'll play the role of the Prof and, you'll note, this will let me stretch out my pennies— two for each presentation.

JOSIANE F. HAMERS

Josiane Hamers focused her attention on the developmental nature of bilingualism. The choice of this frame of reference permitted her to encompass an extremely diversified number of basic issues in the field of bilingualism and to introduce the past and current work of an equally impressive number of research specialists. In fact, her review gives substance to a distinctive field that some of us older researchers really never envisaged. The power of her arguments is enhanced by the multi-cultural examples she brings to bear to document the validity/reliability of any number of issues emerging from the research. Her skill at documentation, so clearly displayed in both the French and the English versions of her work with Michel Blanc, have not at all limited her own work to that of a chronicler of other's research. Instead it has made her own research and that of her students that much richer and more influential.

As one of those involved in the early years when a number of these ideas were emerging, many of them at McGill, I am heartened and encouraged by what has gone on since then. For instance, it was easy for Liz Peal and me in the early 1960s to speculate about the psychological mechanisms that lead bilingual youngsters to outperform monolinguals on tests of cognitive power. The data we had turned up in the base study (Peal & Lambert, 1962) pointed to certain psychometric correlates of possible underlying mechanisms and there wasn't much in the previous literature to restrict our speculations. Vygotsky's brilliant thinking, however, took on a new meaning for us and gave us some direction in how we should theorize. Consequently, it is really exciting to follow Josiane's compilation of new, more searching speculations about the mechanisms that seem progressively more likely to exist, as cross-national replications of studies documenting a cognitive-linguistic advantage to bilingualism keep turning up. The examples of new hypotheses I have in mind are those of Norm Segalowitz (1977), of Bialystok and Ryan (1985a, 1985b) and of Hamers and Blanc (1989), which Josiane reviews.

Similarly, it was relatively easy back in the mid-1960s for Dick Tucker and me to speculate about contrasting forms of bilingualism, those we called "additive" and "subtractive." We had to reconcile the fact that English-Canadian youngsters could develop substantial bilingual skills through French immersion programs without detriment to their English language development, with the results of research on ethnolinguistic minority youngsters in all-English programs in the United States that suggested that many of them were going nowhere in either their L_2 or their L_1. What is significant in the current research is the elaboration and clarification of the additive/subtractive contrast. For example, there is recurring research evidence that language minority children need not only instructional time in L_1, but systematic reading and writing experiences in L_1 in order to transform a subtractive bilingual development into an additive one. Especially important are the studies of Landry and Allard (1987) and Blanc and Hamers (1987) and the schema they propose which combines the *macrologique* of sociology and the *micrologique* of psychology to account for additive/subtractive outcomes for a potentially bilingual child. This model suggests that the key variable is the nature of the child's individual network of linguistic contacts that permits him/her to develop competence in both L_1 and L_2 (or not) as well as socially positive (or negative) beliefs, attitudes, and values associated with the two languages. The social strength of the network both reflects and determines the ethnolinguistic *vitalité* (or weakness) of the social systems associated with L_1 and L_2, and it determines as well the beliefs and attitudes about both languages and the values attached to the child's ultimate competence in one or the other language, or both. In this sense, then, the additive or subtractive nature of the child's bilinguality is fixed. Landry and Allard argued that the affective or attitudinal dimension may have more priority than the cognitive dimension in determining the bilingual outcome for any child; the affective dimension may even control and determine the cognitive/competence dimension. The fact that these (and other) researchers are now able to put such ideas to empirical test in cross-national settings is what gives me hope for the future of this developing field of inquiry.

Finally, it was relatively easy back in the 1960s for Dick Tucker, Fred Genesee, John Macnamara, and me to speculate about the likely impact French immersion experiences would have on anglophone children in Quebec. There wasn't much background research to limit us, and although we had our fingers crossed about giving so much instructional time to French (the L_2) and thus so little to L_1, we slowly saw the possibility, as the early data came in, of youngsters attaining a functional bilingualism by the end of elementary school. Even though so much has transpired in immersion education since that time (see Genesee, 1987, and his chapter in this volume), all of us in it from the start still read the new studies with interest, surprise and, often, amazement.

Josiane's review of immersion provides some valuable new insights. But let me spend my two cents' worth on her statement that French immersion students in Canada don't come up to nativelike standards in spoken French. Why is it that they don't? (At my age, I have no university or political restraints on what I say!) First, a surprising number of anglophone youngsters in Montreal "graduate themselves" out of French immersion classes by enrolling in all-French schools before the end of elementary school. My guess is that this subgroup (and their families) are those most interested in capitalizing on the functional bilingualism which the immersion program opens up to them. Switching to all-French schools provides the peer contact and atmosphere to buttress speaking skills in the L_2. Recent McGill studies (Genesee, Holobow, Lambert, & Chartrand, 1989; Lambert, Holobow, Genesee, & Chartrand, 1990) show that for those who do make this switch, speaking skills in French can come up to nativelike standards with no detriment to English skills.

How about those who stay in regular immersion classes? My guess is that they feel that they have gone as far as they *need* to, or as far as they *want* to, in mastering French speech. Going any further might call for a closer identification with French Canadians than the anglo society is ready to make. In fact, one study (Cziko, Lambert, Sidoti, & Tucker, 1980) suggested that the francophone community wasn't that interested in having immersion Anglos fraternize with their children, especially at that time, when political leaders in Canada talked about French and English relations as a case of "two scorpions in a bottle." So why would anglophone youngsters in immersion programs become any more bilingual than they needed to be?

This line of thought suggests that we would be wise to test the real limits of the immersion experience in other, more "open" societies. We may have to explore further the switch to all-French schools as a valuable sequel to early immersion, especially if a major aim is to develop nativelike speaking skills for immersion students. But I figure that it would be equally valuable to explore the motivations of students (at least in the Canadian setting) *not* to go to nativelike "extremes" with a foreign or second language. Students are more alert to this possibility than one might imagine. I've heard them ask questions of the following sort: "Why should I have to master French if Franco-Canadians in Quebec don't seem to want to learn the basics of English? In Quebec it seems they want to outlaw English. So who wants to get too close to people like that?" They also seem to ask interpersonal questions as well as politically sensitive ones, such as: "Who's interested in 'passing' as a French person? Being too good in French would be confusing or even phoney. My goal is to master that language so that I can understand all that they say or write, and vice versa, but rather than confuse anyone, why not make it clear to everyone that I'm me, using their language comfortably and enjoyably?" This might be an interesting assignment for Josiane before our next seminar?

ROBERT C. GARDNER

Bob Gardner's chapter warmed another cockle of my heart because "only yesterday" we were sharing tea bags (one bag lasted at least a week) all hours of the day and night, not only in Montreal but also in Cambridge (where Bob was on a "pre-doc" with John Carroll) or Cornell (where I was a visiting professor), discussing and arguing about the "underlying factors" that determine foreign language achievement. We also had few restrictions on our speculations since the technical literature was not extensive. His experiences as a part-time worker on an AmerIndian reservation in western Canada gave us some leads: How come some native Canadians were mastering English and others were not, and how come few if any white Canadians ever bothered to learn indigenous languages? We also got ideas from John Carroll and George Ferguson on aptitudes for language learning and from Uriel Weinreich, Charlie Osgood, O. H. Mowrer, and especially Susan Ervin on the role of emotions in the development of bilingual skills. And both of us enjoyed psychometrics, especially factor analysis, as a methodology that helps one organize all sorts of speculations. Once we got rolling, we tested everything that moved: students in numerous high schools, as well as their parents and their teachers; students in McGill's intensive French summer school; college students, in the first matched-guise studies; and Franco-American families, from Maine to Louisiana. A memorable episode was of Bob and my wife, Janine (who helped with most of our early French testing), arguing furiously with the religious sister who directed one school, about the values of our work compared to the religious class we were cutting in on, and the reason why an extra fifteen minutes of testing time was absolutely essential!

The basic idea that got us going was straightforward: Learning a second or foreign language involves more than an ear or aptitude for languages. Attitudes towards the other group that uses the language should also play an essential role, as should the amount and type of motivation the learner brings to the task. Since that time, Gardner has explored this idea in a splendid research fashion, enlisting and training an outstanding group of student-scholars (like Richard Clément, Alain Desrochers, Richard Lalonde, Padric Smythe) to join in the effort. The research approach has been anything but straightforward, because even though the factor analytic data are clear and supportive, they nonetheless beg the chicken-egg question. The Gardner team first had to be certain about their claims of an important associational role played by attitudes and motivation in the learning process. This called for multiple replications across regional sites and age groups. The association is undeniably there. Furthermore, it is now very well established that the attitude-motivation cluster of variables (what Gardner calls the "integrative motive") is statistically independent of the aptitude-verbal intelligence cluster, with both clusters having important impacts on language learning/acquisition. But then the research had to make certain that basic attitudes and motivations played a *causal* role in achievement in L_2 over and above the changes in attitudes and motivation that derive from achieving mastery of the L_2. What is exemplary in the approach of the Gardner team is that they have squarely confronted the problem and, through careful experimentation, have moved on to more exacting associational methodologies, such as path analysis (LISREL), and then to pure experimental designs in order to establish the "construct validity" of the attitude-motivation cluster. This new development in the approach makes the research area itself a more exciting and challenging one, as their work on choice behavior, laboratory analogs, and retention/loss studies nicely illustrates. These new developments are extremely significant, theoretically, practically, and socially.

While waiting for new research to come from this second stage of this program of research, let me dwell a bit on the implications I see in the first stage. Be forewarned that now I may indulge my need to exaggerate a wee bit! Because attitudes and motivation are so involved with second/foreign language achievement, there are grounds to worry about the impact of Quebec's political ideology on Canadian immersion programs and on alternative modes of learning either French or English across the nation. What was said previously in the comments on the Hamers chapter holds here with even more intensity. The ideological polarization of Canada's major ethnolinguistic groups makes the learning of the other group's language, and learning about the other group itself, that much less attractive or interesting (see Lambert, 1988; Esman, 1987). Canada's "two solitudes" seem to be changing into "double alienation." The Gardner team may very likely uncover signs of such an alienation in their current work, making their future research all the more valuable and relevant.

There is, however, a happier connection I see to this line of research; the ideas of the Gardner team are very similar to the powerful ideas of Benjamin Bloom in his study entitled *Developing Talent in Young People* (1985). Consider the following quotation from Bloom:

> What any person in the world can learn, *almost* all persons can learn *if* provided with appropriate prior and current conditions of learning. This generalization does not appear to apply to the 2% or 3% of individuals who have severe emotional and physical difficulties that impair their learning. At the other

extreme, there are about 1% or 2% of individuals who appear to learn in such unusually capable ways that they *may* be exceptions to the theory. At this stage of the research, it applies most clearly to the middle 95% of a school population. (p. 4)

Bloom asked himself whether this conclusion would hold for other types of learning besides the academic. How about piano playing, sculpting, research mathematics, neurology, Olympic swimming, tennis at the championship level? If Bloom's theory holds in these domains as well, it runs totally counter to the theory of "natural gifts and aptitudes," the special stuff that some gifted or talented people are believed to have in their genes. Of course, it might satisfy more egos to think that the great ones in society have natural gifts because that would excuse all of us who don't end up great. But Bloom is convincing, in his careful study of the great ones, in his conclusion that talent (even extraordinary Olympic-level talent) is *developed,* not inborn. It seems not to be in the genes, but in the sweat and, behind the sweat, in the desire and help of various sorts of caretakers and tutors. This follows because the great ones in tennis, piano, mathematics, and so forth (the main data source in the Bloom study) are not spotted as gifted from the start; they *become* gifted if early on they are captivated with their specified field, dedicate themselves to it, have parents or friends who support the dedication by getting them in touch with tutors, who in time relay them on to better, more specialized tutors, until eventually talent *emerges*. If this thesis upsets small egos, it stimulates bigger egos because it opens the door for *all* persons to find a way to develop a talent or two.

The Gardner team has said the same thing, it seems to me, and perhaps, through politeness, they haven't stressed their idea sufficiently. They have fully documented the *independence* of the social-motivational cluster from the aptitude-intelligence cluster. More than that, they have discovered one of the routes by which attitudes affect motivation, which in turn affects achievement (i.e., the first expression of talent).

Gardner could also say it is not a case of having some special talent for languages, but rather that most, if not all, people can acquire a second or foreign language if the attitudes and motivations are optimized. And if this aspect of Gardner's theory holds for language learning, why wouldn't it hold, as Bloom suggests, for any form of talent development? The similarity in approaches here is striking. For instance, Gardner's studies show that when the attitudes and motivation are optimized, the effects are discernible in the interactions of learners and teachers in the classroom, and in the learner's persistence in studying the other language. This is perfectly parallel to Bloom's idea of tutors who patiently help, train, and relay upward to more advanced tutors, so as to develop the talent of learners, even to the point of making them champions.

FRED GENESEE

Two chapters in this book focus on foreign-language immersion education as a new, popular, and robust Canadian innovation which appears to serve the needs of certain ethnolinguistic groups in Canada, and which may prove equally useful in other national settings as well. In fact, a recent book by Anna Lietti (1989) in Switzerland describes how that nation is now suffering from an educational policy that might be called "parallel unilingualism" in that each canton permits education only in its language, thereby making Switzerland far less multilingual than it could or should be. Lietti, who spent a month with us in Quebec in 1989, argues persuasively that Switzerland, like most European nations (other than the Scandinavian countries) about to enter the 1993 European confederation, is in need of a program essentially like the Canadian immersion program, in order to *survive* in multilingual Europe.

No one could be better suited to write these two chapters than Fred Genesee, and Merrill Swain and Sharon Lapkin; they have been directing most of the recent research and developing the majority of the theory concerning the immersion issue, and all have maintained a common research interest, namely, the processes underlying first and second language development. Genesee has worked mainly within Quebec (especially in bicultural Montreal), while Swain and Lapkin have worked mainly in multicultural Toronto and in other centres in Canada.

Genesee started his chapter with a broad summary of immersion programs and the effects they have on children's language development, a summary that has special depth of background because of his recent book on immersion education (Genesee, 1987). In preparing his book, Fred asked Dick Tucker and me many questions about our research on the pioneering St. Lambert immersion studies, since we had been in on those programs from their start. For instance, he asked: "What was your theoretical bias back then? Did you anticipate such and such outcomes?" Fred was dismayed and surprised with our answers because Dick and I were very practical in our approach back then, and made up all sorts of theories only *after* the data were in! With my lack of preoccupation with theory-building, I am impressed with Genesee's integration of a variety of findings as I also am with the efforts of Jim Cummins (1981) and Steve Krashen (1981) when each of them turns to theorizing about immersion education.

Genesee lists three important "lessons" learned so far from research on immersion: 1) "integrating" second language learning with academic content instruction is the most efficient way to master a second language; 2) this integration works best in variations of immersion programs that promote *discourse*, particularly activity-oriented discourse based on students' interests; and 3) time can be wasted or it can be used profitably in integrated immersion programs and much more research is needed to find ways to eliminate wasted time. Each lesson has been learned in the course of years of research, much of it "product-type" research, that is, evaluation research on students' progress in learning to read, write, understand, and speak L2. Up to now, he argues, too little attention has been directed to "process-type" research, that is, studying what actually transpires in the course of teacher-pupil interactions in immersion classes. Clearly, research will eventually become concerned with both product and process because it is now evident that there is a need to generate valuable teacher-pupil discourse so as to optimize time spent in immersion classes.

Although this new direction of research is both necessary and valuable, I am not satisfied with a shift of emphasis merely to conventional forms of process research. There is, I believe, a "deeper" form of process that transpires in immersion programs, not only in the French immersion model in Canada, where parents of the socially dominant, majority anglophone group want their children to become bilingual in the language of a national ethnolinguistic minority group, but also in the United States, where families of linguistic minorities are given the chance to be immersed in their home languages, the heritage languages that are most likely to be neglected or "subtracted out" because of social pressures for assimilation. Genesee didn't have time or space to develop this idea so let me try (see also Lambert, 1989).

By "deeper" forms of processes, I mean more or less what Vygotsky (1934/1962) meant when he wrote:

> It seems to us that [this] phenomenon . . . has not yet received a sufficiently convincing psychological explanation, and this for two reasons: First, investigations have tended to focus on the contents of the phenomenon and to ignore the mental operations involved, i.e., *to study the product rather than the process* [italics added]; second, no adequate attempts have been made to view the phenomenon in the context of other bonds and relationships. (p. 71)

The phenomenon Vygotsky was referring to was the changes that transpire in the normal development of thought from infancy to young adulthood, a progression from thinking in "complexes," to the use of "pseudo-concepts" or "potential" concepts, and finally to the formation of "genuine concepts."

To study this process and to find a potential underlying mechanism led Vygotsky to experiment with children who varied on a continuum of developmental steps. Vygotsky was interested in how children of different ages performed (the product dimension) and how each child in each age group interacted with the experimenter, in terms of the details of what was said by each member of the dyad and what each member meant by what was said (the conventional process concern). More important, he was also interested in *the mental operations involved in each attempted solution of the problems presented*.

It is this last step in Vygotsky's overall approach that I see as a deeper form of process research, a form that is helpful for research in general and particularly for research on second language learning and immersion education. Sometimes the "mental operations" are clearly cognitive in nature; other times they are clearly social in nature. Standard process research can make us aware of what is going on in a classroom and it can help us be certain that the planned treatment offered to pupils in that classroom is or is not transpiring (the "treatment verification" function of process research referred to earlier). The more fundamental processes in foreign language learning, I would argue, are those that take place in students' minds and in the social systems students find themselves, rather than the processes transpiring in classrooms or in the teacher-student interactions. The only way I see to get at these more social-psychological processes is through a combined product-process orientation on the part of the researcher. But to get at the deeper levels— the mental processes— the researcher has to have some relevant theoretical ideas, even if only common-sense hunches, to orient the long-range plan of the research.

Let me illustrate what I mean through an example from Genesee's own research. By way of background: In Montreal, French and English school systems have been, and continue to be, separate; the administration is separate and the schools are in different sites and, consequently, students and staff are kept exclusively in their own linguistic and social worlds. There is, of course, a social-psychological counterpart to this separateness. Ailie Cleghorn and Fred Genesee (1984) were interested in what happens when French- and English-speaking teachers become members of a common teaching staff in English-language schools that have French immersion programs underway. Their hunch was that the social interactions of the two groups of teachers would likely reflect the social realities of distant, separate existences. Data were collected, using observational procedures, over a one-year period. Thus, an observer recorded relevant events in the schools— in classrooms, in principals' offices, and in teachers' rooms (especially at break times and lunch times). It was an unusual situation to have a sizable subgroup of French teachers working in otherwise all-English schools. At first, the English-speaking teachers showed normal amounts of politeness and welcome. In the common teachers' room, for example, small tables were arranged so as to accommodate all staff at lunch period, and initially suggestions were made that French might be made the language of communication from time to time (a type of "French table"), so that the English-speaking teachers could get some experience using French, at the same time (they reasoned) as the French teachers were being made to feel more at home. The Cleghorn and Genesee study is noteworthy because it chronicles, in the teacher-to-teacher contacts, the slow but sure emergence of a microcosm of the deep, longstanding, conflictual nature of English-French relations in the larger society. For instance, there was a gradual separation and segregation of social contacts, including the breaking up of the common table into separate tables, the use of separate burners on the common stove, as well as schedules for French and English usage of the stove. Finally, French teachers slowly switched to English (no matter how poorly they spoke it) for intergroup contacts; for generations, this had been the expected thing for French Canadians to do in the presence of anglophones.

To me, this informative study is a good example of a carefully documented, standard process-oriented study that was designed to go far beyond the structure and content of the interaction between teachers. Instead, the conventional process data were used to explore a fundamental social-context process involving society's impact on the school and on intergroup contacts that take place in the minds of those who had to function in this novel form of mixed-group setting. The impact of this deeper societal process on anglophone children's progress in French (e.g., their reluctance to initiate French conversations outside school and their expectation that francophones are the ones who are more likely to switch to the other group's language than are anglophones) is also evident in the product results of most of the immersion studies. What is more, the type of research interest evidenced by Cleghorn and Genesee's study falls neatly in line with the *macrologique* that Hamers and Blanc, and Landry and Allard, feel to be the next level of research in this area.

MERRILL SWAIN AND SHARON LAPKIN

Merrill Swain and Sharon Lapkin's chapter takes a fresh, new look at bilingualism by asking whether there are demonstrable advantages to being bilingual and, if so, what form they take. Merrill has had a long fascination with this issue. I recall visiting her years ago (too many to mention) in Quebec City where we both sat amazed watching preschoolers who had had "bilingualism as their first language" and who were tricked by Merrill into believing that only they could relay "important" messages from Merrill to another adult who couldn't talk in Merrill's language. It was evident to us that playing this language-mediator role was perfectly normal for them. It was something special to observe, and we were convinced that these youngsters were way ahead in life, clearly profiting from this dual language and dual culture expertise that they had developed so early in their lives.

Since then many of us have teased out various traces of this type of advantage that seems to be associated with being bilingual, contrasting cases of fully bilingual youngsters and adults with cases where the suppression or neglect of one of the two languages/cultures of a person seems to promote equally evident disadvantages, leading us to draw a general contrast between additive and subtractive forms of bilingual experience.

One of the new questions Merrill and Sharon ask in this chapter is whether the additive experience of French immersion students, after six years in the program, would reflect itself in improved competence in English, the students' mother tongue. Merrill and Sharon define "improvement" by comparing immersion students' performance with that of matched, nonimmersion, anglophone children. Drawing on various OISE research studies, they demonstrate a substantial improvement (i.e., advantage of immersion students over the controls) in the area of grammatical usage, that is, a greater sensitivity to number marking, double negatives, past tense forms, and in the use of pronouns in English, even though the immersion group had much less exposure to English in school, over the elementary years, than had the controls. They were not ahead of the controls, however, on cognizance of English words which have French cognates, apparently because the similarities between the words had not been brought to their attention in their education.

For me, the finding of increased grammatical abilities, embedded as it now is in various other supporting results, is important because it points to the possibility of getting "two for one" — that learning through L_2 appears to potentiate L_1 competencies. Furthermore, the finding suggests that immersion programs can be conducted without the need for L_2 specialists since the regular immersion teacher can focus on the teaching of academic content through L_2 with an assurance that it will get through to the students with no difficulty. The L_2 will be progressively developed as a by-product and even the L_1 will be simultaneously benefited in fundamental ways. This, then, becomes an example of "three for one," which will very likely incite further, more comprehensive probes into other repercussions on L_1 competence, and into the mysterious transfer process (from the L_2 instruction to L_1 competence) that must be occurring in the immersion situation.

The second half of the Swain and Lapkin chapter focuses on language minority students and the subtractive form of bilingualism they run the risk of experiencing, because each child in the minority groups had studied a home language other than English or French, and all were attending public schools in Toronto where their home language was not the language of instruction. This set of studies, however, demonstrates nicely how the potentially subtractive experience can be transformed into a clearly additive one. Since we have precious few examples of this type of transformation (see Lambert, 1981), these studies and their outcomes are extremely valuable to theoreticians, and they also are encouraging for anyone with a bias toward multiculturalism and heritage culture/language maintenance. The major outcomes are that, by providing immersion experiences in their L_1, language-minority families can help their children not only compete with anglophones in developing English language skills (L_2) and French skills (L_3), but they can even help them outperform anglophones in French competence. What has to be done, apparently, is to keep L_1 (the heritage language) alive and active at home and/or through Heritage Culture programs. However, the family and community have to push this to the point that the children also develop skills in *reading* and *writing* in L_1. Merely developing oral/aural skills, the findings indicate, is not enough. L_2 has also to be taught in the school, with reading and writing competence in mind, as well. Thus, when all three languages are brought to suprathreshold levels (Cummins, 1979, 1981), the mutually beneficial interplay is assured.

There are several noteworthy implications here. First, the need for specialized training or experience in one's L_1 is nicely illustrated in this work from OISE. I'm reminded of Vygotsky's insistence on "scientific" learning of one's own language in contrast to relying on untutored, "spontaneous" knowledge. Vygotsky argued that mastering a higher level of understanding through "scientific" instruction "raises the level" of spontaneous, untutored comprehension. "Once the child has achieved consciousness and control in one kind of concept through scientific instruction, all the previously formed concepts based on untutored comprehension are reconstructed accordingly" (Vygotsky, 1934/1962, p. 107). Perhaps this is one of the mental mechanisms that underlies literacy and its effect on cognitive competence.

Second, with this study we acquire important new data on the effects of L_1 maintenance on L_2 competencies (cf. Padilla & Long, 1969; Lambert, Giles, & Albert, 1976). More importantly, we discover the multidirectional effects of L_1 maintenance on L_2, L_3, and, in interaction, back onto L_1 itself. A special value of this line of research is that it relates to the typical experiences of many language minority groups in the world.

Third, these studies implicate the motivational zeal of parents and of the ethnic community at large. For instance, one might argue that parents who are motivated enough to have their children become literate in L_1 not only want to maintain their heritage culture/language, but they also want their children to develop similar skill levels in L_2 and L_3 in order that they can keep up with, or even outperform, children in the comparison groups. Thus, perhaps the outcomes of these studies hinge as much or more on a motivational factor as on a cognitive enrichment factor. Interpreted in one way or the other, however, the message to parents and to ethnic communities is the same; they apparently have to bring their children to a level of *literacy* competence in L_1 for the additive benefits of bilingualism or trilingualism to emerge.

HOWARD GILES AND NIKOLAS COUPLAND

Reading Howie Giles and Nikolas Coupland's chapter brought me instantly back to the late 1950s when Bob Gardner, Dick Hodgson, Sam Fillenbaum, and I were getting our "voices" study (now known as the "matched-guise" study) off the ground, with the help of Harry Triandis who was then at McGill. My reaction to the 1989 Giles and Coupland presentation was: "Look what has happened to our little baby!" The baby is still recognizable but she's *much* wiser and much older; in fact in Giles and Coupland's hands she's facing old age and death with dignity and rejuvenation. I was also swiftly brought back to the early 1970s when Howie first came to work at McGill and "eloped" with our daughter, Sylvie, to Madawaska, Maine, to make tapes for and set up a series of Franco-American matched-guise studies (e.g., Lambert et al., 1976).

In their chapter, Giles and Coupland describe the rapid maturation of the matched-guise technique (MGT) and the phases it has passed through, from the descriptive and empirical applications of the 1960s and 1970s to the theoretical and "process" model phase we are now in. The new phase was generated by the critiques and questions asked by socio- and anthropological-linguists, and by an enormously talented group of social psychologists, with Giles and Ellen Ryan as two who have clearly led the way. Not only are the new process models ingenious and interesting, they also have become one of the foundations of a field of study known as the "social psychology of language."

Giles and Coupland explain that researchers now view the MGT with a "discursive" perspective that directs attention simultaneously to a set of interlocking processes—the process of meaning generation, the construction of language attitudes, and the processes involved in the production of vocal stimuli. These models that search for processes stimulate new questions about the nature of "attitudes" as a basic construct in social psychology, and about the ways people interpret what is said and what is not said, what is meant and what is implied in natural and formalized discourse.

With these new developments, the baby has really come a long way. It has, so to speak, also come of age. Giles' current work on the age dimension and its presence in everyday communication is exciting. We all encounter the age factor in interpersonal relations even though we may not register it as such. One episode I've noticed several times recently has to do with automated bank cards, an innovation that can dehumanize the interpersonal transactions of clients and bank personnel, with older clients being left to wonder if the human contacts they have enjoyed in banks are on the way out. Here's the typical scenario, with the bank person saying, "Now let me run over it again to make sure you understand. You don't have to come into the bank at all. Just take your plastic card and put it in the machine outside, anytime, along with your private number— see you have it on this slip— and you can withdraw or deposit what you want. Of course, you *can* come in if you need to, and we'll do it the old way at the teller's window, if you want to." As Giles and Coupland explain, this politeness, this ideational and verbal simplification, this phoney warmth can irritate and anger the elderly who are made "instantly ancient." But one need not focus on the grey generation; just have a baby of your own when you are in your twenties and watch how old that child will soon make *you* feel! The social psychology of these language exchanges— where the "young's conceptions of the elderly's interpretive and cognitive competencies as well as the elderly's construals of their own capacities"— is a new arena into which Coupland, Giles, St. Clair, and colleagues are bringing a newer, more sophisticated version of the MGT. These are exciting and valuable new ventures for young and old alike.

DONALD M. TAYLOR

Don Taylor's chapter is a very carefully thought-through analysis of racial and cultural diversity and the attempts North Americans make to cope with this diversity. The importance of the chapter for me lies in Don's skill at entering a complex sociological and political science literature not normally digested by psychologists and coming out with a convincing argument that psychologists are not only equally competent in systematizing and explaining phenomena like assimilationism and multiculturalism, but they may actually be essential participants in these tasks.

Sociologists led the way in describing in detail how assimilation "works" in the United States. They argued (and apparently many still do argue) that the integration of ethnic minorities into the mainstream (immigrant newcomers as well as established social minorities, like blacks and Jews) was an inevitable process. It might take time and it might develop through stages, but the melting down of minorities would take place (or, as many argue, has taken place) except for some symbolic remnants of the original heritage cultures.

That durable American belief in the inevitability of the assimilation process runs parallel to the idea that the bilingualism of newcomers to America inevitably gives way to linguistic anglicization. In fact, research on the bilingualism issue seemed to be motivated by a desire to prove that bilingualism is a severe personal handicap to be avoided because the negative consequences that would follow would be much like those encountered by those who are slow in assimilating. Worries about early America having too much ethnic and linguistic diversity may have forced researchers to highlight the possibilities of creating a more unified new amalgam of Americans by means of the melting pot process. Whatever the reasons might have been, the hard sell of assimilation was evident even in the research of American social scientists.

Taylor traces this assimilation bias in the theories proposed by sociologists, economists, and political scientists, but he remains unconvinced by the evidence that it is as inevitable or as pervasive as is currently argued. He starts with the question: What motivates members of ethnic minority groups to maintain their heritage cultures and languages? Sometimes they are forced by the dominant groups to stay ethnic in order to find work and thus they find themselves stratified in ethnically lopsided occupations. Sometimes they voluntarily remain ethnic in order to get into risky, low payoff work, or even in respected crafts that become the special domains of particular ethnic workers. Sometimes they want to maintain an ethnic identity as a means of redress against perceived injustices in the past. If this form of maintenance is found effective, the group (e.g., French Canadians in our era) can profit from their ethnicity to gain political, linguistic, and economic control of a sector of a nation; they can also use brinkmanship so as to have their way or else threaten to unconfederate themselves through separation.

Taylor sees affirmative action as a democratic corrective in America that could satisfy the yearnings of ethnic, religious, and sexual minorities. Affirmative action is meant as a temporary solution to injustices and in time it should become unnecessary because, once successful, attention shifts from redressing injustices to rewarding people on the basis of personal merit only. Affirmative action, however, singles out groups and enhances the psychological value and significance of ethnicity and ethnic distinctiveness. This is so, Taylor argues, because membership in a receptive, cohesive cultural group comprised of others of "one's own kind" is often the best possible source of a sense of security about who one is and what value one has. Personal identity generated in this fashion is quite different from being coerced by a dominant group to remain ethnic in order to find certain types of work, or to use ethnicity to explain why one can't find work, or to puzzle over what being "American" really is in order to see how one might begin to shake off one's ethnic identity.

By linking heritage culture maintenance with the psychology of self-identity, Taylor skillfully wrestles the issue of assimilation versus multiculturalism out of the hands of sociologists, economists, and political scientists. Nonetheless, in doing so he challenges the field of social psychology to prove that it can explain ethnic conflict better than others have and do more to improve interethnic group relations.

Many questions come to mind in reading Taylor's chapter: Can one effectively and comfortably *double* one's cultural identity, that is, be both Italian and American? In our joint work (e.g., Lambert & Taylor, 1990), we argue that ethnic minorities in North America can do just that, that minority parents and their children can successfully juggle a heritage culture along with the culture(s) of the adopted land, that they can be "double breeds" rather than "half breeds," that they can have two cultures and two languages for the price of one. But much more research is needed to be sure of this alternative to assimilation. Another challenge for the psychologist who ventures into this domain is the question of blackness in America. As Taylor indicates, blacks have not been assimilated in North America, economically, politically, educationally, or occupationally. And yet they have a distinctive identity and one of the longest residence times in the U.S. and Canada, and their cultural values appear to be as similar to the mainstream norms and as American as anyone else's (Lambert & Taylor, 1990), as do their achievement motivations (e.g., Rosen, 1959). Maybe the trouble is that blacks have gone too far in trying to assimilate, keeping their values too close to American mainstream values, adopting too enthusiastically a peculiarly white Judeo-Christian form of religion, and "keeping their place" by accepting their fate as a minority in the world of work? Maybe they need to find and emphasize their heritage "roots" as African-Americans, and from that base develop a double identity? Thus, Taylor's chapter offers a number of new, powerful ideas for any social psychologist seriously interested in culture, language, and ethnicity.

G. RICHARD TUCKER

Dick Tucker's presentation forces us to change our thinking about bilingualism and multilingualism by taking us, through illustrative examples, to other important parts of the globe— to Nigeria, the Philippines, and China. By means of these setting contrasts, Tucker skillfully brings us back to our local North American concerns with a realization that we are in a position to promote beneficial programs of bilingual skill development with far fewer challenges or obstacles than are most other places in the world. He also makes us ask ourselves: If the effort to preserve languages and cultures is worthwhile in these other settings, why don't we North Americans have a similar appreciation? If bilingualism and its promotion is a natural experience to other peoples, why do we make it so problematic and troublesome?

Tucker's examples are well-chosen and, in a world view, not at all exceptions. In each case, the obstacles are enormous: Each site has numerous indigenous languages to accommodate, much less money than we have to devote to education or language-related research, and much less educational experimentation to draw on. However, in each of the examples, the appreciation and recognized value of *education* seems much higher than is the case in North America where, until recently, we seem to have either taken it for granted or considered it as a necessary routine. In places where education counts, Tucker explains that careful *language planning* (involving parents as well as specialists and policy makers) must be built into innovative programs of study wherein language development and academic content material are *integrated* to meet societal needs.

These needs are met differently in each of the illustrations because the overall plans and aims differ. In China, English is seen as important and it is taught early in schools as a "foreign language" and later more intensively in the form of "English for special purposes." In Nigeria since 1970, Yoruba, a common mother tongue, is used as the central instructional medium for the first six years, and maintained as part of a language arts program thereafter, while English is taught as a second language; this is an interesting switch from before 1970 when English was used as the main medium from Grade 4 on. In the Philippines, English is seen as an important access-to-the-world language and Pilipino as a national language (a delicate choice from among some 150 indigenous language alternatives) and, following a new plan adopted in 1974, both languages are used for primary and secondary education on the basis of "language by subject matter specificity."

The noteworthy issues embedded in these illustrations are: 1) much thought and community-wide collaboration goes into the language plans generated in each site; 2) an appreciation of bilinguality for all citizens is fundamental, including a consideration given to local languages and their maintenance, coupled with a recognition of the usefulness of a world language like English; 3) home language competence is a necessary requirement for the success of second language usage programs; and 4) care is taken to empirically evaluate and test the efficacy of language plans, often with the assistance of specialists from more developed nations. The contrast with developed nations is striking. In the United States, for instance, social movements such as "English Only" or "U.S. English" are prominent in the media, the voting booths, and in people's thinking, and these movements, supposedly in the service of helping language minorities assimilate, make "bilingual" programs of any sort suspect and even dangerous. Just recently, residents of Lowell, Massachusetts, an old textile mill and factory city that has been home to waves of immigrants, decided collectively that the 40% of their residents who are Southeast Asian or Hispanic are such a menace that a vote was taken to make English the city's official language! Residents rationalized this vote as a means of "uniting people" (*E pluribus unum!*). That sort of bunker mentality is a prime example of protective, negative language "planning." Thank goodness there are other positions on this issue in the United States, for example, the fast-growing association called Advocates for Language Learning, a sister organization of a confederation of anglophone parents in Canada called Canadian Parents for French. The main point, however, is that there are few comparable examples of language *planning* in American communities, planning that involves parents, educators, and researchers, that encourages all residents, whether members of language minorities or majorities, to take part in the development of a multifaceted bilingual citizenry. The fact that English is the valued second language in each of Tucker's illustrations suggests that anglophones have been lulled into a belief that English is all anyone needs nowadays. Perhaps we should learn from nations like Japan which, as it surpasses us in industrial productivity, recognizes that English is certainly one of the valuable languages for its citizens in this time period of history, but in no way has Japan jeopardized the bilingual or multilingual development of its citizens by neglecting Japanese languages.

Thus, Dick Tucker's chapter suggests that other nations in the world, including the less developed nations, will teach us a thing or two about bilingualism and multiculturalism. Fortunately there are people like Tucker who are perfectly comfortable working and associating abroad and who are gifted enough to see common, critical themes in widely diversified cultural settings, themes that we may be able to apply at home. Of course, part of Tucker's training and experience came from his involvement in the Canadian immersion programs where, from the start, a lucky combination of factors coincided: 1) community-wide planning (including a research component); 2) a belief in the value of bilingualism and biculturalism; and 3) a tiny group of involved parents. Perhaps Tucker can find the way to make such combinations turn up more often.

ALLAN PAIVIO

Two chapters in this book, those by Allan Paivio, and Jyotsna Vaid and Geoff Hall, take us away from the social worlds of the bilingual and into the bilingual person's mind. One chapter (Vaid and Hall's) very skillfully follows the reductionist path that leads to the neuropsychology of bilingual cognitive processes, and the other (Paivio's) almost purposely stays away from neurology and instead constructs and develops an ingenious new perspective on cognition and language (monolingual or bilingual) he and his colleagues have derived from an impressive body of meticulously designed experiments. One reckless inference I draw from these chapters is that neuroscience models don't seem advanced enough yet to help Vaid and Hall when they run into difficulties in their searchings, whereas Paivio has accumulated enough information and brought it along in such coherent packages that his empirical models of cognition and its effects on processing can very likely be of enormous help to any neuroscientist who might become seriously interested in language and bilingualism. Let's consider Paivio first, and then Vaid and Hall, to explain why I make this inference.

First, a personal note. The conceptualization and development of the dual coding theory is a source of great joy and pride for many of us at McGill. I remember Al, my first PhD student, in the late 1950s as he was changing careers and making up the basic psychology courses he needed for graduate studies. At that time, we collaborated on research on language and memory and began speculating about "conceptual hooks" (like nouns) on which qualifiers (like adjectives) could be hung (see Lambert & Paivio, 1956); both of us at the time were caught up in the power of Don Hebb's views of the mind. Then I recall reminiscing in the early 1980s with Don Hebb who mentioned how appreciative he was of Paivio's line of theorizing and the ever-expanding empirical backups he had developed. Then in the mid-1980s I met Al in Paris, where he was invited to lecture for a spell to staff at the CNRS (a group of advanced scholars in Paris), who were greatly influenced by this new Canadian line of work and thought.

In a nutshell, dual coding theory deals with cognitive systems that have symbolic or representational functions, and Paivio (1986) views these systems as hierarchically organized, but branching into verbal and nonverbal subsystems. The world of words (spoken, heard, or thought about) is subserved by the verbal subsystem while the world of images (generated by the self or relayed from others) is subserved by a separate, although interconnected, subsystem. We're talking about functionally distinct or separate systems here that appear to be "naturally" connected in the sense that humans can employ words to stimulate images just as easily as they can talk about mental images and describe them in words. The connections will be stronger when concrete events or things are referred to because the overlaps of verbal and imaginal representations are more direct in the concrete (word or image) case than the abstract case. Paivio and colleagues have filled in many of the details of how and when the verbal and imaginal systems are differentially brought into play in various forms of cognitive activities. They have also demonstrated the relative power of one system over the other when one shifts from the concrete to the abstract or vice versa. What strikes me is the convincingness of Paivio et al.'s empirical descriptions of these two systems and how they interact in everyday cognitions or in very sophisticated cognitions.

As the theory develops, no reliance is shown on the possible neurological underpinning of these empirically defined systems; rather they are shown to be empirically distinct systems. Don Hebb would approve, I'm sure, because of this next idea: There is a very attractive problem for neuroscientists in all this because they might like *to go find* these systems, or at least signs of their existence, in the nervous system. The parallel that comes to mind is the fascinating current research of Joseph Le Doux and colleagues (e.g., Le Doux, Iwata, Cicchetti, & Reis, 1988) who have recently teased apart in the "central circuitry" two separate systems— one cognitive in nature, the other emotional— that are interconnected when, for example, an animal has to learn a maze trick with the fear of footshock which is classically conditioned. What Le Doux et al. have found are cerebral areas of overlap of the two systems in the central amygdaloid nucleus (ACE) and quite distinct, separate projection targets of the ACE— the lateral hypothalamic area, the midbrain central gray region, and the red nucleus of the stria terminalis! Le Doux demonstrates the distinctiveness of the two systems by microinjections of acid that destroy one projection target or the other; the animals involved demonstrate appropriate responding— in one case, forgetting what was learned but still displaying fear, and in the other case, displaying what was learned but not showing fear. For those with a flair for reductionism, there is a beauty in these outcomes, and they will likely prompt experimental psychologists to explore in more detail how cognition and emotion actually function in behavior. What Paivio's work does is give the empirical details of how his two systems function, and the evidence has now become convincing enough to prompt reductionists to search out the neurophysiological accompaniments of these functionings. This, I find, is just as beautiful an alternative as Le Doux's.

When Paivio and Desrochers (1980) extended the dual system to the bilingual case, things got doubly interesting because we learned more about the development of dual coding theory at the same time as we understood better the bilingual condition itself. In this case, there is not only an imagery system (I), and a verbal system (V) in operation, but two verbal systems (V_1 and V_2) which, depending on language acquisition histories, can be more or less interrelated. When these three components (I, V_1, and V_2) are evoked through empirical tests, very predictable outcomes are brought to light. For instance, in one study (Paivio & Lambert, 1981), English-French bilinguals were to do one of the following: 1) read off a series of concrete English words; 2) translate the translation equivalents of this list into English; or 3) look at a set of drawings of the referents of the original series and write down the appropriate English words that name them. Thus a common set of responses for all conditions is called for and time limits are kept the same; only the options differ since 1) evokes only V_1, 2) evokes V_2 and V_1, and 3) evokes the I component along with V_1. Then, on an unanticipated memory recall task, it turns out that option 1) generates x amount of recall, option 2) 2x, and 3) 3x, just as the bilingual version of the dual coding model predicts (see also Paivio, Clark, & Lambert, 1988).

When Paivio and colleagues confront some of the old chestnuts in the bilingual field, their theory helps resolve many longstanding debates. For example, they are able to deal squarely with the debate about separate memory storage systems for the L_1 and L_2 of bilinguals versus a single, common storage system used for the bilingual's two languages. Similarly, they enter the debate about compound versus coordinate forms of bilingualism. In the latter example, the Paivio team ends up reviewing the research on the issue and this leads them to be sensitive to the importance of language acquisition histories. (Paivio's personal example of confusion about whether his Finnish-English bilingualism is compounded or coordinated is an instructive one. But I wonder how he could have had any really Finnish experiences with church, free from Canadian ones, except for information relays or "assigns" from his Finnish parents?)

Finally, Paivio's chapter provides a very strong argument for the *system specificity* of the bilingual's L_1 and L_2 that shows itself in the separate impact each language has in learning and memory tasks. Bilinguals, by definition, rely on the systemic nature of each of their languages, switching one system off while the other is on, and then, when appropriate to do so, smoothly reversing the on/off process. The more we learn about these functionally related groups of elements that constitute a language, the better we will be able to handle difficult research questions about how two language systems work in the bilingual brain.

JYOTSNA VAID AND D. GEOFFREY HALL

Jyotsna Vaid and Geoff Hall focus on the blood and guts of bilingualism, not as veterinarians or surgeons might, but more as psychometric detectives would. They want to analyze, in one mammoth meta-analysis, all the evidence pro and con the possibility that the putative "bilingual brain" differs in some respect(s) from the brain of the monolingual. Their businesslike approach is called for because the wobble in results from the clinical literature on bilingual aphasics and from the experimental literature on bilingual versus monolingual cerebral lateralization can be confusing and discouraging to specialists in the field. The bilingual phenomenon— a person's ability to switch on and switch off one language system for another with hardly a trace of effort or error— is a charmer that grabs everyone's attention, even admiration, and it seems certain that some time in the future it will be shown that there is a neurochemical accompaniment of the bilingual's special facility with two interrelated verbal systems. It is equally certain that we don't have that accompaniment well understood as of now.

Of interest to me is the fact that Jyotsna came to McGill some time ago and tuned in on a local interest in this question and that Geoff came to McGill very recently and found remnants of the same interest. Before them were two forceful McGill people who were also charmed by the phenomenon: Don Hebb and Wilder Penfield. All of us at McGill listened carefully to these people. For instance, Penfield told me and Dick Tucker on one occasion: "The bilingual *brain* is a better brain; you'll see." And Hebb told us on several occasions something like this: "I'll bet the bilingual *mind* works this way: It's a matter of closely communicating systems of yoked cell assemblies, like a blue system and a red system, related through a common referential network." On another occasion, the same Penfield scolded me and Sam Fillenbaum when we suggested (Lambert & Fillenbaum, 1959) that the "crossed aphasias" we turned up in our early survey of bilingual aphasics might possibly mean that one of a bilingual's two languages would be under the control of a separate hemisphere. Penfield and Brenda Milner were harsh on this point because they had never seen evidence for such a thing in the brains of their bilingual patients. And Hebb was puzzled about that same speculation because he wondered how far apart in the brain his interrelated cell assembly systems could possibly be. Thus, the different hemisphere idea didn't intrigue him either.

It so transpired in that era, however, that Broadbent, followed by Brenda Milner and Doreen Kimura, began to direct attention to the processing possibilities of both hemispheres and, as a consequence, we began to think about bilingual lateralization possibilities, far-fetched as they seemed. Had there been (or if there were now) some other means of exploring interrelated cell assembly systems on *one* side of the brain, most of us never would have got involved in the bilateral exploration. But if we and the many others hadn't become involved, there would not be the wobbly data files for Jyotsna and Geoff to meta-analyze.

Vaid and Hall make it clear that the charm of the bilingual phenomenon needs to be checked on constantly. Is it that special? All of us can shift registers of speech when need be, with fluidity and exactitude, when it is socially appropriate to do so. Could it be that the common (monolingual) capacity to switch registers, or the synonym systems we all have, are the same thing as the bilingual phenomenon, on a monolingual scale? Paivio and others (Paivio & Lambert, 1981; Paivio et al., 1988) have examined part of this possibility and the data available from their studies suggest that the bilingual translation case *is* different from the monolingual synonym case. Thus, the powerful systematicity of two separate but interrelated verbal networks still has its unique charm.

What actually do Jyotsna and Geoff find in their meta-analysis? First, they find little overall evidence (that they are happy with) to support more right hemisphere (RH) involvement (or less LH involvement) in the bilingual brain. Even so, they are aware of many limitations forced on their analysis: very small numbers of studies with basic controls (such as the use of right-handed subjects only); few with monolingual comparison groups for *both* of the bilinguals' languages; few studies available to them that have a language other than English as one of the languages of the bilinguals; and few studies from settings other than North America. Thus, they conclude that the ideal test of the phenomenon is "yet to be done," and they outline very effectively how one might approach the ideal with better research probes. One can anticipate that new meta-analyses will appear including data from various European, Middle East, and Far East areas, and then we may have better grounds to make general conclusions.

Because of a nostalgic link to this issue, I became curious about the basically negative conclusion generated by the meta-analysis. So I tried a few nonparametric tests on the same data Jyotsna and Geoff used to draw their conclusions. Thus, I rely on their selection of studies and their analysis, including the use of correlations (rs) as a summary statistic. When their r is positive, it indicates that the study in question lends support to the main hypothesis, namely, less LH lateralization for bilinguals than for monolinguals; when their r is negative, there is no support for that hypothesis. Many would expect the main hypothesis to hold, especially for the bilingual's second language (L_2), if, of course, the bilingual is not an infant bilingual in which case "bilingualism would be the first language," as Merrill Swain put it.

These homespun reanalyses of mine add some seasoning to the conclusions of Vaid and Hall. The Mann-Whitney test seems appropriate because it ranks outcome scores (rs in this case) and gives weight to both the magnitudes of outcomes and their sign, (when nonsignificant lateralization outcomes are reported in a study with no backup statistics, I assigned an outcome score of zero). In fact, the Mann-Whitney tests are perhaps safer to use because one does not have to make the various assumptions necessary when the rs in a meta-analysis are combined for one final overall effect.

The upshot of this is that the Mann-Whitney U test shows no significant difference in hemispheric lateralization patterns between monolinguals and bilinguals when measurement is made in L_1. However, there *is* a significant difference when bilinguals are functioning in their L_2 (the same finding that emerged from the meta-analysis). Thus, for the data available (and granted that English was the monolinguals' language in the majority of studies), there is still a significant difference found between bilinguals and monolinguals in the parts of the brain used for cogitating on verbal materials, and this difference seems to be traceable to the bilingual's second language. Because all bilinguals, by definition, have a second language at their command, this difference is intriguing. Even though this difference turns up in the meta-analysis, its significance there (statistical as well as scientific) is made secondary. But it is not secondary for those who may still have a hunch that the bilingual *brain* and the bilingual *mind* may be significantly different from those of the monolingual.

There is another significant finding which could be given more attention; in their test of the age hypothesis, there is a statistically reliable "age of bilingualism" effect such that "early" bilinguals are more right-lateralized than either "late" bilinguals *or* monolingual controls. Thus, the bilingual brain may become different when one's bilingualism starts early in life.

Together, these are not insignificant possibilities, and I'm sure Jyotsna and Geoff now have brought the whole issue back for reconsideration since they provide extremely valuable clues as to how one should conduct "good" lateralization research— what controls are needed and what aspects of language are most/least likely to show lateralization effects. Incidentally, since most of the McGill-based studies are the more useful ones in the meta-analysis (i.e., those with the necessary controls) and since Jyotsna's work, is in my mind, the most carefully done and the most inventive of all, it may turn out that McGill would be wise to gear itself up for a continuation of interest in this issue.

But the Vaid/Hall chapter has another important message, namely, that the lateralization probes have so far not proved predictable, dependable, or straightforward; perhaps researchers should shop around for other approaches to explicate or reject the putative bilingual-monolingual difference. In fact, if the lateralization data were clearly supportive of a difference in the brain organization of bilinguals versus monolinguals, what would that mean to those of us also interested in how the bilingual *mind* works and how the bilingual *person* functions? Looking for new approaches is always a good idea, and my guess is that attention might profitably shift to the study of double versus single language *systems*. Paivio may have valuable suggestions to make in this instance, with his bilingual dual coding theory. Similarly, the experimental work of Stanislav Dornic (1977) on bilingual language systems is exciting. Dornic's emphasis reminds me of the period when Leon Jakobovits, Rabi Kanungo, and I were struggling with "semantic satiation." We tried to develop a means of neutralizing the meaning of words by satiating them (overusing them through repetition). With bilinguals, we could satiate words in one language and measure cosatiation of translated equivalents in the bilingual's second language (e.g., see Jakobovits & Lambert, 1961). Thus we asked ourselves, if we satiate the meaning of the concept *mother*, what effect would this have on the concept *mère*? There is much we still don't understand about semantic satiation, but it is an exciting area and it might be one of the new candidates for attention that Jyotsna and Geoff suggest we now consider.

ALLAN G. REYNOLDS

I've placed Al Reynolds' chapter last in the series for several reasons: It looks back critically on several of the earlier chapters; it fits with the Vaid/Hall chapter because it finds shortcomings in the work up to the present and suggests new directions for future research; and, incidentally, it was the last chapter to be finalized for this volume. It is not only well-written but it is also well thought-through; Reynolds writes clearly and he thinks clearly. In fact, he is logical and *demanding* and he conveys clearly the message that he wants us eager, bushy-tailed investigators to slow down and think more deeply before moving into research. There is nothing wrong with reflection before jumping into a study, but his telling design criticisms may dishearten and even overwhelm researchers, and thus discourage further valuable research. Actually that would be an unfortunate result because he is calling for more research on the cognitive consequences of bilingualism, not less, and what he suggests as valuable alternative theoretical approaches— a McClelland need-achievement model, a Bloom or a Sternberg model— are actually loose, carefree alternatives, not at all muscle-bound with design details. As I see it, the Reynolds chapter is written to challenge and provoke, and even though I have no basic criticism with his details, I'll take up certain of his challenges just to make him happy, and then I'll introduce certain emphases for future work that are different from those he favors.

What is Reynolds' main message? He wants to "help improve the quality" of future work in a "theoretically, personally, and politically important area of research." Improvement is called for because the research to date on the cognitive consequences of bilingualism has promoted "a state of false complacency, because the designs used have all been preexperimental or quasi-experimental" in nature "with all their attendant dangers." Reynolds wants researchers to strive for trouble-free designs, and to develop process-type theoretical models to orient their particular research explorations. He is convinced that the various themes emerging in the study of the cognitive consequences of bilingualism are unmistakably important ones, but we should now move from approximate models and designs to first class ones.

Reynolds doesn't just preach; he also very clearly lays out the design weaknesses in nearly all relevant studies, the newer ones as well as the older ones. His excellent review of trouble-prone designs and theory-deprived interpretations will be extremely useful for future research, and it could help move the field of bilingual research closer to mainstream science. Reynolds' suggestions for the application of a theory like Sternberg's to bilingualism and the application of David McClelland's research strategies to test the long-range societal effects of widespread bilingualism (supported in Canada, for example, by Federal Government bilingualism policies and the growth of immersion education in schools) are fascinating examples of what can be done to strengthen the scientific base of the field.

There are nonetheless other ways of evaluating what has been done in this field and how one should proceed from here. The Reynolds chapter, because it holds no punches, almost asks for a rebuttal of some sort. Here's mine: Reynolds gives convincing arguments for tightening things up. However, there may be value in the opposite strategy— keeping things loose. One can view design issues as little more than matters of common sense; as well, statisticians can be viewed as if they were referees in a hockey game, who have to be tested periodically for their watchfulness, their perspicacity, and their flexibility (see Lambert, 1989). This is not an advocation for cheating when the ref isn't looking, but rather a suggestion to keep statistical treatments as simple and uncomplicated as possible, while experimenting with less conventional, often homespun methods, even using nonparametric statistics as often as possible, or using growth curves whenever possible or even d-scores for measures of change, even though sophisticated referees might blow the whistle in each case. I see a need for this uncomplicated experimental approach to social-psychological research (which includes much of bilingualism and biculturalism) because the "big problems" in society can't meet tight-design demands. For instance, we can't randomly assign people to black/white, rich/poor, or male/female categories, and we might need to do so if we wanted to really understand how membership in these categories affects various types of performance and behavior. Similarly for theory, perhaps "hunches" or "best guesses" in our field may be as rich as most of the "theories" that can be drawn on. In fact, in the long run, it could be that hunch-rich, loosely designed research provides the best leads for explaining the bilingual condition, and when these types of research outcomes recur from one study to another, they could then be systematized in a more formal theoretical manner. In my mind, theory construction is easy since it usually knits together findings that show trends and recurrence. In contrast, hunches are harder to come by and they contain potentially useful new ideas.

Consider again the laid-back, commonsense approach of Lev Vygotsky (1934/1962) mentioned earlier with reference to the Genesee chapter. Vygotsky was searching for deep-lying "processes," something more than the processes referred to in debates about "product versus process" research, or the process-oriented theory Reynolds advocates. To study "processes" and to search for potential "mechanisms" of the sort Vygotsky referred to led him to conduct experiments using the now-famous Vygotsky blocks, or pneumatically monitored rubber balls to be pressed in tests of same/different. I see two important features of this "deeper type" of process research or this "Vygotsky-style" search for underlying processes. First, all such research makes use of a hypothetico-deductive schema (cf. Underwood, 1957; or Hull, 1952) that starts with "hypothetical constructs" or "intervening variables" (see MacCorquodale & Meehl, 1948). These hypothetical constructs are often simply the product of sophisticated guesses on the part of a researcher. Their importance lies in the fact that they can be linked, through experiments, with particular input variables (the "independent variables") that are systematically related to one or several output variables (the "dependent variables"). Second, the basic schema also implies *multiple* hypothetical deductions and multiple, varied testings of the central construct; thus, there is an implied requirement that the researcher-theoretician strive for "construct validity" as his only means of enhancing the believability of the basic construct (see Cronbach & Meehl, 1955; Underwood, 1957). This old, dependable model gets new names and new twists from time to time, but never any substantive modifications. And its value is unmistakably recognized today (see Edwards, 1990; Howard, 1990; Nicholson & Hogan, 1990; Walsh, 1990.) The constructs or basic processes explored can be psychological in nature, group- or community-oriented, or even culture-oriented.

In summary, what I see as a viable alternative to Al Reynolds' important suggestions is a wide variety of tests of constructs (such as the idea that bilinguals may be advantaged in cognitive activities and in social outlooks) that are based on strongly felt hunches which in turn can be tested in as well-controlled conditions as is possible. Each study's impact will then be much less than the combined effect of a network of studies, especially if the *variety* of hypothetico-deductive guesses explored in the network is wide open to differences in the perspectives and experiences of the hunch-makers.

Nonetheless, it is difficult to escape the intent of Al Reynolds' message: Let's no longer be satisfied with incomplete, approximate designs; the issues of bilingualism are too important in the field of behavioral sciences to be only half-studied; relevant modern designs and theories are available and our field should be mature enough now to apply them.

Still, there are questions about the reality of what is available. For instance, if there are limitations to the validity of the Peabody and Raven tests (which many of us find useful), what are the better tests we might try? (Perhaps Al Reynolds should check out Jerome Sattler's, 1988, evaluation of these two tests!) If the limitation of the Peabody test is its questionable relation to other measures of IQ, it should be emphasized that none of the studies done at McGill used it as an IQ measure; rather, it was a convenient vocabulary test, with pictures for use with young subjects, and with alternate forms that makes it valuable for assessing vocabulary level in both of the languages of bilingual children. If a limitation of the original Raven test was its peculiarly small norm base, we never really use the norms because we favor matched control groups wherever possible; and the nonverbal feature of the Raven test is important for cross-cultural research. When comparing "natural" bilinguals and monolinguals, no researcher can assign youngsters at random to these classifications; they come one way or the other. With these real world restrictions, most researchers then try, with as much care as possible, to get comparable, if not matched, groups. For instance, Peal and Lambert (1962) tried their best to keep all bilinguals in their sample if they were "balanced," whether they were high performers in both languages or, as many readers of that paper failed to appreciate, *low* in both; similarly, Balkan (1970) did an even better job with his comparison groups in Switzerland— with essentially the same overall outcomes. Thus, one has either not to experiment at all or limp along with the nonrandom design feature and wait for multiple probes from other research sites to test the basic idea from as many perspectives as possible.

While limping along, one can try at least to approximate the elegance of random assignment, by a variety of techniques. For instance, on the matter of the cognitive consequences of bilingualism, Sheridan Scott (1973), working with Dick Tucker and me, examined the cognitive performance and speaking skills of two groups of Grade 5 and 6 students. One group had become functionally bilingual because they had been enrolled in a French immersion program since kindergarten; a second sample of monolingual anglophone children comprised a control group. It is important to note that many of these children had been candidates for the early immersion program but, by chance, did not get into it; thus, this subset of the control group was similar to the "waiting list" sample proposed by Reynolds. In order to further ensure comparability between the two groups on the important variables of IQ, family, socio-economic status, and home environment, a covariance adjustment was applied. The differences in the cognitive gymnastics of the "manufactured" bilinguals (measured through two tests of divergent thinking) in contrast to the monolingual controls in that study were impressive. The Scott study suggests to me that becoming bilingual has a causal and favorable impact on cognitive flexibility. Interestingly, Dick Tucker (1991) has summarized a recent batch of studies that either explicitly or implicitly argue for the same causal link between bilingualism and cognitive performance (Bamford & Mizokawa, 1989; Cleghorn, Merritt, & Abagi, 1989; Diaz, 1985; Secada, 1989). Incidentally, this network of studies constitutes a multimeasure attempt to validate the construct of cognitive enrichment due to bilingualism (see Campbell & Fiske, 1959; Howard, 1990). Furthermore, this network of studies would also add substance to a meta-analysis directed to this important issue, if Vaid and Hall became interested in extending their meta-analytic skills.

One can take another step while limping along, namely, asking oneself questions about the motivations of parents who assist in making their children bilingual (in the home, through enrollment in immersion education, etc.) versus those who try their best to keep their children monolingual. Without a random assignment design, a recurrent criticism one encounters, whenever the intelligence of these children is compared, is that the bilingual children are brighter because they are the offspring of parents who chose the bilingualism alternative, and thus are presumed to be brighter than parents who didn't. Many readers of this literature worry about this possibility. But I'm not so sure about the logic involved; there are many bright parents with solid values and ideologies who choose the nonbilingual alternative. In fact, one can easily argue that in Quebec today there are many very perceptive francophone parents who are bilingualism-shy for what they see as very solid reasons. So is it a sure thing that when bilingual and monolingual children are compared, the brighter parents are necessarily those who promote bilingualism in their children?

Clearly, we have much more work to do before our hypothetical constructs about the positive effects of bilingualism are convincing enough to have a real social and political force, but I'm very optimistic on that score. Happily, Al Reynolds is now getting personally interested in going further into the matter, and the research will be all that much better because of his involvement.

CONCLUSIONS

Whoops! Time's up. And I've spent all my pennies. Just before breaking the seminar up, what can I conclude from all this? My conclusions are multiple. The study of bilingualism and multiculturalism is by its nature a very hot topic not only for us as insiders (we who have the luxury of contemplating, researching, and theorizing about the topic), but also for outsiders (those who are not in the research field itself, but whose life experiences with the underlying issues are as real and insightful as anyone else's). The topic is hot also because it touches many fields of study, from neurology to psychology to sociology to politics. At the same time as it is a serious, real-world domain of study, making it much more than an academic exercise, it is also a fun topic, as these chapters have so admirably demonstrated. In addition, it now has a good start, as the research details introduced here have made so clear, even though only the surfaces of the basic issues have been scratched. Finally, there is a splendidly educated cadre of young people who are now guiding the new directions the field is taking. Their involvement is certain to make it even hotter and more fun in the future. Like Rip Van Winkle, I'd love to wake up in thirty-five years and sit in on a follow-up seminar to see where the field is then!

ACKNOWLEDGMENTS

I have several longstanding acknowledgments to make: first, to the friends/colleagues who presented chapters for this volume and who have brought me along over the years as a coresearcher on projects of mutual interest; second, to McGill University, and especially the Psychology Department, comprised as it is of colleagues mainly in other specialty areas, who have nonetheless encouraged and contributed their ideas to the peculiar line of research in which my students and I persisted; third, to the granting agencies who helped us financially, in particular the old Defense Research Board of Canada, the Social Sciences and Humanities Research Council of Canada, the Carnegie Corporation of New York, and, most recently, the Spencer Foundation of Chicago; and finally, and most important of all, to my wife Janine, my daughter

Sylvie, and my son Philippe, who not only introduced me to the underlying issues that became mainstays of my research, but who also showed me, through their lives, how real and important affection, language, culture, and identity are.

REFERENCES

Balkan, L. (1970). *Les effets du bilinguisme français-anglais sur les aptitudes intellectuelles.* Brussels: AIMAV.

Bamford, K. W., & Mizokawa, D. T. (1989, April). *Cognitive and attitudinal outcomes of an additive bilingual program.* Paper presented at the meeting of the American Educational Research Association, San Francisco, CA.

Bialystok, E., & Ryan, E. B. (1985a). Toward a definition of metalinguistic skill. *Merrill-Palmer Quarterly, 31,* 229-251.

Bialystok, E., & Ryan, E. B. (1985b). A metacognitive framework for the development of first and second language skills. In D. L. Forrest-Pressley, G. E. MacKinnon, & T. G. Waller (Eds.), *Metacognition, cognition, and human performance.* New York: Academic Press.

Blanc, M., & Hamers, J. F. (1987). Preface. In M. Blanc & J. F. Hamers (Eds.), *Theoretical and methodological issue in the study of languages/dialects in contact at macro and micrological levels of analysis* (Report No. B-160). Québec: International Center for Research on Bilingualism.

Bloom, B. (1985). *Developing talent in young people.* New York: Ballantine Books.

Campbell, D. T., & Fiske, D. W. (1959). Convergent and discriminant validity in the multitrait-multimethod matrix. *Psychological Bulletin, 56,* 81-105.

Cleghorn, A., & Genesee, F. (1984). Languages in contact: An ethnographic study of interaction in an immersion school. *TESOL Quarterly, 18,* 595-625.

Cleghorn, A., Merritt, M. W., & Abagi, J. D. (1989). Language policy and science instruction in Kenyan primary schools. *Comparative Education Review, 33,* 21-39.

Cronbach, L. J., & Meehl, P. E. (1955). Construct validity in psychological tests. *Psychological Bulletin, 52,* 281-302.

Cummins, J. (1979). Linguistic interdependence and the educational development of bilingual children. *Review of Educational Research, 49,* 222-251.

Cummins, J. (1981). The role of primary language development in promoting educational success for language minority students. In *Schooling and language minority students: A theoretical framework.* Los Angeles: California State Department of Education, Evaluation, Dissemination and Assessment Center.

Cziko, G. A., Lambert, W. E., Sidoti, N., & Tucker, G. R. (1980). Graduates of early immersion: Retrospective views of grade 11 students and their parents. In R. N. St. Clair & H. Giles (Eds.), *The social and psychological contexts of language.* Hillsdale, NJ: Lawrence Erlbaum Associates.

Diaz, R. M. (1985). Bilingual cognitive development: Addressing three gaps in current research. *Child Development, 56,* 1376-1388.

Dornic, S. (1977). *Information processing and bilingualism* (Rep. No. 510). Stockholm: The University of Stockholm, Department of Psychology.

Edwards, A. L. (1990). Construct validity and social desirability. *American Psychologist, 45,* 287-289.

Esman, M. J. (1987). Ethnic politics and economic power. *Comparative Politics, 19,* 395-418.

Genesee, F. (1987). *Learning through two languages.* Cambridge, MA: Newbury House.

Genesee, F., Holobow, N., Lambert, W. E., & Chartrand, L. (1989). Three elementary school alternatives for learning through a second language. *Modern Language Journal, 73*, 250-263.

Hamers, J. F., & Blanc, M. (1989). *Bilinguality and bilingualism.* Cambridge: Cambridge University Press.

Howard, G. S. (1990). On the construct validity of self-reports: What do the data say? *American Psychologist, 45*, 292-294.

Hull, C. (1952). *A behavior system.* New Haven: Yale University Press.

Jakobovits, L., & Lambert, W. E. (1961). Semantic satiation among bilinguals. *Journal of Experimental Psychology, 62*, 576-582.

Krashen, S. (1981). The theoretical and practical relevance of simple codes in second language acquisition. In R. Scarcella & S. Krashen (Eds.), *Research in second language acquisition.* Rowley, MA: Newbury House.

Lambert, W. E. (1981). Bilingualism and language acquisition. In H. Winitz (Ed.), *Native language and foreign language acquisition.* New York: The New York Academy of Sciences.

Lambert, W. E. (1988, May). *"Minority" language rights and education in Québec.* Paper presented at the Conference on Minority Language Rights and Minority Education, Cornell University, Ithaca, NY.

Lambert, W. E. (1989, October). *Pros, cons, and limits to quantitative approaches in foreign language research.* Paper presented at the Conference on Foreign Language Research, University of Pennsylvania, Philadelphia.

Lambert, W. E., & Fillenbaum, S. (1959). A pilot study of aphasia among bilinguals. *Canadian Journal of Psychology, 13*, 28-34.

Lambert, W. E., Giles, H., & Albert, A. (1976). Language attitudes in a rural city of northern Maine. *La Monda Linguo-Problemo, 15*, 129-192.

Lambert, W. E., Holobow, N., Genesee, F., & Chartrand, L. (1990). *School-based alternatives for learning a second language: A longitudinal evaluation.* Unpublished manuscript, McGill University, Department of Psychology, Montreal.

Lambert, W. E., & Paivio, A. (1956). The influence of noun-adjective order on learning. *Canadian Journal of Psychology, 10*, 9-12.

Lambert, W. E., & Taylor, D. M. (1990). *Coping with cultural and racial diversity in urban America.* New York: Praeger.

Landry, R., & Allard, R. (1987). *Contact des langues et développement bilingue: Un modèle macroscopique.* Paper given at the conference on Contact des langues, Nice, France.

Le Doux, J., Iwata, J., Cicchetti, P., & Reis, D. J. (1988). Different projections of the central amygdaloid nucleus mediate autonomic and behavioral correlates of conditioned fear. *The Journal of Neurosciences, 8*(7), 2517-2529.

Lietti, A. (1989). *Pour l' éducation bilingue.* Lausanne: Favre, S.A.

MacCorquodale, K., & Meehl, P. E. (1948). On a distinction between hypothetical constructs and intervening variables. *Psychological Review, 55*, 95-107.

Nicholson, R. A., & Hogan, R. (1990). The construct validity of social desirability. *American Psychologist, 45*, 290-291.

Padilla, A. M., & Long, K. K. (1969). *An assessment of successful Spanish-American students at the University of New Mexico.* Paper given at the annual meeting of the American Association for the Advancement of Science, Colorado Springs, CO.

Paivio, A. (1986). *Mental representations: A dual coding approach.* New York: Oxford University Press.

Paivio, A., Clark, J., & Lambert, W. E. (1988). Bilingual dual-coding theory and semantic repetition effects on recall. *Journal of Experimental Psychology, 14*, 163-172.

Paivio, A., & Desrochers, A. (1980). A dual-coding approach to bilingual memory. *Canadian Journal of Psychology, 34*, 390-401.

Paivio, A., & Lambert, W. E. (1981). Dual coding and bilingual memory. *Journal of Verbal Learning and Verbal Behavior, 20*, 532-539.

Peal, E., & Lambert, W. E. (1962). The relation of bilingualism to intelligence. *Psychological Monographs, 76*, 1-23.

Rosen, B. C. (1959). Race, ethnicity, and the achievement syndrome. *American Sociological Review, 24*, 47-60.

Sattler, J. M. (1988). *Assessment of children*. San Diego: J. M. Sattler.

Scott, S. (1973). *The relation of divergent thinking to bilingualism: Cause or effect?* Unpublished manuscript, McGill University, Department of Psychology, Montreal.

Secada, W. G. (1989, April). *The relationship between degree of bilingualism and arithmetic problem-solving performance in first-grade Hispanic children*. Paper presented at the meeting of the American Educational Research Association, San Francisco, CA.

Segalowitz, N. (1977). Psychological perspectives on bilingual education. In B. Spolsky & R. Cooper (Eds.), *Frontiers of bilingual education*. Rowley, MA: Newbury House.

Tucker, G. R. (1991). Cognitive and social correlates of bilinguality. In R. L. Cooper & B. Spolsky (Eds.), *Language, society, and thought: Essays in honor of Joshua A. Fishman's sixty-fifth birthday*. Berlin: Mouton de Gruyter.

Underwood, B. J. (1957). *Psychological research*. New York: Appleton-Century-Crofts.

Vygotsky, L. S. (1962). *Thought and language*. (E. Hanfmann & G. Vakar, Eds. and Trans.). Cambridge, MA: MIT Press. (Original work published 1934)

Walsh, J. A. (1990). Comment on social desirability. *American Psychologist, 45*, 289-290.

Author Index

Italics denote pages with bibliographic information.

Subject Index

Italics denote French language entries.